D0699478

THE SUPREME COURT IN AMERICAN LIFE

Volume 5

The Fuller Court *1888-1910*

Howard B. Furer

ASSOCIATED FACULTY PRESS, INC.
Millwood, N.Y. • New York City • London

Associated Faculty Press, Inc.

The Supreme Court in American Life Series

George J. Lankevich, Editor

George J. Lankevich, *The Federal Court, 1787-1801.*
Adrienne Siegel, *The Marshall Court, 1801-1835.*
Martin Siegel, *The Taney Court, 1836-1864.*
Robert Fridlington, *The Reconstruction Court, 1864-1888.*
Howard Furer, *The Fuller Court, 1888-1910.*
Norman Bindler, *The Conservative Court, 1910-1930.*
Robert Mayer, *The Court and the American Crises, 1930-1952.*
Arnold S. Rice, *The Warren Court, 1953-1968.*
Arthur L. Galub, *The Burger Court, 1968-1984*

Photographs of the Supreme Court justices provided by the Supreme Court Historical Society, Washington, D.C.

Manufactured in the United States of America

Library of Congress Cataloging in Publication Data

Furer, Howard B., 1934-
The Fuller Court, 1888-1910.

(The Supreme Court in American life series; v. 5)
Bibliography: p.
1. United States. Supreme Court—History. 2. Judges—United States—History. 3. Fuller, Melville Weston, 1833-1910. I. Title. II. Series.
KF8742.F87 1986 347.73'26 84-2873
ISBN 0-86733-060-0 (pt. 5) 347.30735
ISBN 0-86733-065-1 (9 v. set)

Dedication

To My Wife
Marlene
for Devotion, Patience, Understanding

Contents

Part III

Introductory Note

The Supreme Court of the United States is an effective and very human institution, but it also stands as a symbolic, almost sacred, icon of the American nation. Almost every school child knows that the Constitution established the judiciary as an independent third branch of government, yet few mature citizens can confidently assert that they understand how the Supreme Court became the respected final arbiter of American life that it is today. And rationally, how is it possible that an institution composed of unelected men serving for life and deliberating in secrecy, is accorded the authority to bend the other branches to its will? By what alchemy have independent Americans become submissive to Court decisions which are as final as the ukase of a tsar? To study the human and institutional development of the Supreme Court in terms free of legal jargon, and to relate the history of the Court to the wider concerns of American life, is the purpose of these volumes.

The Founding Fathers who wrote America's Constitution were wise and prudent men. It took them eight times as long to define the powers of Congress (Article I), and three times the space to create the Presidency (Article II), than to organize the judicial branch (Article III). The Fathers were concerned with potential abuse of power, and devoted most of their efforts to devising intricate mechanisms to limit the exercise of government authority. Showing more faith in the judiciary, they did not set qualifications for Supreme Court Justices, mandate a Chief Justice or establish a court system. Once the Court's jurisdiction was defined at Philadelphia, the only limitations placed upon the Justices were the Senate's right to reject candidates (a right since exercised twenty-six times), Congress' power to impeach, the people's right to amend the Constitution and the Justices' own sense of self-restraint and wisdom. Yet from such meager origins developed a Supreme Court which has, on over one hundred occasions, invalidated acts of Congress and set aside well over a thousand statutes passed by state legislatures. The Court has thus displayed awesome power throughout our history, perhaps far more than the Fathers ever suspected it would enjoy. The successive volumes of this series will trace the development of the Court's judicial power, introduce the men who interpreted the Constitution, and study the society that inspired and surrounded the decisions of the Justices.

The Court has become central to our national life because it is the arena in which two basic American attitudes contend. Americans revere and respect the law, yet they also believe in the determining nature of the will of the people. Congress legislates in the name of the people, but the Court has the responsibility of testing statutes against American ideals and the words of the Constitution. That such a task has political ramifications is hardly surprising. As often as the Court has seized the opportunity to decide major cases, it has as frequently avoided controversial issues. Powerful as it can be, the Court is often important for what it chooses not to decide. If the Court sometimes appears to "follow the election returns," does that not imply judicial sensitivity to public opinion? A central theme of these volumes is the unending tension between the desires of the people, the dictates of the Constitution, and the decisions of the Justices. "We are under a Constitution," wrote Justice Hughes, "but the Constitution is what the judges say it is." One of the enduring marvels of American society is that the people have been so willing to admit the Justices' right to determine the meaning of our fundamental law and permit them to say "no" to the initiatives of the elected representatives of the people.

These volumes emphasize biography because the decisions of the Court are produced by the experience, prejudices and convictions of its changing membership. America's Supreme Court asserts that it does not make the law, it only decides what the law is; yet the attitudes of the men and one woman who have had the final word in our political process are critical to that discovery. As a kind of reward for their even-handed efforts, Justices seem far more likely to be labeled "great" than are Presidents or members of Congress. This accolade appears to be more freely given precisely because the nation believes its Justices act on a more rigorous and unforgiving standard. The law, more so than the practice of politics, seems to make greater demands of men. During our history as a nation, the Justices of the Supreme Court have invalidated acts of Congress, accepted slavery, dissolved trusts, ordered reapportionment and given their approval to abortion; such actions invariably shook the nation. Yet our Justices have no monopoly on wisdom or competence. The Constitution awards authority to the Court, but not omniscience. Understanding the Court demands that we know its membership, as well as the law they are sworn to uphold.

American history has given to our Supreme Court enduring prestige, but the willingness of society to accept Court decisions testifies as well to the national faith in law and the Constitution. The people, the law and the Court mutually support each other. Although the members of each Court temporarily enjoy the right to decide questions of law, they are keenly aware that they must protect broadly-held moral principles, legal precedent, and unspoken tradition as well. The interaction between the Justices and the society that called them to serve remains one of the enduring dramas of American history. If that relationship becomes clearer for readers, the authors of these volumes will have created the useful tool and reference work they intended.

Editor's Foreword

In the constitutional history of the United States, the years from 1888 to 1910 may be referred to as the period of the Fuller Court, for, to a very great extent, the history of this country was determined in the chambers of the highest tribunal in the land. During these years, a revolution took place in every phase of American society as the United States changed from an agricultural country to an industrialized nation, painfully adjusting to a machine civilization. It was a period during which America's true political rulers were captains of business who had no wish to solve the pressing problems facing the United States. Instead, their major concern was the perpetuation of a laissez faire system which left them free to amass huge profits, yet, at the same time, to win special favors from government for business enterprise. In their drive to achieve these goals, businessmen were most ably assisted by the Fuller Court, which became a sanctuary of final appeal for them. It was there that the conservative tenets of economic exploitation were protected from interference, whether by individual state legislatures or by the Congress of the United States.

The Fuller Court, as William F. Swindler wrote, "stood upon a watershed" in American history with a very powerful pull of "ideological gravity toward the past." When Melville Weston Fuller was appointed Chief Justice of the Supreme Court in 1888, at least three of his colleagues, Justices Joseph P. Bradley, Stephen J. Field, and Samuel F. Miller dated from the "constitutional golden age," and all eight of the Justices occupying seats on the bench predated his appointment. Most of these men were tied to an earlier age when life had been less complex and when the constitutional questions facing them were not as economically, politically or socially profound. Fuller's appointment to the Court marked the conclusion of the first hundred years of American history under the Constitution, and the beginning of its modern interpretation. Despite a rapidly changing America, the Chief Justice and the majority of his colleagues were not personally or philosophically prepared to cope with the new propositions of economics, society or government which came before the Court during these years. The nation demanded new definitions of individual and property rights, definitions which the Fuller Court proved unable or unwilling to provide. As industrial America moved inexorably forward, often detrimentally to the interests of farmers and workers, a turbulent era of protest ensued. From the Populist outburst of the

1890's to the first decade of the Progressive Period in the twentieth century, the Fuller Court made constitutional history favorable to industry. The conservative businessmen who dominated this country's economy and politics, continually looked to the Supreme Court to protect them from the threats posed by radicals and reformers.

Farmers and workers, driven to rebellion by the growing power of big business, organized to support a new theory of government. They held that the state should assume a more positive role in men's lives. If railroad rates were too high, they argued, the government should protect shippers by forcing the carriers to lower their charges; if a corporation became so monopolistic that it could completely control the market in its products, the government should intervene to break it down into competing units; and if harmful social effects resulted from long working hours, dangerous and unsanitary conditions, and exceedingly low wages, the state should take action to remedy these conditions. The Fuller Court, however, did not share this expansive view of government. Instead, it adopted or developed new principles to protect the rights of property and the individual's freedom of contract from legislative interference. Fuller and his colleagues undertook to create a jurisprudence applicable to questions never dreamed of by the men who wrote the Constitution, or their early predecessors on the bench. Among the new constitutional issues dealt with by the Court were substantive due process under the Fourteenth Amendment, freedom of contract, the myth of fair value, the separate but equal concept, restrictions on the commerce power, the legality of an income tax, and the constitutional aspects of the imperial interlude that arose out of the Spanish-American War. The Fuller Court's decisions in cases concerned with these questions indicated the Justices's inflexible attitudes toward the wide range of problems created by the impact of industrialism. In each of these constitutional questions, the Fuller Court placed property rights above human rights.

To a great extent, the Fuller Court represented a judicial lag in American history. The men who sat on the supreme bench during these years reminded the nation that, despite their high position, they were only men, and that their personal ideology very often colored their "constitutional alchemy." They were disturbed by the growth of governmental authority, and were seeking to protect individuality in a society in which the individual was becoming less and less important. They came to believe that the safeguarding of individualism was essentially a judicial task and therefore, during these two decades, they facilitated a constitutional power shift from Congress to the Supreme Court. Since many parts of the American public were demanding a wide variety of regulatory legislation, lively encounters among the Justices over proper judicial interpretation sometimes ensued. Moreover, because of the complexity of the constitutional questions that came before it, the Fuller Court, on occasion, appeared inconsistent in its decisions. The Judges often found it difficult to reconcile the limits of governmental interference with the demands of private property. As a result, judicial decisions were based upon an individual Justice's personal philosophy rather than past Court action or legal precedent. More often than not, however, the approach was conservative. To be sure, during the final few years of Chief Justice Fuller's tenure, several new, liberal appointees donned the black robes of the high tribunal, but they consistently found themselves in the minority. Despite the arrival of that turn of the century reform movement known as progressivism, the majority of the Justices continued to subscribe to the conservative philosophy that had characterized the Court since Fuller's ascendency in 1888, a view best expressed by the Court's arch-conservative, Justice Stephen J. Field. In an address given upon the centennial anniversary of the federal judicial system (1890), Field said: "The limitations upon legislative power, arising from the nature of the Constitution and its specific restraints in favor of private rights, cannot be disregarded without conceding that the legislature can change at will the form of our government from one of limited to one of unlimited powers."

When Fuller's term came to an end with his death in 1910, the country looked much the same as it did when he had been appointed to head the supreme bench. For the most part, conservatism still reigned supreme. By 1910, labor unions had been rendered powerless by the use of the injunction; the Sherman Anti-Trust Act and the Interstate Commerce Act reduced to virtual uselessness by the hostile Court; and farmers and workers so decisively beaten at the polls that they were ready to abandon their battle for economic equality. Yet, during the Chief Justice's last years, progressivism made some important inroads. The American people regained partial control of their nation's government and economy but the Court, however, remained steadfastly committed to the protection of private property and laissez faire. Fuller and his associates believed that conservative due process decisions were the necessary legal accompaniment to the industrial conquest of this country. During Fuller's twenty-two years at the center of the Court, decisions exalting property rights over human rights seemed logical in the wake of the massive economic developments transforming the United States.

This book does not presume to be a definitive history of the Supreme Court during the Chief Justiceship of Melville Weston Fuller. It attempts, rather, to summarize the history of the United States and the role the Court played in that history between 1888 and 1910. In order to fulfill that purpose, this volume has been divided into four sections. The first part of this work consists of a detailed chronology including the major events in United States history during this twenty-two year period, brief descriptions of the landmark Court decisions, the various changes that occurred in Court personnel, the important events that led to later Court decisions, and the principle statutes enacted by Congress which helped to shape the incredible changes taking place in the nation. Section two includes a series of documents drawn largely from the most important decisions and dissents delivered by the Fuller Court. In addition, the documents section contains several selections dealing with commentary on the Court's role in American society and government. The third section of the book presents concise biographical data on each Justice who served on the Court during these years. A lightly annotated bibliography has been compiled including general historical works on this period of American history, general studies on the history of the Supreme Court and constitutional law, biographies of the Justices, scholarly articles, and legal analyses of the Court, its philosophy and its work.

A broad spectrum of facts and sources have been cited to provide the reader with the widest possible coverage of the Fuller Court's history and development within the confines of a small volume. This work, then, is a handy research tool for those students interested in this crucial period in the Court's history.

I want to make special acknowledgment of very real assistance to my daughter, Cara, who helped with the research and typed parts of the manuscript. I am also indebted to the staffs of the Kean College Library and the Teaneck Public Library whose gracious help made the task of obtaining some of the necessary material easier and more affable. Finally, my appreciation goes to Gloria Santucci, secretary to the Kean College of New Jersey History Department, whose cooperation in photocopying the many documents used in this volume was invaluable.

Howard B. Furer

PART I

The Supreme Court in American Life

▪ ▪ ▪ ▪ ▪

Chronology 1888-1910

Chronology

1888

July 20	Melville Weston Fuller (Illinois) is appointed the eighth Chief Justice of the United States Supreme Court by President Cleveland to replace Chief Justice Morrison R. Waite who died on March 23, 1888. Fuller would serve as Chief Justice for twenty-two years.
July 21	The Mills Bill, enacting a tariff reduction of seven percent passes the House of Representatives. The Senate does not act on the measure.
August 21	The United States Senate rejects the Bayard-Chamberlain Treaty. However, the United States retains certain privileges in Canadian ports, primarily the use of the fisheries. The Canadian government removes these privileges in 1923.
October 24	The so-called Murchison Letter written by the British minister to the United States, Lord Lionel Sackville-West, is made public. It is damaging to the Democrats and hurts Cleveland's chances for reelection by costing him the votes of many Irish-Americans.
October 29	In *Georgia Railroad and Banking Company v. Smith,* 128 U.S. 174, an early opinion of the Fuller Court, the majority declares that a state charter giving a railroad condemnation power "clothed the railroad with a public use subject to legislative regulation."
November 6	Harrison defeats Cleveland for the presidency, although Cleveland receives the greater popular vote. In the electoral college, however, Harrison has 233 votes to Cleveland's 168.

Louisville, Kentucky introduces the use of the Australian (secret) ballot in elections in the United States.

1889

January 14	The Supreme Court in *Stoutenbourgh v. Hennick,* 129 U.S. 141, voids an act of Congress which had licensed commission salesmen in the District of Columbia since the statute is a burden on interstate commerce.
February 11	The Department of Agriculture is given Cabinet status, and Norman J. Coleman (Missouri) is appointed the first secretary.
February 22	Congress passes an Omnibus Bill providing for the admission of North Dakota, South Dakota, Washington, and Montana into the Union.
March 4	Benjamin Harrision (Indiana) is inaugurated the twenty-third President of the United States.
March 7	President Harrison appoints William H.H. Miller attorney general of the United States.
March 22	Supreme Court Justice Stanley Matthews dies. He had been appointed to the Court by President James A. Garfield on May 12, 1881.
April 22	The Oklahoma Territory is thrown open to settlement. By nightfall, almost the entire area is claimed by "Boomers" and "Sooners." Two towns, Guthrie and Oklahoma City with populations of 15,000 and 10,000 respectively, are immediately laid out.
April 29	The Berlin Conference on Samoa opens. A tripartite agreement providing for the independence and autonomy of the Samoan Islands under a protectorate of the United States, Great Britain, and Germany is signed on June 14, 1889.
May 13	The Supreme Court rules in *Chae Chan Ping v. United States,* 130 U.S. 581, known as the *Chinese Exclusion* case, that expelling Chinese immigrant laborers, does

not violate the treaties made with China in 1868 and 1880, and does not contravene the rights vested in them under law.

May 29 — Orlow W. Chapman is appointed solicitor general of the United States by President Harrison.

October 2 — The First International Conference of American States opens in Washington, D.C., hosted by Secretary of State James G. Blaine.

October 13 — Kansas becomes the first state to enact an antitrust law. By 1893, fifteen other states and territories follow suit.

November 2 — North and South Dakota are admitted to the Union.

November 8 — Montana is admitted to the Union.

November 11 — Washington is admitted to the Union.

December 18 — David J. Brewer (Kansas) is appointed to the Supreme Court by President Harrison to replace Justice Matthews. Brewer would serve on the Court for twenty-one years.

1890

The population of the United States reaches 63, 056,000, a total rapidly increasing due to massive immigration from Central, Eastern, and Southern Europe.

February 4 — William Howard Taft is appointed solicitor general of the United States by President Benjamin Harrison.

March 24 — In *Chicago, Milwaukee, and St. Paul Railroad Company v. Minnesota,* 134 U.S. 418, the Court strikes down a Minnesota statute of 1887, which had established a state commission with the power to fix railroad and warehouse rates without having to appeal to the courts for review; such act violates the Fourteenth Amendment's due process clause. This decision opens the door to judicial review of rates set by state regulatory commissions.

April 14 — The Court, in *In re Neagle,* 135 U.S. 1, sustains the decision of a Federal Circuit Court which had ruled that the bodyguard of a federal official who kills an individual who is believed to be threatening the life of that official cannot be tried for murder in a state court because the bodyguard was carrying out his duty "in pursuance of a law of the United States." The public official in this case was Supreme Court Justice Stephen J. Field, who had been attacked in a California restaurant, and whose bodyguard, David Neagle, had killed the attacker on the spot.

April 28 — In *Leisy v. Hardin,* 135 U.S. 100, Chief Justice Melville W. Fuller introduces the concept of the "unbroken package"; in this instance, liquor shipped into a state in its original containers. The Court holds that these are items in interstate commerce and therefore exempt from a state prohibition law despite the absence of specific congressional legislation.

May 2 — The Territory of Oklahoma is created by congressional enactment.

May 19 — The Court rules in *McGahey v. Virginia,* 135 U.S. 662, that state laws authorizing the refinancing, reducing, or extinguishing of the original obligations of state bonds impairs the contracts represented in the bonds in violation of the federal Constitution's contract clause.

In *The Late Corporation of the Church of Jesus Christ of Latter-Day Saints v. United States,* 136 U.S. 1, also known as the *Mormon Church* case, the Court rules that Mormon property and buildings should be used for the benefit of the common schools in the Utah Territory. Congress had previously revoked the Mormon Church's charter and ordered the disposal of its lands, properties, and structures as a result of the Church's refusal to give up the practice of polygamy.

The Court invalidates a San Francisco license tax that had been levied upon a local ticket agency of a Chicago to New York railroad line on the ground that it is an unnecessary state burden on interstate commerce. The local agency's primary function was to solicit passengers traveling from California to New York via Chicago. The Court reasons, therefore, that the ticket office is engaged in interstate commerce and is not subject to state regulations or taxes. This case, *McCall v. California,* 136 U.S. 104, sets a precedent for the judicial negation of state taxation of agencies engaged in interstate commerce.

The Court in *Norfolk and Western Railway Company v. Pennsylvania,* 136 U.S. 114, strikes down a state tax placed upon interstate carriers on the ground that it is an unwarranted restraint upon interstate commerce, and thus violates the commerce clause of the Constitution.

In *Hans v. Louisiana,* 134 U.S. 1, the Court rules that a state cannot be sued in a federal Circuit Court by one of its citizens upon a suggestion that the case is one that arises under the laws or the Constitution of the United States.

The Court, in *Minnesota v. Barber,* 136 U.S. 313, holds unconstitutional a Minnesota statute which makes it illegal to offer for sale any meat other than that taken from animals passed by Minnesota inspectors within twenty-four hours of slaughter. The Court believes that the law patently discriminates against outside of state meat products and places an undue burden upon interstate commerce.

June 16 — The first Madison Square Garden opens in New York City. It is designed by the architect Stanford White.

June 27 — Congress passes the Dependent Pensions Act granting pensions to Union veterans with at least 90 days of service, who are for any reason disabled and unable to earn a living. The initial appropriation for the pensions is $81,000,000.

July 1 — The director of the census announces that a discernible frontier line in the West no longer exists.

July 2 The Force Bill providing for the supervision of federal elections in the South by the national government is passed by the House of Representatives. Its objective is to protect black voters in the Southern states against measures which would deprive them of their vote. It is subsequently defeated in the Senate.

Congress passes the Sherman Anti-Trust Act sponsored by Senators George F. Hoar (Massachusetts), George F. Edmunds (Vermont), and John Sherman (Ohio). The act declares that "every contract, combination in the form of a trust or otherwise, or conspiracy, in restraint of trade or commerce among the several states, or with foreign nations" is illegal. The attorney general of the United States is empowered to bring suits in circuit courts against violators of the statute. Unfortunately, the act's wording is too vague to make it totally effective, and between 1890 and 1901, only eighteen antitrust suits are initiated by the federal government under the Sherman Anti-Trust Act; four of these were directed against labor unions.

July 3 Idaho is admitted to the Union.

July 10 Wyoming is admitted to the Union.

July 14 Congress passes the Sherman Silver Purchase Act authorizing the United States Treasury to make monthly purchases of silver amounting to 4.5 million ounces, and to issue silver certificates, redeemable in gold, as currency.

October 1 Congress enacts the McKinley Tariff sponsored by Congressman William McKinley (Ohio). This new tariff raises duties to an average of about fifty percent, an all-time high up to this time in American history.

October 13 Justice Samuel F. Miller (Iowa) dies after serving on the Supreme Court for twenty-eight years. Appointed by President Abraham Lincoln on July 16, 1862, Miller is usually considered one of the greatest Justices in the history of the Court.

November 4 In the mid-year elections, the Democrats gain control of the House of Representatives, but the Republicans narrowly retain control of the Senate. The unpopularity of the McKinley Tariff is blamed for the tremendous gains achieved by the Democratic party.

December — Meeting in Ocala, Florida, a number of farmer organizations issue a petition of grievances directed against the Harrison administration and the so-called billion-dollar Congress.

December 29 — Henry Billings Brown (Michigan) is appointed to the Supreme Court by President Harrison to replace Justice Miller.

The Ghost Dance War in the Black Hills of South Dakota comes to an end with the Indian massacre at the Battle of Wounded Knee. The massacre ends all effective Sioux resistance to the encroachment of white settlers into their lands.

1891

January 19 — According to the Court in *Brimmer v. Rebman,* 138 U.S. 78, the principle established in *Minnesota v. Barber* (1890) applies to a Virginia statute concerned with the sale and inspection of meat products.

February — Dr. James Naismith, a physical education professor at Springfield College, invents the game of basketball to give his classes something to do during the long winter months in Massachusetts.

March 3 — The Circuit Court of Appeals Act is passed by Congress. The first important reform in the federal judicial system since it was created, the act grants review power to intermediate appellate courts, established by the statute, over all trial court decisions. Only those cases designated by law are entitled to direct review by the Supreme Court.

Congress repeals the Preemption and Timber Culture acts.

The International Copyright Law is enacted by Congress.

The Forest Reserve Act is passed by Congress. It is a conservation measure authorizing the President to set aside any part of the public domain as national forest reserves.

May 25

In *In re Rahrer,* 140 U.S. 545, the Court validates an 1890 congressional statute making interstate shipments of alcoholic beverages subject to state prohibition regulations. This decision modifies Chief Justice Melville W. Fuller's "unbroken package" dictum issued in *Leisy v. Hardin* (1890).

In the case of *In re Ross,* 140 U.S. 453, the Court upholds the constitutional power of Congress to create consular courts overseas having extraterritorial jurisdiction over Americans residing on foreign soil.

In *Pullman Palace Car Company v. Pennsylvania,* 141 U.S. 18, the Court substantially changes the doctrine established in *Norfolk and Western v. Pennsylvania* (1890), when it attempts to create some acceptable method of state taxation to apply to interstate railroads.

In *Crutcher v. Kentucky,* 141 U.S. 47, the Court holds that interstate express lines are not subject to a rigid state license law since the statute infringes upon the congressional commerce power.

October 16

A mob in Valparaiso, Chile, attacks a group of American sailors on shore leave, killing two, after the United States government angered the rebel Congressionalist party in Chile by seizing a Chilean ship that the Congressionalists had sent to San Diego, California in early 1891, in order to purchase arms. During the following year, the Chilean government officially apologizes and pays a $75,000 indemnity to the United States.

1892

January 1 — Ellis Island in New York Harbor is officially opened as the nation's primary immigrant depot.

January 11 — In *Counselman v. Hitchcock,* 142 U.S. 547, the Court holds that testimony could be compelled in the face of the Fifth Amendment guarantee only by granting a witness "transactional immunity"; that is, immunity from subsequent prosecution for any offense thus disclosed. The government could later develop a case independent of the witness's testimony.

January 22 — Justice Joseph P. Bradley (New Jersey) dies. He had been appointed by President Ulysses S. Grant on March 21, 1870, and served for twenty-two years on the Court. Bradley will always be remembered as the man who cast the deciding vote at the specially convened Electoral Commission which decided the disputed election of 1876, in favor of Rutherford B. Hayes (Ohio).

February 22 — The People's or Populist party of the United States of America is founded at St. Louis, Missouri, when representatives of the National Alliance, the Northern Alliance, the Knights of Labor, Prohibition party members, and representatives of the Greenback party assembled. The origins of this new party dated back to May 18, 1891, when a national convention of farmers and other associations met in Cincinnati, Ohio, and conceived the idea for the formation of a third party.

February 28 — In *Field v. Clark,* 143 U.S. 649, the Court gives formal recognition to Congress's right to delegate power to the executive. Congressional procedure concerned with the enactment of legislation is declared a "political question" outside the jurisdiction of the Court.

February 29 — The United States and Great Britain settle their differences over sealing rights in the Bering Sea when Secretary James G. Blaine and the British Foreign secretary, Lord Salisbury, sign an arbitration treaty.

In a landmark case, *Budd v. New York,* 143 U.S. 517,

	the Court affirms the public interest doctrine which had been established in the *Granger* case of *Munn v. Illinois,* 94 U.S. 113. A "practical" as well as a legal monopoly could be endowed with a public interest and thus be subject to regulation.
March	The Ohio Supreme Court orders the Standard Oil Trust, organized in 1879, to be dissolved.
March 21	Charles H. Aldrich is appointed solicitor general of the United States by President Benjamin Harrison.
April 4	The Court rules in *Logan v. United States,* 144 U.S. 263, that suspects in the custody of United States officers have to be protected from violence, and that any attempt to seize them or harm them would be considered a conspiracy against government authority and would be an indictable offense.
April 12	The United States pays an indemnity of $25,000 to the government of Italy as a result of a mob lynching of three Italian nationals in New Orleans. The murdered Italians had been acquitted in connection with the slaying of a New Orleans police chief who had been investigating the activities of the secret Black Hand (Mafia) Society.
May 5	Congress passes the Chinese Exclusion Act to halt the importation of cheap coolie labor. The origins of this measure dates back to 1862, and between 1882 and 1904, nine different laws concerned with this problem were enacted.
June 10	The Republican National Nominating Convention, meeting in Minneapolis, Minnesota, nominates Harrison (Indiana) for President and Whitelaw Reid (New York) for Vice-President.
June 21	The Democratic National Nominating Convention meets in Chicago and nominates Grover Cleveland (New York) for the presidency and Adlai E. Stevenson (Illinois) for Vice-President.
July 2	The Populist National Nominating Convention, meet-

ing in Omaha, Nebraska, nominates James B. Weaver (Iowa) for President and James G. Field (Virginia) for Vice-President. On July 4, the convention adopts the Omaha Platform calling for the free and unlimited coinage of silver at the legal ratio of 16 to 1. Among the other planks on the platform were a graduated income tax; a subtreasury plan of loans to farmers; government ownership of railroad, telegraph, and telephone lines; an eight-hour day for labor; and the restriction of immigration.

July 6 — The Homestead Massacre takes place at the Carnegie Steel Plant at Homestead, Pennsylvania. During a strike workers fire on Pinkerton detectives who had been brought in to break the strike by the company's manager, Henry Clay Frick. Three detectives and ten strikers are killed in the ensuing melee.

July 11 — During a strike at the Coeur d'Alene silver mines in Idaho, fighting breaks out between striking miners and strikebreakers. Federal troops are brought in on July 14, to quell the disorders.

July 26 — George Shiras, Jr. (Pennsylvania) is appointed to the Supreme Court by Harrison to replace Justice Bradley. Shiras would serve on the Court for eleven years and is chiefly remembered as the Justice who switched his vote in the rehearing of the Income Tax case in 1895.

September 8 — James J. "Gentleman Jim" Corbett knocks out John L. Sullivan in the twenty-first round in New Orleans to win the heavyweight boxing championship of the world.

October 17 — The Court, in *McPherson v. Blacker,* 146 U.S. 1, declares the selection of presidential electors an exclusive prerogative of a state, when it validates a Michigan law providing for district rather than statewide election of electors.

November 8 — Cleveland regains the presidency by defeating Harrison by an electoral vote of 277 to 145 and by a popular vote of 5,555,426 to 5,182,690. The Populist party candidate, James B. Weaver, garners 22 electoral votes and more than a million popular votes. The unpopularity of the Harrison administration's policies also allow the Democrats to gain control of both houses of Congress.

1893

January 16 — Led by Sanford B. Dole, American sugar planters in Hawaii revolt against Queen Lydia Liliuokalani to facilitate the annexation of the Hawaiian Islands to the United States. The American minister to Hawaii, John L. Stevens, favoring annexation, orders United States marines landed, recognizes the revolutionary government, raises the American flag, and signs a treaty of annexation with the planter government on February 14.

January 23 — Justice Lucius Quintus Cincinnatus Lamar (Georgia) dies. He had served on the Supreme Court for only five years.

February 9 — Congress passes the District of Columbia Court of Appeals Act which establishes a separate intermediate trial court within the district.

February 15 — Outgoing President Benjamin Harrison presents the Hawaiian annexation treaty before the Senate. However, the Senate fails to act on the treaty before Harrison leaves office.

February 18 — Howell E. Jackson (Tennessee) is appointed to the Supreme Court by Harrison to replace Justice Lamar. He was to serve for only two years on the Court.

March 4 — Grover Cleveland is inaugurated the twenty-fourth President of the United States.

March 6 — Richard Olney is appointed attorney general of the United States by President Cleveland.

March 9 — President Cleveland withdraws the Hawaiian Annexation Treaty from the Senate.

March 27 — The Court, in *Monogahela Naval Company v. United*

States, 148 U.S. 312, rules that the Monogahela Naval Company deserves "reasonable" compensation from the federal government because the government had appropriated certain facilities constructed by the company on Pennsylvania's navigable waters. The Court delcares that in this particular case, it rather than Congress has the authority to judge "reasonableness."

March 30 Thomas F. Bayard is confirmed by the Senate as ambassador to Great Britain, the first American to hold that rank.

April 3 In *Virginia v. Tennessee,* 148 U.S. 503, the Court rules that interstate agreements require Congressional consent, but that when Congress accepts an agreement among the states, congressional consent is implied.

May 1 The Chicago World's Fair, known as the World's Columbian Exposition, opens.

May 5 The Panic of 1893 begins as security prices on the New York Stock Exchange suddenly drop. Among the primary causes is the continuing agricultural depression, the withdrawal of European investments from American business, and the drain placed upon the government's gold reserve precipitated by the Sherman Silver Purchase Act. The reserve fell from about $190,000,000 in 1891, to less than $100,000,000 by the beginning of 1893. Severe unemployment and a serious depression struck the nation for about four years.

May 15 In *Fong Yue Ting v. United States,* 149 U.S. 698, the Court sustains a federal statute of 1892, requiring all Chinese laborers, then lawfully residing in the United States and entitled to remain, to secure within one year governmental certificates of residency. Failure to do so is deemed a federal offense that could result in deportation.

May 19 In *United States v. Workingmen's Amalgamated Council of New Orleans et al,* 54 Fed. 994, a Federal District Court in Louisiana decides that the Sherman Anti-Trust Act applies to labor unions as well as business corporations, thereby establishing a precedent for

	future decisions in labor disputes.
May 29	Lawrence Maxwell, Jr., is appointed solicitor general of the United States by President Cleveland.
June 6	Governor John P. Altgeld (Illinois) frees three convicted Haymarket Riot (1886) prisoners maintaining that their trial had been unfair.
July 7	Justice Samuel Blatchford (New York) dies. He had been appointed to the Supreme Court by President Chester A. Arthur on March 27, 1882 and served on the Court for eleven years.
September 19	President Cleveland nominates William Hornblower (New York) to the Supreme Court to replace Justice Blatchford.
November 1	The Great Northern Railroad reaches Seattle, Washington.
	The Sherman Silver Purchase Act is repealed to stem the drain on the gold reserve. The repeal came after three months of debate in Congress between gold Democrats supported by President Cleveland and silver Democrats backed by farming and mining interests.
December 30	The United States gold reserve drops below $80,000,000.

1894

January	President Cleveland, because of the declining gold reserve, floats a loan of $50,000,000 in gold by means of a government bond issue.
January 15	The Senate, by a vote of 24 to 30, refuses to confirm William Hornblower's (New York) nomination to the Supreme Court. The opposition is led by Senator David Hill (New York) as part of Hill's attempt to control the Democratic party in New York State.

January 22	President Cleveland now nominates Wheeler H. Peckham (New York) to the Supreme Court.
February 8	The Force acts of 1870 and 1871, which allow federal troops to supervise congressional elections in the Southern states, are repealed by Congress.
February 16	The Senate refuses to confirm Cleveland's nomination of Peckham to the Supreme Court by a vote of 32 to 41. Once again, Senator Hill, joined by the junior senator from New York, Edward Murphy, opposes the President's choice because of the Hill-Cleveland patronage struggle. Peckham had shown militant independence of the regular Democratic party organization in New York in opposition to Hill and Murphy.
February 19	To avoid any further embarrassment, President Cleveland breaks from past precedent and appoints Edward D. White (Louisiana) to the so-called New York seat on the Supreme Court. Senators Hill and Murphy do not oppose the appointment and White is easily confirmed. White would serve as an Associate Justice until 1910, when, upon the death of Melville Fuller he would be elevated to Chief Justice by President William Howard Taft. In all, White would serve on the Court for a total of twenty-seven years.
March 6	Congress passes an act making the first Monday in September an annual legal holiday (Labor Day).
March 25-May 1	"Coxey's Army," a mass of unemployed men from the Midwest led by self-styled Populist "General" Jacob Coxey, begins a march on Washington, D.C., to demand relief from the national government. About five hundred of them arrive in the capital on April 30.
April 1	The Immigration Restriction League is organized in Boston. Its primary goal is to strictly curtail foreign immigration by means of a literacy test.
May 14	In *Lawton v. Steele,* 152 U.S. 133, the Court rules that a New York State law designed for the protection of fisheries does not deprive the plaintiff in this case of his property without due process of law. Steele, a New

York State game warden, had destroyed fifteen fish nets used by Lawton for illegal fishing.

In *Brass v. North Dakota ex rel. Stoeser,* 153 U.S. 391, the Court validates both *Munn v. Illinois* (1877) and *Budd v. New York* (1892) by accepting as constitutional the regulation of a business where no practical or legal monopoly existed. The public interest dictum is once again confirmed by the Supreme bench.

The Court holds, in *Mobile and Ohio Railroad v. Tennessee,* 153 U.S. 468, that a state law subjecting the property of a railroad corporation to taxation, where the company's charter contains an exemption clause, is unconstitutional. This decision reveals a very narrow interpretation of tax exemption clauses by the Supreme Court at this time.

May 26 In *Covington and Cincinnati Bridge Company v. Kentucky,* 154 U.S. 204, the Court rules that when a bridge has been built subject to an interstate agreement, neither state involved can unilaterally regulate its fees.

The Court, in *Regan v. Farmers' Loan and Trust Company,* 154 U.S. 362, sustains judicial scrutiny over rate-fixing by a state commission, acting under state law, and gives the courts the right to declare rates fixed by a commission as unreasonable. The decision lays the groundwork for conservative control of the Court for the next ten years.

In *Interstate Commerce Commission v. Brimson,* 154 U.S. 477, the Court rules that while the Interstate Commerce Commission can compel witnesses to testify, the commission does not have the authority to punish those who refuse to appear before the ICC. However, the Court declares that Congress might ask the judiciary to enforce a commission summons.

June A Niagara Falls, New York, plant begins the hydroelectric industry in the United States.

June 21 The Pullman Strike begins. Members of the American Railway Union, led by Eugene V. Debs, strike because of salary cuts imposed by George S. Pullman, the owner of the Pullman Palace Car Company of Chicago. The strike spreads, paralyzing rail transportation throughout the mid- and far-west.

July 2 Attorney General Richard Olney secures an injunction against the Pullman strikers despite the opposition of Governor John P. Altgeld (Illinois).

July 4 President Cleveland sends two thousand federal troops to Chicago to restore order in the wake of the Pullman strike.

July 20 The Pullman Strike ends and Debs is arrested and jailed for contempt of court when he violates the federal injunction brought against the strike. He is later tried in Circuit Court for violating the Sherman Anti-Trust Act by disobeying the federal injunction. He and the union are convicted on the ground that they had unlawfully restrained trade in the face of the antitrust statutes.

August 7 President Cleveland recognizes the American sugar planter government of the Republic of Hawaii.

August 18 Congress passes the Carey Act, a conservation measure which authorizes the President to grant up to a million acres of public lands to states in which the lands are to be used for reclamation purposes.

August 28 Congress passes the Wilson-Gorman Tariff, sponsored by Senator Arthur P. Gorman (Maryland) and Congressman William L. Wilson (West Virginia). The act lowers duties to about forty percent, and one of its clauses contains a modest two percent income tax provision.

September 10 A treaty that imposes a ten-year exclusion period for the emigration of Chinese laborers to the United States is signed by the United States and the Chinese government. This agreement all but ends Chinese immigration to this country.

November 1 President Cleveland negotiates a second gold loan from New York bankers as the nation's gold reserves drops to $50,000,000.

November 6 — In the congressional elections Republicans increase their numbers in the House by 117 seats and in the Senate by 5 seats. The Populists garner 40 percent more votes than they did in the election of 1892.

December 10 — In *Plumley v. Massachusetts,* 155 U.S. 461, the Court validates a state's police powers, when is sustains a Massachusetts act forbidding the sale of artificially colored oleomargarine.

December 16 — The United States Golf Association is organized.

1895

January 21 — In *United States v. E.C. Knight Company,* 156 U.S. 1, the Court makes its first ruling in a case concerning the Sherman Anti-Trust Act as applied to corporations. E.C. Knight Company is charged with a near monopoly of the sugar refining industry in the United States in violation of the antitrust laws. However, the majority decision in this case finds that this corporation, which controls at least ninety-five percent of the nation's sugar supply is not a conspiracy in restraint of interstate commerce. Chief Justice Melville W. Fuller gives a narrow interpretation to the meaning of the word *commerce,* drawing a distinction between commerce and manufacturing and the Court declares that a manufacturing monopoly does not necessarily violate the Sherman Anti-Trust Act. This decision seriously limits the effectiveness of the act, places most monopolies outside the scope of the law, and clearly indicates the Court's conservatism.

January 30 — The nation's gold reserve falls to $41,000,000.

February 7 — Holmes Conrad is appointed solicitor general of the United States by President Cleveland.

February 8 — Because the nation's gold reserve had dropped to $41,000,000, Secretary of the Treasury, John G. Carlisle, enters into an agreement with a banking syndicate headed by J. Pierpont Morgan and August Belmont to purchase 3,500,000 ounces of gold, half of which the syndicate would purchase from outside the United States. This deal produces profits of $2,000,000 for the financiers, who had loaned the government only $62,000,000. As a result, President Cleveland is subjected to much public criticism and is labeled "a tool of Wall Street."

February 20 — The United States proposes the arbitration of the boundary dispute between Venezuela and British Guiana (Great Britain).

February 24 — A revolt against Spanish rule on the island of Cuba breaks out. The American people sympathize with the Cuban people's desire for freedom.

March 5 — Congressman Richard P. Bland (Missouri) and William Jennings Bryan (Nebraska) write the "Appeal of the Silver Democrats." Signed by all Democratic congressmen who favor bimetalism, the document calls for the free and unlimited coinage of silver at the legal ratio of 16 to 1.

March 17 — The National Association of Manufacturers is organized.

March 30 — The Anti-Saloon League of America is founded.

April 8 — The *Income Tax* case, *Pollock v. Farmers' Loan and Trust Company,* 157 U.S. 429, is heard. This case involves the constitutionality of the income tax clauses of the Wilson-Gorman Tariff of 1894. In the first hearing of the case the Court, by a 6-2 decision, strikes down one section of the tax clause which had placed a tax on income from real estate and municipal bonds. The Court views this type of levy as a direct tax which, in order to be considered constitutional, had to be apportioned among the states. On the question of the constitutionality of the income tax itself, the Court divides, 4-4 (Justice Howell E. Jackson is ill and does not participate). Since no decision resulted on the issue of whether the income tax as a whole was constitutional or not, a rehearing of the case is scheduled. The rehearing would prove to be one of the most controversial cases of the Fuller Court.

April 29 — In *Gulf, Colorado, etc. Railroad Company v. Hefley,* 158 U.S. 98, the Court rules that the Interstate Commerce Act takes precedence over state laws concerned with the same subject. State laws, the Court declares, are limited to intrastate commerce.

May — The first United States Open Golf Championship is played at Newport, Rhode Island.

May 20 — Upon rescheduling the Income Tax case and hearing reargument on the constitutional issue, the Court by a 5-4 majority declares the entire tax law unconstitutional on the ground that taxes on personal property are direct taxes and subject to apportionment among the states. In this rehearing, *Pollock v. Farmers' Loan and Trust Company,* 158 U.S. 601, Justice George Shiras, Jr., allegedly shifts his vote favoring the income tax in the original hearing of the case to opposition in the rehearing. The Court kills the income tax for the time being and necessitates the passage of the Sixteenth Amendment to the Constitution authorizing an income tax.

May 23 — New York City combines several libraries to found the New York Public Library.

May 27 — In *In re Debs,* 158 U.S. 564, the Court sustains the conviction of Eugene V. Debs for his actions in the Pullman Strike of 1894. The Court refuses to accept Debs's writ of habeus corpus holding that the use of a federal injunction to prevent forcible interference with the mails or interstate commerce is a warranted exercise of governmental power. Justice David J. Brewer's opinion asserts, "The entire strength of the nation may be used to enforce in any part of the land the full and free exercise of all national powers and the security of all rights entrusted by the Constitution to its care."

June 8 — Judson Harmon is appointed attorney general of the United States by President Cleveland.

July 20	Secretary of State Richard Olney accuses Great Britain of violating the Monroe Doctrine in regard to settlement of the Venezuela Boundary dispute, and issues what is known as the Olney Doctrine. "Today the United States is practically sovereign on this continent, and its fiat is law."
August 8	Justice Jackson dies.
September 8	Long-distance telephone lines are established between New York and Chicago.
November 26	Prime Minister Salisbury rejects the Olney Doctrine stating that the Monroe Doctrine does not apply to the Venezuelan Boundary dispute; he rejects as well the United States's offer of arbitration. Angry feelings begin to develop on both sides of the Atlantic.
December 9	Rufus W. Peckham (New York) is appointed to the Supreme Court of the United States by President Cleveland to replace Justice Jackson. This time, Senator David Hill (New York) does not object to the appointment and Peckham is confirmed without dissent. He would serve on the Court for fourteen years.
December 17	President Cleveland sends a chauvinistic message to Congress requesting the appointment of an independent American commission to draw the demarcation line in the Venezuelan Boundary dispute. Great Britain eventually backs down and signs a treaty of arbitration with Venezuela on February 2, 1897.

1896

January 4	The Utah Territory is admitted to the Union.
January 6	President Cleveland floats another loan for $100,000,000 as the gold reserve dips once again to $79,000,000. This time, however, the loan comes from public subscription.
February	Rural Free Delivery (RFD) is established.

February 10 — Suppression of the Cuban revolt is assigned to General Valeriano "Butcher" Weyler, who establishes concentration camps where Cubans are indiscriminately incarcerated. The American people, who had already expressed sympathy for the Cuban cause are infuriated by this callous action by the Spanish government.

February 28 — Concurrent resolutions recognizing Cuban belligerency are passed by the Senate and the House, but President Cleveland refuses to follow suit. The Yellow Press in New York City led by William Randolph Hearst's New York *Journal* and Joseph Pulitzer's New York *World,* fan American sympathy for the Cuban rebels.

March 2 — In *Greer v. Connecticut,* 161 U.S. 519, the Court rules that since Congress has not exercised its preemptive authority, a state game bird conservation act is constitutional even though it affects interstate commerce.

March 16 — Representative Henry Cabot Lodge (Massachusetts) urges Congress to adopt a literacy test for all immigrants.

March 23 — The Court, in *Brown v. Walker,* 161 U.S. 591, validates the Interstate Commerce Act's immunity provision amendment.

March 30 — In *Cincinnati, New Orleans, and Texas Pacific Railway Company v. Interstate Commerce Commission,* 162 U.S. 184, the Court strips the Interstate Commerce Commission of all positive rate-fixing power, but declares that the commission could regulate an intrastate carrier that was engaged in carrying interstate traffic.

April 13 — In *Gibson v. Mississippi,* 162 U.S. 565, the Court invalidates a state act denying blacks the right to serve on juries exclusively on the basis of race. However, the Court also declares that a state could prohibit persons from jury duty for other reasons. Cases of this type, moreover, are not eligible for appeal in a federal court.

April 22 — The greatest pacer of all time, Dan Patch, is foaled at Shebanse, Indiana.

April 23 — The first motion picture commercially exhibited is shown at Koster and Bial's Music Hall in New York City.

May 18 — In another *Chinese Exclusion* case, *Wong Wing v. United States,* 163 U.S. 228, the Court delcares one section of the Chinese Exclusion Act of 1892 unconstitutional. This section of the act had subjected violators of the statute to a year of hard labor before deportation. A unanimous Court finds that Congress could not add to the exclusion and expulsion punishment of Chinese persons by imprisonment at hard labor without a jury trial. The Court holds that this constituted "infamous punishment."

In one of the most celebrated cases of the Fuller Court, *Plessy v. Ferguson,* 163 U.S. 537, the majority by a vote of 7 to 1 sustains a Louisiana law requiring segregated railroad facilities for blacks and whites on the ground that "separate but equal" accommodations do not constitute discrimination and that blacks were not deprived of equal protection under the Fourteenth Amendment. The decision states that the statute in question is a "reasonable regulation" and that "established usages, customs, and traditions, as well as the preservation of public peace and good order had to be considered in declaring the constitutionality of the Louisiana law." Justice John Marshall Harlan in a ringing dissent makes the famous remark, "Our Constitution is color-blind." The Harlan position is revived in the desegregation cases beginning in 1953, especially in *Brown v. Board of Education of Topeka* (1954). Mr. Justice Harlan (Kentucky) is appointed to the Supreme Court on November 29, 1877, by President Rutherford B. Hayes and serves a total of thirty-four years, the second longest tenure of any Supreme Court Justice.

May 25 — The Court rules, in *United States v. Perkins,* 163 U.S. 625, that Congress possesses implicit control over the removal of inferior officers whose appointment it had lodged with department heads.

June 16 — The Republican National Nominating Convention

meeting in St. Louis, nominates William McKinley (Ohio) for President and Garret A. Hobart (New Jersey) for Vice-President. Its platform defends the gold standard and the protective tariff. Senator Henry M. Teller (Colorado) leads the "Silver Republicans" out of the convention, and on July 22, they hold their own nominating convention which endorses the Democratic party's candidates and platform.

July 7 — The Democratic National Convention meets in Chicago and draws up a platform endorsing free silver at the legal ratio of 16 to 1, an income tax, and downward tariff reform. On July 8, William Jennings Bryan (Nebraska) makes his famous "Cross of Gold" speech. His rhetoric, "You shall not press down upon the brow of labor this crown of thorns; you shall not crucify mankind upon a cross of gold," so sways the delegates that as a result of his oratory, they nominate the thirty-six-year-old Nebraskan for the presidency. Arthur Sewall, a conservative banker from Maine, is given second place on the ticket. "Gold Democrats," opposing the platform, form the National Democratic party, which meets in September and nominates its own candidates, John M. Palmer (Illinois) for President and Simon B. Buckner (Kentucky) for Vice-President.

July 22 — The Populist National Nominating Convention meets in St. Louis and, not wishing to split the silverite vote, endorses Bryan's candidacy. However, the convention selects one of their own, Thomas E. Watson (Georgia) for Vice-President. The platform that they write is essentially that of the Democrats, but contains a number of planks taken from their "Omaha Platform" of 1892.

August 16 — The Klondike gold rush in Canada begins. The discoveries are so vast that they increase the gold supply in the United States and the nation's gold reserve is rescued. An inflationary trend sets into the economy and finally relieves the depression in existence since 1892.

November 3 — Colorado and Idaho grant women the right to vote in state elections.

Despite much support from reform groups in the country and an extremely energetic campaign which takes him some 18,000 miles across the width and breadth of the nation, Bryan is defeated by McKinley for the presidency, 271 electoral votes to 176. The popular vote is 7,102,246 for McKinley to Bryan's 6,492,559. McKinley's campaign manager, Marcus A. Hanna, a millionare Ohio industrialist, raises a vast campaign fund of more than $3,000,000 from fellow businessmen who, in turn, hint to their employees that if Bryan is elected they might have to shut down their companies.

November 30 — In *Fallbrook Irrigation District v. Bradley,* 164 U.S. 112, the Court declares unconstitutional a California law which had permitted groups of California landowners living in the same area to form irrigation districts which, in turn, had the power to place assessments upon all landowners in the district.

The Court, in *Missouri Pacific Railway Company v. Nebraska,* 164 U.S. 403, strikes down a statute which had given a state commission the power to force a railroad to construct additional grain elevators along its tracks on similar terms as it had done for its best customers.

1897

January 18 — In *Gulf, Colorado and Santa Fe Railway Company v. Ellis,* 165 U.S. 150, the Court declares unconstitutional a Texas statute requiring railroads to pay court costs and attorney's fees for plaintiffs who successfully wage legal battles against the railroads.

January 30 — Congress passes the Indian Liquor Sales Prohibition Act, forbidding the sale of intoxicating beverages to Indians living on government supervised reservation land. The constitutionaltiy of the law is later challenged in 1905, and in 1916.

February 15 — The Library of Congress opens in a new building constructed at the cost of $6,000,000.

March 1 In *Allgeyer v. Louisiana,* 165 U.S. 578, the Court strikes down a Louisiana law which forbids non-state insurance companies from operating in Louisiana if they had not complied with the laws of the state. The Court declares that the law infringes upon substantive due process. "Freedom of contract" under the Fourteenth Amendment is given its broadest interpretation up to that time by this case.

The Court, in *Chicago, Burlington, and Quincy Railroad v. Chicago,* 166 U.S. 226, sustains an Illinois law requiring carriers to pay for the construction of crossing facilities and the services of flagmen along its tracks, as a constitutional use of a state's police powers.

March 2 On the eve of his last days in office, Cleveland vetoes a Literacy Test Bill whose purpose was to severely restrict foreign immigration.

March 4 William McKinley is inaugurated the twenty-fifth President of the United States.

March 5 Joseph McKenna (California) is appointed attorney general of the United States by President McKinley.

March 17 Bob Fitzsimmons becomes heavyweight boxing champion of the world when he knocks out James J. Corbett in the fourteenth round in Carson City, Nevada.

March 22 In *United States v. Trans-Missouri Freight Association,* 166 U.S. 290, the Court by a 5-4 majority holds that an association of 18 railroads formed to fix rates violated the Sherman Anti-Trust Act. The attorney representing the railroads argues a "rule of reason" to distinguish between reasonable and unreasonable restraints of trade, but the Court rejects his argument that only unreasonable combinations are illegal. However, the principle introduced by the counsel for the defense is, several years later, enunciated by Justice Edward D. White in the *Standard Oil and Tobacco Trust* cases heard in 1911.

April 27 Grant's Tomb in New York City is opened and

dedicated by President McKinley.

May 25 — The Court once again denies the Interstate Commerce Commission rate-fixing powers in *Interstate Commerce Commission v. Cincinnati, New Orleans, and Texas Pacific Railway Company,* 167 U.S. 479, by ruling that a quasi-legislative function cannot be granted to an administrative body.

June 8 — The Tea Inspection Act is passed by Congress. This statute gives the secretary of the treasury the power to appoint a Board of Tea Inspectors who are authorized to recommend certain standards in tea-grading, and to inspect and grade all imported tea.

July 1 — John K. Richards is appointed solicitor general of the United States by President McKinley.

July 7 — The Dingley Tariff is passed by Congress raising duties to an all-time high of fifty-seven percent.

September 1 — Boston opens the first underground subway system in the United States.

November 18 — In *Interstate Commerce Commission v. Alabama Midlands Railway Company,* 168 U.S. 144, the Court substantially modifies the Interstate Commerce Act's "long haul-short haul" clause, originally discussed in *Wabash, St. Louis, and Pacific Railway Company v. Illinois* (1886). The Court also declares its right of judicial review over the Interstate Commerce Commission's findings, and as a result, the commission's rate-fixing powers are severely restricted.

November 25 — General Valeriano "Butcher" Weyler is recalled from Cuba by a new liberal ministery in Spain. The Spanish government's concentration camp policies are substantially changed, thereby mollifying American sentiments.

December 1 — Justice Stephen J. Field (California) retires after more than thirty-four years on the bench, then the longest tenure in the history of the Supreme Court. Field had been appointed by President Lincoln on March 10,

1863. This arch-conservative dies two years later on April 9, 1899.

1898

January 21 — Joseph McKenna (California) is appointed to the Supreme Court by President McKinley to replace Justice Stephen J. Field (California). Probably the least qualified and least prepared Justice in the history of the Supreme Court, this old friend of the President serves on the bench for twenty-seven years until his death on November 21, 1926.

January 25 — John W. Griggs is appointed attorney general of the United States by President McKinley.

February 8 — The De Lome Letter written by the Spanish minister to the United States, Dupuy de Lome, is published in William Randolph Hearst's New York *Journal.* It had been stolen from a Havana, Cuba, post office and called President McKinley "a spineless politician interested only in the plaudits of the crowd."

February 15 — The United States battleship *Maine,* anchored in Havana Harbor, blows up with a loss of 260 American lives. America's Yellow Press blames the explosion on the Spanish although conclusive proof is lacking. Remember the Maine becomes a popular slogan as war fever runs high.

February 25 — Commodore George Dewey, commander of the United States Pacific fleet, is ordered by the assistant secretary of the navy, Theodore Roosevelt, to attack and capture the Spanish-owned Philippine Islands in the event that war breaks out with Spain.

February 28 — In *Holden v. Hardy,* 169 U.S. 366, the Court by a vote of 7 to 2, sustains an 1896 Utah law limiting maximum working hours for miners. The Court holds that this statute is a reasonable exercise of the state's police powers, and does not violate the Fourteenth Amendment. Furthermore, the Court states, the Utah act does not abridge the privileges or immunities of United

States citizens, and does not deprive either the employer or the laborer of his property without due process of law. Uncharacteristically, the normally conservative Fuller Court declares that freedom of contract has to be qualified when health and safety principles are involved.

March 7 The Court, in *Smyth v. Ames,* 169 U.S. 466, strikes down a Nebraska statute of 1893, which fixes railroad rates in the state on the ground that it violates the due process clause of the Fourteenth Amendment. The majority opinion states that in order to be "reasonable," the rates established by the law had to assure the companies involved a "fair return" on a "fair value" of the properties involved. The rule is so vague that it places virtually all rate-making by state commissions under the determination of the courts to insure the equity of any disputed rate. This decision further negates the principle established in *Munn v. Illinois* (1877).

March 27 In a formal note to the Spanish government, President McKinley proposes that Spain establish an armistice in Cuba, abandon her concentration camp policies, and grant Cuba independence. While the Spanish accept the first two conditions, they adamantly reject the last point.

March 28 The Court holds in *United States v. Wong Kim Ark,* 169 U.S. 649, that American-born children of Chinese nationals who have a permanent residence in the United States and who are not employed in any official diplomatic capacity for the emperor of China are American citizens by virtue of the Fourteenth Amendment's citizenship clause. The Court declares that Wong Kim Ark had become a citizen of the United States at birth. "All persons born or naturalized in the United States and subject to the jurisdiction thereof, are citizens of the United States and of the state wherein they reside."

April 11 President McKinley sends a war message to Congress requesting American intervention in Cuba in order to restore and establish peace in that country. McKinley is

	undoubtedly influenced by the warlike sentiment in the nation and asks for a declaration of war on rather spurious grounds.
April 18	By a 6 to 3 vote, the Court in *Hawkes v. New York,* 170 U.S. 189, rules that a New York statute does not violate the constitutional prohibition against bills of attainder by denying convicted criminals their right to obtain a professional license in the state.
April 19	In a joint resolution, Congress recognizes the independence of Cuba, empowers the President to use force to expel the Spanish from the island, and adopts an amendment proposed by Senator Henry M. Teller (Colorado) renouncing any American intention to annex Cuba.
April 20	President McKinley signs the joint resolution drafted by Congress concerning Cuban independence.
April 24	Spain officially declares war against the United States.
April 25	The United States retaliates and issues a declaration of war against Spain.
	In *Williams v. Mississippi,* 170 U.S. 213, the Court rules that a Mississippi law that stipulates that local officials are given the authority to require voters to read and interpret any part of the Constitution of the United States is a valid use of state regulation of local elections. In the same case, the majority sustains the payment of a poll tax as a prerequisite for the franchise.
	The Court rules in *Galveston, Harrisburg, etc. Railroad Company v. Texas,* 170 U.S. 226, that a state legislature can legally change a land grant clause in a state granted railroad charter, if the railroad has not undertaken any developments or improvements on the land in question. The Court declares that such alteration is not an impairment of the original contract under these circumstances.
May 1	Having departed Hong Kong on April 27, Commodore Dewey's Pacific fleet sails into Manila Bay and destroys

the Spanish fleet consisting of 10 ships that are anchored there. More than 380 Spanish sailors are killed in this first battle in the Philippine Islands; no American casualties are sustained and no American ships lost.

May 12 The state of Louisiana adopts a new constitution which contains several clauses disenfranchising its black citizens by means of a "grandfather clause" as well as by property and literacy tests.

May 19 A Spanish fleet commanded by Admiral Pascual Cervera sails from Spain, eludes the American blockade of Santiago de Cuba, and drops anchor in that city's harbor.

May 23 In *Schollenberger v. Pennsylvania,* 171 U.S. 1, the Court reverses the decision in *Plumley v. Massachusetts* (1894), when it resurrects Chief Justice Melville W. Fuller's "original package" principle. It rules that a state cannot forbid the importation and sale of artifically colored oleomargarine.

June 1 The Erdman or Railroad Labor Disputes Act is passed by Congress. It establishes a mediation service composed of the Interstate Commerce Commission chairman and the commissioner of the Bureau of labor. The act represents a significant breakthrough for the federal government as it develops machinery for the arbitration of disputes between labor and management in the railroad industry. One important part of the act provides for the outlawing of "yellow dog" contracts, which railroad employers had used in their attempts to break the American Railway Union. These contracts specify that prospective railroad employees, as a condition of employment, would not join a labor union.

June 14 American military forces under General William R. Shafter, leave Tampa, Florida, for Cuba. These units land at Santiago de Cuba on June 22-26.

July 1 In order to provide the Supreme Court of the United States with some relief from the massive volume of appeals from bankruptcy cases, Congress passes the

Uniform Bankruptcy Act, which reasserts exclusive original jurisidction in the federal circuit courts, with appeal to the newly created intermediate courts. Final review would go to the Supreme Court only in cases where the Court decides to issue writs of certiorari.

The land battle of Santiago de Cuba begins when American military contingents occupy the high ground outside of the city. In engagements at El Caney and San Juan Hill, a volunteer cavalry unit known as the Rough Riders under the command of Colonel Theodore Roosevelt participate.

July 3 — In the naval battle of Santiago de Cuba, Admiral William T. Sampson destroys the Spanish fleet attempting to escape from Santiago Harbor. The Spanish suffer casualties when 474 men are killed while the Americans only lose one sailor.

July 4 — Wake Island in the South Pacific is captured by an American naval squadron on its way to the Philippine Islands. It is formally occupied by the United States in 1900.

July 7 — President McKinley signs the Hawaiian Annexation Treaty which had been negotiated with the Hawaiian-American sugar planter government on June 16, 1897. Congress, on the same day, approves the treaty by a joint resolution.

July 17 — Fighting in Santiago de Cuba ends as American military forces occupy the city.

July 25 — American military forces under General Nelson A. Miles occupy the Spanish-owned island of Puerto Rico in an almost bloodless action.

August 13 — United States troops aided by Philippine insurrectionists under Emilio Aguinaldo capture the city of Manila.

October 1 — A peace conference between the United States and Spain opens in Paris. On October 25, President McKinley instructs the American delegation at the conference to demand the cession of the Philippines to the United States.

December 10 — The Treaty of Paris ending the Spanish-American War is signed. By its terms, the United States receives the Philippine Islands, Puerto Rico, and Guam, and, at the same time, relinquishes all claims to Cuba. Spain is awarded $20,000,000 as compensation for the Philippines and the United States has acquired a colonial empire.

December 12 — In *Blake v. McClung,* 172 U.S. 239, corporations are denied the rights of citizenship, when the Court by a 7 to 2 vote makes a distinction between the words persons and citizens in the Fourteenth Amendment. As a result of this decision, it is now possible to sue foreign based companies that maintain offices in the United States.

1899

January — A heated debate begins in the Senate over the ratification of the Treaty of Paris. Antiimperialists argue that the creation of an American overseas empire runs contrary to democratic traditions, while expansionists led by Senator Albert Beveridge deplore "hauling down the flag."

February 4 — The Filipino Insurrection, led by Emilio Aguinaldo, begins. American forces are unable to subdue the rebels until late 1899, when an American army of 70,000 men are in the field. Sporadic guerrilla attacks continue until 1902, when comparative calm is restored by the American army of occupation.

February 6 — The Senate ratifies the Treaty of Paris by a vote of 57 to 27 although antiimperialists continue to oppose the establishment of an American empire.

February 27 — In *Ohio v. Thomas,* 173 U.S. 276, a unanimous Court strikes down a statute prohibiting the purchase and use of artificially colored oleomargarine in federal institutions within the state as an unconstitutional exercise of state police power.

June 1 — A report issued by the specially appointed Philippine Commission recommends eventual independence for the islands, but also approves American rule until the Filipinos are "ready" for self-government.

June 9 — James J. Jeffries becomes the new heavyweight boxing champion of the world by knocking out Bob Fitzsimmons in the eleventh round.

July 29 — The Permanent Court of International Arbitration is established at the First Hague Conference meeting at the Hague in Holland. Twenty-six nations, including the United States, attend this international convention where a number of problems of international concern, including disarmament, are discussed.

September 6 — Secretary of State John Hay proposes the Open Door policy whereby the other great powers are asked to respect Chinese territorial integrity and to assure commercial equality for all nations by opening their spheres of influence and treaty ports to all countries interested in trading in China. Although the replies of the great powers are vague and somewhat contradictory, Hay announces on March 20, that the Open Door Policy is in effect. The primary reason for this action is the fear that the newly acquired Philippine Islands would be useless as a gateway to the trade of the Asian mainland if the great powers refuse to open their Chinese ports to American commercial and business interests.

December 2 — A second Samoan Treaty, in which Great Britain relinquishes her earlier treaty claims in the islands for concessions elsewhere, is signed by the United States, Great Britain, and Germany. The United States receives the lion's share of the Samoan Islands including the excellent harbor of Pago Pago.

December 4 — In *Addyston Pipe and Steel Company v. United States,* 175 U.S. 211, a unanimous Court declares a scheme to control the market, similar to the one attempted by the Trans-Missouri Freight Association, a violation of the Sherman Anti-Trust Act. Validating the conviction of the owners of the Addyston Pipe and Steel Company restores a measure of credibility to the statute emasculated by the decision in the *E.C. Knight* case of 1895.

In *Bradfield v. Roberts,* 175 U.S. 291, the Court renders its first decision in a case involving the First Amendment's "establishment" clause concerning freedom of religion. By a unanimous vote, the Court sustains a contract entered into by a Washington, D.C., religious order and the District of Columbia Board of Commissioners providing for the construction of a charity clinic, attached to a public hospital in the District, but owned and operated by the religious order. The opinion delcares that this arrangement is not a violation of separation of Church and state.

December 18 — By a unanimous vote, the Court, in *Cumming v. Board of Education,* 175 U.S. 528, validates a state court ruling which reiterates the "separate but equal" doctrine of *Plessy v. Ferguson.* It declares that a school board could not be forced under the Fourteenth Amendment to withhold, from an all-white high school, money appropriated for its maintenance and operation until matching funds are also provided for an all-black high school. It is interesting to note that the opinion of the Court is delivered by Mr. Justice John Marshall Harlan, who had dissented so vigorously only three years earlier in *Plessy.*

December 21 — Standard Oil Company of New Jersey is established by John D. Rockefeller. This giant holding company is eventually dissolved in 1911.

1900

The population of the United States reaches 76,094,000.

January 10 — The National Civic Federation is established in Chicago.

March 14 — The Currency or Gold Standard Act is passed by Congress as a method for developing an efficient national currency. This measure places the United

States firmly on a gold standard, defines the gold content of the dollar, and makes all other forms of money redeemable in gold. It also establishes a gold reserve of $150,000,000.

April 7 — William Howard Taft is named by President McKinley chairman of the United States Philippine Commission; the purpose of this commission is to establish a civilian government in the Islands.

April 12 — Puerto Rico is made an unincorporated Territory of the United States when Congress passes the Foraker Act whereby a civil government is established on the island. Puerto Ricans are made citizens of Puerto Rico but not of the United States. The Dingley Tariff is extended to the island and the President is authorized to appoint a governor-general and council. United States citizenship is granted to Puerto Ricans in 1917.

April 30 — The Hawaiian Islands are granted full territorial status by Congressional enactment. The Navy Department is ordered to administer Guam.

May — The first Davis Cup matches between the United States and Great Britain are played at the Longwood Club in Brookline, Massachusetts.

May 14 — Galveston, Texas, introduces the commission form of municipal government; a commission of experts replaces the traditional mayor-council type of urban administration.

In *Knowlton v. Moore,* 178 U.S. 41, the Court modifies the principle it had established in the Income Tax case of 1895, by ruling that the "requirement of uniformity of indirect taxes was geographic not intrinsic." In a 5-3 decision, the majority sustains the constitutionality of excise taxes levied upon "the incidents of ownership."

June 19 — The Republican National Nominating Convention meeting in Philadelphia renominates William McKinley for President, but turns to Theodore Roosevelt (New York) as its nominee for Vice-President. The platform includes support for the gold standard and endorsement for an American-built and -controlled interoceanic canal; it also praises the administration's foreign policy.

June 20 The Boxer Rebellion in China begins. Aggressive, antiforeign Chinese nationalists wishing to drive all the "foreign devils" out of China, lay seige to the foreign legations in Peking.

July 3 Secretary of State John Hay issues a second Open Door note since he feared that the great powers might not honor their obligations to preserve Chinese territorial integrity in the wake of the Boxer Rebellion.

July 4 The Democratic National Nominating Convention meets in Kansas City and nominates William Jennings Bryan (Nebraska) for the presidency once again. Second place on the ticket goes to Adlai E. Stevenson (Illinois), who had been elected with Cleveland in 1892. The Democratic platform denounces both the Republican administration's imperialist policies and the gold standard. The Populists are divided in their choice of candidates, and as a result gather at two separate conventions. The Fusionists name Bryan as their standard bearer along with Charles A. Towne (Minnesota) for Vice-President. The Anti-Fusionists choose Wharton Barker (Pennsylvania) for President and Ignatius Donnelly (Minnesota) for Vice-President. On March 6, the Social Democratic party is formed at Indianapolis and nominates Eugene V. Debs (Indiana) for the presidency and Job Harriman (California) for Vice-President.

August 6 The so-called First Gentleman's Agreement is reached between the United States and Japan, whereby the Japanese government is to initiate a policy of voluntary emigration restriction.

August 14 A multinational army, which includes contingents of United States armed forces, rescues the foreign legations in Peking thereby causing the collapse of the Boxer Rebellion.

September Dr. Walter Reed is named the head of the United States

Army Yellow Fever Commission. Due to his medical experiments, the incidence of yellow fever is eliminated in the United States, Cuba, and the Panama Canal Zone.

November 6 — McKinley and Roosevelt defeat Bryan and Stevenson, 292 electoral votes to 155. The popular vote is 7,218,491 for the incumbent McKinley and 6, 356,734 for Bryan. The Republicans retain control of both houses of Congress.

November 19 — In *Stearns v. Minnesota,* 179 U.S. 223, the Court holds constitutional a clause in the act admitting Minnesota to the Union, whereby Congress reserved the right to determine subsequently the disposition of federal public lands in the state.

In *Austin v. Tennessee,* 179 U.S. 344, the Court reverses its decision in *Schollenberger v. Pennsylvania* (1898), when, by a 5 to 4 vote, it validates a state law which forbids the importation and sale of cigarettes. By its action, the Court temporarily abandons Chief Justice Melville W. Fuller's "original package" dictum.

1901

February — The American League achieves major league status in the baseball world.

February 15 — Congress passes an act which establishes a licensing system for the use of water power on public lands.

March 2 — The Platt Amendment, sponsored by Senator Orville H. Platt (Connecticut) is passed by Congress. Under its terms, the President is authorized to withdraw American troops from Cuba, as soon as the Cuban government agrees to a series of conditions that virtually make the island-republic a protectorate of the United States. Cuba is not allowed to make any treaties that might threaten her independence; she could not borrow money beyond her ability to repay the loans; the United States is granted permission to intervene in her affairs in order to protect her territorial sovereignty; and she is compelled to sell or lease several naval bases, including Guantánamo, to the United States. The Cubans are forced to incorporate the obnoxious Platt Amendment into their newly drawn constitution on June 12, 1901.

March 4 — William McKinley begins his second term as President of the United States.

April 9 — Philander C. Knox is appointed attorney general of the United States by President McKinley.

April 15 — The United States Steel Corporation is organized by J. Pierpont Morgan and Elbert H. Gary.

May 27 — In the first of the so-called *Insular* cases, *DeLima v. Bidwell,* 182 U.S. 1, the majority rules 5-4 that Puerto Rico ceases to be a foreign nation at the end of the Spanish-American War. As a result, the Court holds that duties could not be placed upon goods imported to the United States from the island without congressional approval. However, the Court also declares that the inhabitants of colonial possessions are not automatically American citizens and hold only those rights extended to them by Congress.

In the second *Insular* case, *Dooley v. United States,* 182 U.S. 222, the Court again by a 4-5 majority rules that products shipped to Puerto Rico from the United States are duty free.

In the third of the *Insular* cases, *Downes v. Bidwell,* 182 U.S. 244, the Court somewhat changes its position when it declares that Puerto Rico is not part of the United States for revenue purposes. In other words, the Constitution does not automatically and immediately extend to the peoples of a newly annexed territory, and that all the rights and privileges of United States citizenship does not necessarily apply to them. The Court emphatically declares that Congress alone might grant such constitutional provisions as it sees fit. "The United States government," the Court states, "has the power to acquire and hold territory without immediately incorporating it into the United States." The three *Insular* cases, therefore, give Congress the sole power to administer the government of such territory. The Court has made it very clear that the Constitution does not necessarily follow the flag.

September 6 — President McKinley is shot by Leon Czolgosz, an anarchist, while attending the Pan American Exposition in Buffalo, New York. He dies on September 14.

September 7 — The Boxer Protocol is announced. It provides a total indemnity of $333,000,000 of which the United States' share is $24,500,000. The United States eventually reduces this to $12,000,000, and remits the entire unpaid balance in 1924.

September 14 — Immediately following McKinley's death, Theodore Roosevelt is sworn in as the twenty-sixth President of the United States.

October 1 — The Five Civilized Indian Tribes are granted United States citizenship.

October 21 — In *Knoxville Iron Company v. Harbison,* 183 U.S. 13, the Court sustains a Tennessee statute permitting company employees to redeem, for cash, coal certificates which they have been paid in lieu of salary. The majority opinion declares that the law does not deny Knoxville Iron Company of its due process under the Fourteenth Amendment.

November 18 — The Hay-Pauncefote Treaty with Great Britian is signed. It abrogates the Clayton-Bulwar Treaty of 1850, and now permits the United States to build, control, and fortify an interoceanic canal across Central America.

November 25 — In *Cotting v. Kansas City Stockyards,* 183 U.S. 79, the Court strikes down a Kansas stockyard regulatory law as a violation of the equal protection clause of the Fourteenth Amendment, since the law is not applicable to all stockyards in the state.

November 27 — The United States Army War College, headed by General Tasker H. Bliss, opens.

December 3	President Roosevelt, in his first annual message to Congress, asks that body to take immediate action in the area of trust regulation.

1902

January 4	The French-owned New Panama Canal Company offers to sell its rights to build an interoceanic canal across the Isthmus of Panama to the United States for $40,000,000.
January 18	The United States Isthmian Canal Commission recommends to Congress a canal route across Panama. It had originally been in favor of a Nicaraguan route, but when the French Canal Company reduces its price, the commission changes its opinion.
January 29	Congress passes a new Chinese Exclusion Act, but no terminal date is specified in this statute.
March 10	Attorney General Philander C. Knox files suit against the Northern Securities Company, a giant holding company, for violation of the antitrust laws.
May 1	The Pan American Exposition opens in St. Louis.
May 12	The Anthracite Coal Strike begins when the United Mine Workers Union walks out demanding higher wages and recognition for their union. Led by their president, John Mitchell, the strikers walk picket lines for more than five months.
May 20	United States military forces are finally withdrawn from Cuba.
June 1	Maryland enacts the nation's first state workmen's compensation law.
June 2	Oregon becomes the first state to adopt the progressive reforms of initiative and referendum.
June 17	Congress passes the Newlands Reclamation Act, also known as the National Reclamation Act. It is spon-

sored by Senator Francis G. Newlands (Nevada), and becomes the nucleus of President Roosevelt's conservation program. Proceeds from public land sales in sixteen western states are reserved for the construction of irrigation projects in those states.

June 28 — By congressional enactment the Spooner Act goes into effect. It creates the Isthmian Canal Commission, which begins operations the following year, and empowers the President to buy the New Panama Canal Company's rights in the Isthmus for $40,000,000. The President is also authorized to negotiate the conditions for building the canal across the Isthmus of Panama with Colombia, the owner of the area. If a successful arrangement cannot be reached with Colombia, the President then has the authority to negotiate with Nicaragua for the construction of a canal there.

July 1 — Congress passes the Philippine Government Act, which makes the Philippine Islands an unorganized territory and its inhabitants citizens of the Philippines. The statute is also known as the Organic Act.

July 9 — Justice Horace Gray (Massachusetts) resigns his seat on the Supreme Court because of a debilitating illness. He had been appointed by President Chester A. Arthur on December 20, 1881, and served a total of twenty-one years on the bench. Some Supreme Court scholars believe that it was Justice Gray who switched his vote in the rehearing of the Income Tax case in 1895, and not Justice George Shiras, Jr., as usually assumed.

August 11 — Oliver Wendell Holmes (Massachusetts) is given an interim appointment to the Supreme Court by President Roosevelt. His name is to be resubmitted after Congress reconvenes.

August 19 — President Roosevelt launches progressivism on a national level, when he begins a tour of New England and the Midwest to explain his new Square Deal program of reform to the American people.

September 15 — Justice Gray dies.

October — This month's issue of *McClure's Magazine* features Lincoln Steffens's article, "Tweed Days in St. Louis," which details political corruption in that city. It begins another series of articles highlighting and attacking corruption and injustice in American society, business, and politics and may be called the start of the Muckraking era. Other works of this genre were David Graham Philips's "The Treason of the Senate," Ida Tarbell's *The History of the Standard Oil Company,* Thomas Lawson's *Frenzied Finance,* and Ray Stannard Baker's "The Railroads on Trial." This literature of protest contributes substantially to the reform movements in cities and states throughout the nation.

October 3 — President Roosevelt calls a White House conference on the Anthracite Coal Strike inviting representatives of labor and management to Washington in an attempt to settle their differences.

October 16 — A special mediation commission is appointed by President Roosevelt to arbitrate the Anthracite Coal Strike.

October 21 — John Mitchell, head of the United Mine Workers Union, calls off the strike as negotiations begin. In March of the following year, the commission awards the union a ten-percent salary increase, but recognition of the union is not accorded.

December 1 — In a case concerning a state's public health authority over imported cattle, *Reid v. Colorado,* 187 U.S. 137, the Court rules that a state may protect the health and safety of its residents by prohibiting the admittance of cattle into the state if they are suspected of being diseased. Under such conditions, the Court states, the statute in question is a reasonable exercise of a state's police powers and does not violate due process of law under the Fourteenth Amendment.

December 8 — Holmes, soon to be the liberal leader of the Fuller Court, takes his seat as an Associate Justice of the Supreme Court. President Roosevelt's interim appointment of Holmes is made permanent by the Senate, and the "great dissenter" from Massachusetts begins his twenty-nine years on the bench. He retires at the age of ninety-one on January 12, 1932, and dies three years later on March 6, 1935.

December 29 — Dr. Luis M. Drago, the Argentinian foreign minister, issues the doctrine that bears his name; a foreign nation is prohibited from invading the Americas to collect debts owed to its nationals by any American country. The Roosevelt administration wholely subscribes to the Drago pronouncement because it reinforces the Monroe Doctrine of 1823.

1903

January 22 — The Hay-Herran Convention is signed. Secretary of State John Hay and Tomas Herran, the Colombian minister to the United States, sign an agreement which provides that in return for an initial payment of $10,000,000 and a yearly rent of $250,000, the United States would be granted a ninety-nine year lease, with renewal options, over a six-mile wide canal zone across the Isthmus of Panama.

February 11 — Congress passes the Expediting Act which gives precedence in the federal trial courts to any suits arising out of antitrust prosecutions and the injunction petition. The statute also declares that appeals in such litigation could be taken directly to the Supreme Court. The law is passed to speed up the long delays in trial procedure that had developed as a result of renewed efforts on the part of the Justice Department to enforce the Sherman Anti-Trust Act.

February 14 — The Department of Commerce and Labor is established by Congress. This new cabinet-level department also includes a Bureau of Corporations whose function it was to investigate the operations of all corporations engaged in interstate commerce except common carriers. Labor and Commerce are separated on March 4, 1913, when a new Department of Labor is created by Congress.

Congress creates the Army General Staff Corps at the

suggestion of Secretary of War Elihu Root. This new body is placed in charge of the preparation and execution of military plans and is a major part of the reorganization of the War Department.

February 16 George B. Cortelyou is appointed the Department of Commerce's first secretary by President Roosevelt.

February 19 The Elkins Act, reinforcing the Interstate Commerce Act of 1887, is passed by Congress. A major revision of the earlier statute, it redefines unfair discrimination against shippers engaged in interstate commerce, especially concerning the rebate practice, and sets penalties for railroads that deviate from published rate schedules as well as for those both giving and receiving rebates. The act empowers the federal courts to issue injunctions against violators and establishes a precedent for expanding the Interstate Commerce Commission's powers in subsequent congressional statutes in 1906, 1910, and 1920.

February 23 Justice George Shiras, Jr., resigns his seat on the Supreme Court at age seventy-one. He lives in retirement in Florida until his death on August 21, 1924, at the age of ninety-two.

By congressional enactment a law in 1895, prohibits the sale of lottery tickets through the mails, and provides a prison term for violation of the statute. Charles Champion violates the act, is arrested, and found guilty. He appeals, charging in his petition that the law is unconstitutional since the commerce clause of the Constitution grants Congress the power to regulate but not to prohibit. In the Supreme Court action that follows known as the *Lottery* case, *Champion v. Ames,* 188 U.S. 321, the Court by a 5-4 majority sustains the federal act of 1895, ruling that the commerce clause implies the power to prohibit as well as regulate. The opinion asserts a federal police power not fully recognized by the courts prior to the case.

March 2 William R. Day (Ohio) takes his seat as an Associate Justice of the Supreme Court. He had been appointed by President Roosevelt on February 19, 1903, to replace Justice Shiras. Day is another liberal appointed to the bench by Roosevelt in his effort to reconstitute the conservative Fuller Court. Day would serve for nineteen years until he retires from the Court in May 1923. He dies a few months later on July 9, 1923.

March 3 — Congress passes an Immigrant Inspection Act providing for the inspection of immigrants at European ports of embarkation by United States inspectors. The act also gives the federal government the power to deport immediately any immigrant who enters the country illegally.

March 11 — An act is passed by Congress placing a head tax of two dollars on all entering immigrants.

March 16 — Henry M. Hoyt is appointed solicitor general of the United States by President Roosevelt.

May 22 — A United States-Cuba Treaty is signed which includes the Platt Amendment. The treaty is ratified by the United States Senate on March 22, 1904.

May 23 — Wisconsin becomes the first state to adopt the direct primary, another progressive reform.

June 1 — In another Insular case, *Hawaii v. Mankichi,* 190 U.S. 197, the Court is asked to resolve the question: "Did the rights to grand jury indictment and jury trial under the Constitution apply in Hawaii?" The Court by a 5-4 vote rules that these rights do not apply to Hawaii because Congress had not indicated its intention to incorporate Hawaii, and, as a result, the formal provisions of the Constitution, including those regarding grand and petit juries, do not apply there. Using, what Justice Henry B. Brown called the extension concept,the Court holds that Congress has not acted to extend certain benefits of the Bill of Rights, including the Fifth and Sixth amendments to Hawaii. The Bill of Rights, therefore, is not applicable in this case, which involves an appeal from a manslaughter conviction in a Hawaiian criminal court. The Supreme Court once again emphatically states that the Constitution does not automatically follow the flag.

August 12	The Colombian Senate rejects the Hay-Herran Treaty and decides to delay confirmation of the convention signed in January until the construction rights of the French Panama Canal Company expire. This would enable the Colombian government to collect the entire $40,000,000 the United States is willing to pay the French for its construction concession, which is due to expire in October 1904.
September 21	The great Italian tenor, Enrico Caruso, makes his American debut at the Metropolitan Opera House in New York City.
October 1-13	The first baseball World Series is played between the Boston Red Sox and the Pittsburgh Pirates with the Red Sox winning five games to three.
October 20	The Alaskan Boundary Dispute between the United States and Canada is settled in favor of the United States. The dispute had been precipitated by the Klondike gold rush in 1897. In January 1903, the United States and Great Britain agree to submit their dispute to an Anglo-American Arbitration Commission, which nine months later decides in favor of the United States on all points.
November 3-5	A revolution breaks out in Panama. The rebels are guided and assisted in their struggle for independence from Colombia by the agent of the French Panama Canal Company, Philippe Bunau-Varilla. The Panamanians announce their independence from Colombia, while an American warship, on the pretext of maintaining the United States's right of transit across the Isthmus as well as protection of United States mails, stop Colombian military forces from entering Panama to crush the revolution.
November 13	Full recognition is extended to the newly established Republic of Panama by the United States and Bunau-Varilla is welcomed as the new Panamanian minister.
November 18	A convention providing for the construction of an interoceanic canal across the Isthmus of Panama is signed by the United States and the Republic of

Panama. It is called the Hay-Bunau-Varilla Treaty and grants the United States sovereign rights, in perpetuity, to a 10-mile wide canal zone across the Isthmus in return for an initial payment of $10,000,000 and annual payments of $250,000. In addition, the United States is granted the right to intervene in the internal affairs of Panama in order to maintain the peace and security of the canal zone.

November 30 — In *Atkin v. Kansas,* 191 U.S. 207, the Court validates a Kansas law which had established an eight-hour day for construction workers engaged in public works within the state as a lawful exercise of the state's police powers. The statute in question is not a violation of "freedom of contract" under the Constitution.

December — Orville and Wilbur Wright make the first successful airplane flight at Kitty Hawk, North Carolina.

1904

January 23 — In *Buttfield v. Stranahan,* 192 U.S. 470, the Court accepts as constitutional the delegation of a large amount of administrative discretion to the President. It agrees that Congress might lawfully delegate to the executive certain minor policy-making decisions.

March 14 — In 1902, the Northern Pacific and the Great Northern Railroad companies purchase the majority interest in the Burlington Railroad Company, creating a giant holding company known as the Northern Securities Company. As a result, President Roosevelt orders his attorney general, Philander C. Knox, to begin a suit against the Northern Securities Company charging it with violating the antitrust laws. In *Northern Securities v. United States,* 193 U.S. 197, also known as the *Merger* case, the Court, by a narrow 5-4 decision holds in favor of the government, ruling that this giant railroad holding company is restraining trade among the several states and thus is in violation of the Sherman Anti-Trust Act. The Court reasons that "the mere existence of such a combination and the power acquired by the holding company as its trustee constituted a menace to, and a restraint upon, that freedom of commerce which Congress intended to recognize and protect, and which the public was entitled to have protected." For the time being, the decision in this case temporarily rejuvenates the Sherman Anti-Trust Act of 1890.

April 4 — The Court rules, by a vote of 8 to 0, in *National Building and Loan Association v. Brahan,* 193 U.S. 635, that any out-of-state insurance firm wishing to establish offices in Missouri must adhere to all state business and insurance laws.

April 17 — The Kincaid Home Act, providing free grants of 640 acres to Nebraska settlers who live on the land for 5 years and make improvements valued at $800, goes into effect.

April 30 — The Louisiana Purchase Exposition begins in St. Louis, dedicated by President Roosevelt.

May 1 — The Socialist party's (formerly the Social Democratic party) National Nominating Convention, meeting in Chicago, nominates Eugene V. Debs (Indiana) for President and Benjamin Hanford (New York) for Vice-President.

May 31 — In *Public Clearing House v. Coyne,* 194 U.S. 497, the Court declares constitutional, a congressional statute making fraudulent use of the federal mails a crime.

The Court, in *McCray v. United States,* 195 U.S. 27, sustains an 1886 congressional act which places a tax upon artifically colored oleomargarine that was made to look like butter. By a 6-3 decision, the majority rules that the tax is a valid exercise of the federal taxing power as an instrument of social control, and paves the way for the use of the federal tax power as a means for federal social regulation.

In another so-called *Insular* case, *Dorr v. United States,* 195 U.S. 138, the Court again rules that the Constitution does not automatically follow the flag. A libel trial in the Philippines is heard by a federal Circuit Court without a traditional indictment or a twelve-man jury, but the Court holds that trial without jury does not deprive the plaintiff of his rights under the Constitution because the Philippines are not a part of the United States, and therefore, the Constitution does not apply to them. Justice William R. Day, who delivers the opinion of the Court, states, "that if the United States acquires territory where trial by jury is not known but where, due to customs and preferences, the people have another method—are these considerations to be ignored and they coerced to accept a system of trial unknown to them and unsuited to their needs?"

June 21 The Republican National Nominating Convention, meeting in Chicago, nominates President Roosevelt for reelection and names Charles W. Fairbanks (Indiana) to be his running mate.

July 1 President Roosevelt appoints William H. Moody (Massachusetts) attorney general of the United States.

July 4 The Populist National Nominating Convention, meeting in Springfield, Illinois, nominates Thomas E. Watson (Georgia) for President and Thomas H. Tibbles (Nebraska) for Vice-President.

July 6 The Democratic National Nominating Convention, meets in St. Louis, and in an attempt to project a more conservative image, turns from William Jennings Bryan and nominates a conservative New York judge, Alton B. Parker for President. Henry G. Davis (West Virginia) runs on the Vice-Presidential slate.

November 8 In the presidential election Roosevelt wins a smashing victory over Parker, 336 electoral votes to 140. The popular vote is 7,628,461 for Roosevelt to 5,084,223 for Parker. The Republicans retain control over both houses of Congress.

December 6 President Roosevelt, in his annual message to Congress, announces what later became known as the Roosevelt Corollary to the Monroe Doctrine. He states that "chronic wrongdoing, or an impotence which results in a general loosening of the ties of civilized society, may in America, as elsewhere, ultimately require intervention by some civilized nation, and... might force the United States to exercise an international police power to prevent this kind of intervention."

1905

January 21 — The United States government, by executive agreement with the government of Santo Domingo, accepts the responsibility for the management and administration of the Dominican customs service and debt payments. Santo Domingo's territorial integrity is also guaranteed.

January 30 — As part of the Roosevelt administration's attempt to regulate big business and curb the excesses of the giant trusts, the Justice Department brings suit against a number of meat-packing corporations who are charged with attempting to monopolize the fresh meat market in the United States. In the *Beef Trust* case, *Swift and Company v. United States,* 196 U.S. 375, a unanimous Court decides that this giant combination is an illegal monopoly in violation of the Sherman Anti-Trust Act. Justice Oliver Wendell Holmes, who delivers the opinion of the Court, introduces his "current of commerce" concept in which he states, "When cattle are sent for sale from a place in one State, with the expectation that they will end their transit, after purchase, in another, and when in effect they do so, with only the interruption necessary to find a purchaser at the stockyards, and when this is a typical, constantly recurring course, the current thus existing is a current of commerce among the States, and the purchase of the cattle is a part and incident of such commerce."

February 20 — In *Jacobson v. Massachusetts,* 197 U.S. 11, the Court sustains a Massachusetts compulsory vaccination statute which imposes a $5 fine on any person refusing to submit to free vaccination. In a 7-2 decision, the Court limits personal liberty by approving the social purpose of the legislation in question under the state's police powers.

March 4 — Theodore Roosevelt is inaugurated President of the United States in his own right.

April 10 — In the case *Matter of Heff,* 197 U.S. 488, the Court approves of the principle of a federal prohibition law, but at the same time, limits the application of the Indian Liquor Sales Act of 1897, which had prohibited the sale of alcoholic beverages to Indians on lands held in trust by the United States government. The Court, in giving its decision, cites the Constitution's commerce clause as a means of implementing the federal police power.

Utilizing the "incorporation" concept once more, the Court, in *Rasmussen v. United States,* 197 U.S. 516, rules that since Alaska had been almost completely incorporated within the United States, it is unconstitutional for the territorial courts to use six-member juries rather than the traditional twelve-member juries because the former violated the Fifth, Sixth, and Seventh amendments; the Court, therefore, voids the verdict. The use of the "incorporation" concept in this case was a complete turnabout from the Court's interpretation of the same principle in the earlier Insular cases involving Puerto Rico, Hawaii, and the Philippines. Some critics of the Court charge that the racial attitudes of the judges conditioned their decisions.

April 17 — In one of the most controversial cases heard by the Fuller Court, the so-called *freedom of contract* case, *Lochner v. New York,* 198 U.S. 45, the Court declares unconstitutional a New York State statute which had established a maximum ten-hour day or sixty-hour week for bakers or those engaged in the confectionary business. The Court, by a narrow 5-4 vote, rules that the act in question violates the Fourteenth Amendment's "liberty of contract" clause and is an unwarranted and excessive use of the state's police powers. It is, the Court declares, "an illegal interference in the rights of individuals, both employers and employees, for reasons entirely arbitrary." A vigorous dissent from Justice Oliver Wendell Holmes states that the Constitution is not intended to embody any specific economic theory, especially laissez faire.

May 7 — A Japanese and Korean Exclusion League is formed in California and subsequently spreads up the west coast.

May 15 — The Court rules in *Delaware, Lackawanna, and Western Railroad Company v. Pennsylvania,* 198 U.S. 341, that a state tax on the capital stock of a railroad, where the state includes $1,700,000 in coal, located outside of the state, but owned by the railroad, as part of the capital stock in question, is unconstitutional on the ground that it is an excessive and illegal use of the state's taxing power.

June — The Industrial Workers of the World (IWW) is founded on the West Coast by William D. "Big Bill" Haywood and Eugene V. Debs.

July 29 — A Memorandum is signed by Secretary of War William Howard Taft and Japanese Prime Minister Taro Katsura, in which Japan promises to keep out of the Philippine Islands in return for United States recognition of Japanese hegemony over Korea.

July 31 — President Roosevelt endorses the Taft-Katsura Memorandum despite his earlier pronouncements in which he favored an Open Door policy with respect to the Far East.

August 9-September 5 — President Roosevelt serves as mediator at the peace negotiations between Russia and Japan at Portsmouth, New Hampshire, bringing to an end the Russo-Japanese War of 1904-5.

November 13 — In *Union Refrigerator Transit Company v. Kentucky,* 199 U.S. 194, the Court invalidates a law which is levying a tax on property belonging to the Union Refrigerator Transit Company, a business located outside of the state. The Court holds that such property is beyonds the state's jurisdiction and that the tax on it constitutes "extortion."

December 4 — The Court, in *South Carolina v. United States,* 199 U.S. 437, is asked to rule if a state-owned and -operated chain of liquor stores should be granted immunity from federal taxation because it is an agency exercising the sovereign power of the state. In a 6-3 decision, the majority holds that the proprietary activities of a state as distinguished from its governmental activities are subject to federal internal revenue taxes. Justice David J. Brewer, who delivers the opinion of the Court, states: "Whenever a state engages in a business which is of a private nature, that business is not withdrawn from the taxing power of the nation."

1906

January 16 — President Roosevelt is instrumental in arranging a conference at Algeciras, Spain, which settles the first Moroccan crisis between France and Germany.

January 31 — The federal government's Bureau of Immigration is organized to keep records and statistical information.

May 28 — Associate Justice Henry B. Brown retires from the Court after serving sixteen years. He lives in retirement until his death on September 4, 1913.

June 11 — Congress passes the Forest Homestead Act which permits the secretary of the interior to open for settlement forest lands that contain agricultural value, under the terms of the Homestead Act of 1862.

By congressional enactment, the Employers' Liability Act becomes law. This statute places the liability for injuries or death to railroad workers upon the employers.

June 29 — The Hepburn Act, calling for more comprehensive railroad regulation is passed by Congress. Under its provisions the Interstate Commerce Act of 1887, is substantially overhauled and strengthened. This statute gives the Interstate Commerce Commission maximum rate-making authority; expands its jurisdiction to include pipelines, ferries, express companies, and bridges; and increases the membership on the commission from five to seven members. The act makes the ICC's decisions binding until successfully challenged in the courts, and in court cases, involving violation of the statute, the burden of proof is now placed upon the carriers. Finally, the act contains a commodities clause which authorizes the ICC to order the railroads to divest themselves of the controlling interest in certain companies which include products that are transported in interstate commerce.

Congress authorizes the Army Corps of Engineers to build an interoceanic canal across the Isthmus of Panama. Colonel George W. Goethals is placed in charge of construction.

All coal lands in the public domain are withdrawn from private use by order of the President so that they could be accurately surveyed and appraised.

June 30 Congress passes the Pure Food and Drug Act which prohibits the manufacture and sale of adulterated foods and drugs in interstate commerce. In a number of subsequent legal cases, the courts declare the act constitutional, paving the way for an increased use of federal police power under the commerce clause. This statute is the highpoint of President Roosevelt's Square Deal.

The Meat Inspection Act is passed by Congress, providing for strict federal inspection of the meat-packing industry; it also attempts to eliminate the dangerous and unsanitary conditions then prevailing in the companies engaged in selling and processing meat in interstate commerce. The publication of Upton Sinclair's *The Jungle,* a devastating exposé of the meat-packing industry, plays a major role in the passage of the act.

Congress passes the Immunity of Witnesses Act which denies corporation officials the right to invoke immunity pleas in cases involving company operations and conduct.

July 23 The Third International Conference of American States meets at Rio de Janeiro, Brazil.

September 29 United States military forces are sent into Cuba to establish and operate a provisional government following an abortive rebellion on the island. The troops remain until 1909.

October 11 — The San Francisco School Board issues a segregation order establishing a separate Oriental school for all Japanese, Chinese, and Korean children in the city.

October 25 — The Japanese government protests San Francisco's school segregation order, and prompts President Roosevelt to convene a White House meeting with San Francisco School Board officials. The conference takes place in February 1907; as a result San Francisco school officials rescind the segregation order upon Roosevelt's promise that the government would act promptly on the problem of Oriental immigration.

November — The Territory of Alaska is permitted to elect a territorial delegate as its representative in Congress.

December 12 — William H. Moody (Massachusetts) is appointed to the Supreme Court of the United States by President Theodore Roosevelt to replace the retired Justice Henry B. Brown. Moody would serve for only four years on the Supreme bench.

December 17 — Charles J. Bonaparte is appointed attorney general of the United States by President Roosevelt.

1907

March 1 — Congress increases the head tax on all immigrants entering the country to four dollars.

March 13 — The Panic of 1907 begins when a precipitous drop in the stock market occurs. The Knickerbocker Trust Company in New York suspends operations in October, and many businesses throughout the nation declare bankruptcy. However, the Panic is short-lived and no serious depression results.

March 14 — The Inland Waterways Commission is appointed by the President.

April 15 — The Court, in *Patterson v. Colorado,* 205 U.S. 454, sustains the concept that the judiciary possesses "inherent power" to find offenders in contempt. This case reverses the statutory limitations that had been placed on that power for nearly a century.

May 8 — Tommy Burns defeats "Philadelphia" Jack O'Brien at Los Angeles to become heavyweight boxing champion of the world. Burns, in turn, is knocked out by Jack Johnson on December 26, 1908, and thus America had its first black heavyweight boxing champion.

May 27 — In *Kansas v. Colorado,* 206 U.S. 46, a unanimous Court rules that the reclamation of arid lands is not one of the powers granted to the federal government by the Constitution. This case stems from an attempt by Colorado to divert the Arkansas River's water for the purposes of irrigation, thus preventing the natural flow of the river into Kansas. Kansas sues Colorado to stop this action. The federal government intervenes, claiming the power to reclaim arid lands by the use and control of inland water, but the Court states: "It may well be that no power is adequate for their reclamation other than that of the national government. But, if no such power has been granted, none can be exercised." The decision reflects a narrow interpretation of the implied powers clause of the Constitution.

The Court in *Buck v. Beach,* 206 U.S. 392, reaffirms substantive due process under the Fourteenth Amendment when it rules that the state of Indiana could not legally collect a personal property tax placed upon certain notes deposited in an Indiana vault because the owners of the notes were New York residents and the borrowers of the notes were Ohio residents. The Court declares that "the debt had no actual relationship to the jurisdiction of the State of Indiana and that the enforcement of such a tax would be the taking of property without due process of law."

June 15-October 18 — The Second Hague Conference meets in Holland, but fails to solve any of the growing world problems.

July 31	The United States withdraws its military forces from Santo Domingo.
October 23	Congress passes an act making it illegal to harbor any alien woman for immoral purposes within three years after her arrival in the United States.
November 14-December 20	The Central American Peace Conference, made up of six Central American nations and the United States, meets in Washington, D.C. Eight separate agreements are signed including a general peace treaty which the United States refuses to sign. In addition, the Central American Court of Justice is established.
November 16	The Territory of Oklahoma is admitted to the Union.
December 16	America's "Great White Fleet" is sent around the world by President Roosevelt on a goodwill mission. The actual purpose of the voyage is to enhance the United States's presence in the Pacific and the Far East. It is a spectacular example of Roosevelt's Speak softly, but carry a big stick philosophy.

1908

January 6	The Court in the *First Employer's Liability* case, 207 U.S. 463, declares that the Employers' Liability Act of 1906, is unconstitutional on the ground that it is an unwarranted invasion into the sphere of intrastate commerce. As a result of this 8-1 decision, Congress amends the law in both 1908 and again in 1910, and the *Second Employers' Liability* case, 223 U.S. 1, in 1912, upholds the validity of the amended statute.
January 27	In *Adair v. United States,* 208 U.S. 161, the Court strikes down that portion of the Erdman Act of 1898, which outlaws "yellow dog contracts" as a condition of employment and makes it a criminal offense to force a prospective worker to sign one, on the ground that it is an unreasonable violation of "freedom of contract." The Court holds that the act is beyond the power of Congress to regulate interstate commerce.

February 3 — A unanimous Court rules in the Danbury Hatters' case, *Loewe v. Lawlor,* 208 U.S. 274, that a secondary boycott engaged in by the United Hatters of North America constitutes an illegal combination in restraint of interstate commerce under the Sherman Anti-Trust Act. Chief Justice Melville W. Fuller, who delivers the opinion of the Court, states that, "the use by this organization of such means as boycotts, labor controls, intimidation of dealers, and other oppressive and coercive measures to gain control of the hat industry is definitely a restraint and a hindrance of interstate commerce."

February 18 — President Roosevelt and the emperor of Japan conclude a Gentlemen's Agreement whereby the Japanese government agrees to restrict the issuance of passports to Japanese laborers wishing to emigrate to the United States. This is another attempt of the United States to eliminate Oriental emigration to this country.

February 24 — The Court, by unanimous vote, sustains an Oregon act which makes it illegal to employ women in any "mechanical establishment, factory, or laundry" for more than ten hours per day. This case, *Muller v. Oregon,* 208 U.S. 412, sees the Court modify its position of *Lochner v. New York* since the Oregon statute does not violate "freedom of contract" under the Fourteenth Amendment. The case is also notable because of the brilliant defense prepared by the counsel for the state, Louis D. Brandies, later, himself a Supreme Court Justice. His famous "Brandies Brief" utilizes sociological, economic, historical, and physical data to justify the Oregon Maximum Working Hours Law for women. The arch-conservative of the Court, Justice David J. Brewer, not only votes to validate the legislation, but also writes the decision, literally overawed, some scholars say, by the masterful Brandies presentation. Brewer declares that when a woman's "physical well-being becomes an object of public interest and care in order to preserve the strength and vigor of the race," then the "special legislation restricting or qualifying the conditions under which she should be permitted to toil" is justified.

March 16 — By a 7 to 1 decision, the Court in *Armour Packing Company v. United States,* 209 U.S. 56, validates that portion of the Elkins Act (1903), that gives the Interstate Commerce Commission power to conduct railroad rate investigations concerned with the imposition of unfair and discriminating rate differentials by the carriers upon the shippers.

March 23 — In *Ashbell v. Kansas,* 209 U.S. 251, the Court declares constitutional a Kansas Livestock Inspection Act which requires a clean bill of health document as a prerequisite for the transportation of cattle into the state.

April 2 — The Populist party National Nominating Convention meeting in St. Louis, nominates Thomas E. Watson (Georgia)—for President and Samuel W. Williams (Indiana) for Vice-President.

April 6 — In *Hudson Water Company v. Mc Carter,* 209 U.S. 349, the Court, by a vote of 8 to 1, validates a state's police powers, when it approves the right of a state to forbid diverting its waters for use in another state. The Court's opinion declares that the contract of the company constructing this project is not impaired by the state's actions.

April 22 — Congress passes the second Employers' Liability Act; the law now applies solely to interstate commerce.

May 9 — The Court in *Berea College v. Kentucky,* 211 U.S. 45, sustains a Kentucky statute which prohibits the admission of blacks and whites to the same private schools. This case uses as its precedent the "separate but equal" doctrine established in *Plessy v. Ferguson* (1896).

May 10 — The Socialist party convention, meeting in Chicago, once again chooses Eugene V. Debs as their standard bearer and gives second place on the ticket to Benjamin Hanford.

May 13-15 — President Roosevelt hosts a White House Conference on Conservation. Cabinet members, congressmen, Supreme Court Justices, and governors from thirty-four states attend.

May 18 — In *St. Louis and Iron Mountain Railway Company v. Taylor,* 210 U.S. 281, the Court sustains the constitutionality of the Safety Appliance Act of 1905, as a legitimate exercise of the federal government's police powers in regard to the health and safety of workers on or involved with common carriers.

May 30 — Congress passes the Aldrich-Vreeland Act, a currency measure, which attempts to restrict paper money in circulation to notes issued by national banks or by federally secured state banks. The act also establishes the National Monetary Commission which is authorized to study international banking and monetary systems. Senator Nelson W. Aldrich (Rhode Island) is named chairman.

June 1 — In *Londoner v. Denver,* 210 U.S. 373, the Court declares a Denver street assessment unconstitutional because the city council had passed the law without providing an opportunity for a full hearing to the landowners assessed, thus violating due process under the Fourteenth Amendment.

June 8 — President Roosevelt appoints the National Conservation Commission with Gifford Pinchot as chairman. Its primary purpose is to make recommendations for the conservation and preservation of the nation's resources. By 1909, Roosevelt withdraws almost two million acres of the public domain from private use.

June 16 — The Republican National Convention, meeting in Chicago, nominates William Howard Taft (Ohio) for President and James S. Sherman (New York) for Vice-President.

July 7 — The Democratic National Convention, meeting in Denver, returns to the more liberal William Jennings Bryan and nominates him for President. John W. Kern (Indiana) is named as the Vice-Presidential candidate.

November 3 — Taft with 321 electoral votes and 7,675,320 popular votes defeats Bryan who receives 162 electoral votes and 6,412,294 popular votes for the presidency. In addition, the Republicans retain control of Congress.

The state of Oregon adopts the progressive reform known as recall.

November 9 — In *Twining v. New Jersey,* 211 U.S. 78, the Court rules that exemption from compulsory self-incrimination is not an immunity or privilege of national citizenship guaranteed by the due process clause of the Fourteenth Amendment from abridgement by the states. By an 8 to 1 decision, the Court declares that the personal rights enumerated in the first eight amendments do not automatically apply to the states through the Fourteenth Amendment.

November 30 — The Root-Takahira Agreement is concluded between Secretary of State Elihu Root and the Japanese ambassador to the United States, Baron Kogoro Takahira. Its provisions include a promise by both nations to maintain the Open Door policy in China and to respect each other's territorial possessions in the Pacific and the Far East.

1909

February 19 — Congress passes the Enlarged Homestead Act to satisfy western cattle interests.

March 3 — Congress enacts a new and enlarged Criminal Code as the initial phase of a comprehensive program to streamline and update all statutory provisions of the federal judicial procedure.

March 4 — William Howard Taft is inaugurated the twenty-seventh President of the United States.

March 5 — George W. Wickersham is appointed attorney general of the United States by President Taft.

April 1 — President Taft names Lloyd W. Bowers solicitor general of the United States.

April 5	In *Keller v. United States,* 213 U.S. 138, the Court invalidates the act of 1907, making it a punishable offense to harbor an alien woman for immoral purposes within three years after her entry into the United States. The act attempts to regulate prostitution on a local level, and is an invasion of state power violating the Tenth Amendment.
July 12	The Sixteenth Amendment, which authorized the imposition of an income tax, is sent to the respective states by Congress. The amendment is ratified by the requisite number of states in February 1913.
July 15	Admission of United States banking interests into a European consortium planning to build a railroad in China is requested by President Taft.
August 5	Congress, after five months of debate, enacts the Payne-Aldrich Tariff which lowers duties to about thirty-eight percent. Tariff reform advocates are less than satisfied with the new statute.
August 25	The First National Conservation Congress is convened in Seattle, Washington.
September 15	The so-called Ballinger-Pinchot Controversy begins. President Taft announces his support of Secretary of the Interior Richard A. Ballinger's decision to open certain previously withdrawn water power sites to public sale. The chief forester, Gifford Pinchot, who had been appointed by Roosevelt, vigorously opposes both Taft and Ballinger for their actions which he called a sellout of the conservation movement.
Septembner 17	President Taft, speaking at Winona, Minnesota, declares that the Payne-Aldrich Tariff is the best tariff ever enacted by the Republican party. His statements anger all those who favor genuine tariff reform.
October 24	Justice Rufus W. Peckham dies after thirteen years of service on the Supreme Court.
December	A new Chinese railroad consortium is initiated by Secretary of State Philander C. Knox and includes, in

addition to the United States, Russia, Japan, and Great Britian. The consortium fails.

December 20 — President Taft appoints Horace H. Lurton (Tennessee) to the Supreme Court. Lurton takes his seat on January 3; he serves for only five years until his death on July 12, 1914.

1910

The population of the United States increases to 92,407,000.

January 7 — President Taft removes Gifford Pinchot as head of the United States Forest Service because of Pinchot's continuing criticism of Interior Secretary Richard A. Ballinger, this time for permitting coal lands in Alaska to be sold to private interests.

January 10 — In *Interstate Commerce Commission v. Illinois Central Railroad Company,* 215 U.S. 452, the Court sustains the ICC's policymaking functions, and declares that it would not usurp the commission's authority under the pretext of reviewing its decisions.

February 8 — The Boy Scouts of America is chartered in Washington, D.C.

March 19 — Speaker of the House, Joseph G. "Uncle Joe" Cannon is stripped of his authority to appoint the House Rules Committee as well as his other dictatorial powers. Congress adopts an amendment to its rules, proposed by Representative George W. Norris, which also removes the Speaker himself from the committee.

March 26 — Congress amends the Immigration Act (1907) to exclude paupers, criminals, and anarchists.

March 28 — Justice David J. Brewer dies after serving for almost twenty-one years on the Supreme Court.

April 4 — The Court in *Missouri Pacific Railway Company v. Nebraska,* 217 U.S. 196, strikes down a statute which requires railroad companies to extend tracks to any private grain elevator, if the elevator owner made such a request. The Court, by a 7-2 decision, declares that the law in question is a denial of due process.

April 5 — Congress passes an amendment to the Employers' Liability Act of 1906, which substantially strengthens the statute.

April 21 — In *International Textbook Company v. Pigg,* 217 U.S. 91, the Court invalidates a Kansas law which requires a foreign company to file a financial statement with the state prior to doing business within the state on the ground that the act is an unwarranted invasion of the federal commerce power.

May 19 — United States military forces are sent to Nicaragua to protect American lives and property when a revolution breaks out in that Central American nation.

May 31 — The Court in *Interstate Commerce Commission v. Chicago, Rock Island, and Pacific Railway Company,* 218 U.S. 88, validates the new rate-fixing powers of the ICC by sustaining a commission order, which in effect asserts ICC right of control over the railroad rate system.

June — The National Collegiate Athletic Association (NCAA) is organized.

June 18 — Congress passes the Mann-Elkins Act, sponsored by Senator Stephen B. Elkins (West Virginia) and Congressman James R. Mann (Illinois). This statute grants the ICC broad rate-fixing powers and strengthens the long haul-short haul clauses within the Interstate Commerce Act of 1887. In addition, the new law places telephone, telegraph, cable, and wireless companies under the rate-fixing jurisdiction of the ICC and establishes a commerce court to review commission rulings.

June 25 — The Postal Savings Bank system is passed by Congress.

Congress passes the Corrupt Practices Publicity Act

which requires congressional candidates to file statements detailing their election campaign contributions.

The Mann (White Slave) Act is passed by Congress. This statute makes it a crime to transport women across state lines for immoral purposes.

The Amended Expediting Act provides for the calling of a three-judge trial court, upon a request from the attorney general, to facilitate the judicial process in antitrust cases. Direct appeal for review in these cases is under the jurisdiction of the Supreme Court.

July 4 — Chief Justice Melville W. Fuller dies after serving for almost twenty-two years on the Supreme Court. He had led the Court during one of its most controversial and exciting periods in its history. For the most part, the Court under Fuller is decidedly conservative.

PART II

The Fuller Court

▪ ▪ ▪ ▪ ▪

Decisions and Documents

Justice Samuel F. Miller: The Judicial Branch of Government

1880

One of the greatest judges in Supreme Court history was Samuel Freeman Miller. A staunch Republican, he was appointed to the Court by President Abraham Lincoln in 1862. On the Court, Miller was labeled a "moderate," and during his twenty-eight years on the bench, he was involved in the development of what he called ordered liberty. A pragmatic man, he became a dominant personality on the bench and contributed great statesmanship to the Supreme tribunal. He wrote the majority opinion in the *Slaughterhouse Cases* (1873), which became the first important interpretation of the Fourteenth Amendment, ruling that the amendment did not inhibit the reasonable exercise of a state's power to regulate private enterprise. The selection that follows, part of a series of law lectures given by Miller in 1880, expresses his views concerning the law and the judicial branch of government. Lectures on the Constitution (1880; reprint ed., Washington, D.C.: Morrison: New York: Rothman Publishers, 1981), pp. 24-29.

The judicial branch of the government is, of all others, the weakest branch. It has no army; it has no navy; it has no press; it has no officers except its marshals, and they are appointed by the President and confirmed by the Senate; and the marshals that we send our processes to cannot be removed by us, but they may be removed any day by the executive. The clerks whom they permit us in some form or other to appoint, have salaries and compensations regulated by the legislature; and a clerk who gets $20,000 in fees, pays all but $3,500 into the Treasury of the United States. We are, then, so far as the ordinary forms of power are concerned, by far the feeblest branch or department of the government. We have to rely—I beg pardon for using the personal pronoun in this discussion—but the judiciary have to rely on the confidence and respect of the public for their weight and influence in the government; and I am happy to say that the country, the people, and the other branches of the government have never been found wanting in that respect and in that confidence. It is one of the best tributes to the American nation—a tribute which it deserves above all others even of the Anglo-Saxon race—a tribute which can be paid to no other race like the Anglo-Saxon race—that they submit to the law as expounded by the judiciary.

Under all the excitement of wealth; of money; of the contest of railroads; of political existence—everything which can be got before the court—everything which can come fairly within judicial cognizance—our people seem to think is safe. And whatever may be said or felt about the recent trouble in the State of Maine, there is no grander phenomenon to be found in the history of this country than a body calling itself a legal legislature and government quietly laying down its functions and dispersing at the mere opinion of a court that they were not the proper government.

Of course. . . there are nice questions between these various departments of the government as to the lines of demarkation; and it has always been an anxious question, and always must be one, where there is a conflict in the claims of these branches of government. While it is the duty of the court to construe the great instrument, the Constitution, whenever it shall come before it in a fair judicial proceeding, and it can construe it in no other way—for it is a delusion, it is a mistake, the idea that the Supreme Court of the United States was created with one of its special functions to interpret and construe that instrument,—I say while, however, it is the special function of the courts to construe the Constitution in a judicial proceeding, with parties properly before them, it is equally the duty of each member of Congress and of the executive to make that construction for himself when he is called to act within the sphere of his duty. And I think myself I have changed one of my beliefs of early life, when I used to think that when a Marshall and his compeers had decided that the Bank of the United States was a financial institution authorized by the Constitution of the United States, the legislative and executive branches should also concede that fact. I am prepared to admit, that while they are bound to consider that in that particular—that is, its execution of the law as between the parties—all the other branches of the government must yield, yet when it comes to the conscience of any member of Congress or any executive to say, "Can I sign a bill?" or "Can I vote for a measure?" it is for him to decide, on the best lights he has, whether the act he is going to do is within the constitutional power of the body of which he is a member. Therefore you see the difficulty in getting a settled construction of this instrument. And since every branch of the government, when called on to act originally, is bound to act on the judgment it forms of its own powers, you can understand the reason that for eighty or ninety years the question of the relations of the States to the Federal government should remain an open and undecided question.

We are, however, getting a body of decisions of recognized principles. The instrument is being construed by the judicial branch more than the others, but largely by all others, in the light of the events which have arisen to test it. The construction which was put upon the Constitution during the recent insurrection—the powers that could be exercised in such an emergency by the President, by the War Department, by the Legislature, by the Judiciary, all have been tested—all have undergone investigation; and while no man can say that all the decisions have been correct, because they have been varying, it must, in the light of any impartial mind, be clear that we are completing a construction and are deciding a great many things that will remain forever, with regard to the Constitution.

It is very desirable that it should be so. All loose construction of authority is dangerous; all construction of authority too limited to serve the purpose for which it is given is injurious. You must look at that instrument in the light of the purposes which it was intended to answer; in the light of the evils it was intended to remedy; in the light of the fact that we were a dissolving people, and the instrument was intended to bind us anew forever; in the light of the fact that the government was going to pieces for want of power to protect itself, and we must consider that one of the purposes of the Constitution was to give the government that power; in the light of the fact that the Confederacy—the government under the Articles of Confederation—could only request the States to do a great deal that was necessary to carry on the Federal government, and it was desirable to give the new government the power of operating directly upon the people without going through the instrumentality of the States, and that instead of laws which before the constitution was made were intended to have effect through the State legislatures, the government should now have direct effect through the legislation of Congress—the action of the legislative branch—and the judiciary, upon the people themselves, without the consent, and even against the wishes, of the States, if it were necessary.

In all these ways, when you come to construe this instrument like a remedial statute, like a contract between individuals, it must be construed in the light of the times in which it was made—of the evils to be remedied, of the good to be effected, and, above all, in the light of the idea that it was made to create a perpetual government of the people, among the people, and by the people.

Chicago, Milwaukee, and St. Paul Railroad v. Minnesota, (Minnesota Rate Case)

134 U.S. 148

1890

In 1887, a Minnesota statute created a state railroad commission with power to establish "final and conclusive" maximum rate schedules. Chicago, Milwaukee, and St. Paul Railroad sued the state, claiming that the commission's rate schedules violated the due process clause of the Fourteenth Amendment. When the Supreme Court of Minnesota found for the defendant, the railroad appealed the case to the Supreme Court of the United States. Known as the *Minnesota Rate Case,* the Court reversed the decision of the state court and held the statute in question unconstitutional, because it did not provide for the judicial review of the commission's rate decisions. This verdict effectively negated the principles established in *Munn v. Illinois* (94 U.S. 113, 1890). What follows is the majority opinion delivered by Justice Samuel Blatchford.

. . . It is contended for the railway company that the State of Minnesota is bound by the contract made by the Territory in the charter granted to the Minneapolis and Cedar Valley Railroad Company; that a contract existed that the company should have the power of regulating its rates of toll; that any legislation by the State infringing upon that right impairs the obligation of the contract; that there was no provision in the charter or in any general statute reserving to the Territory or to the State the right to alter or amend the charter; and that no subsequent legislation of the Territory or of the State could deprive the directors of the company of the power to fix its rates of toll, subject only to the general provision of law that such rates should be reasonable.

But we are of opinion that the general language of . . . the charter of the Minneapolis and Cedar Valley Railroad Company cannot be held to constitute an irrepealable contract with that company that it should have the right for all future time to prescribe its rates of toll, free from all control by the legislature of the State.

It was held by this court in *Pennsylvania Railroad Co. v. Miller,* 132 U.S. 75, in accordance with a long course of decisions both in the state courts and in this court that a railroad corporation takes its charter, containing a kindered provision with that in question, subject to the general law of the State, and to such changes as may be made in such general law, and subject to future constitutional provisions and future general legislation, in the absence of any prior contract with it exempting it from liability to such future general legislation in respect of the subject matter involved; and that exemption from future general legislation, either by a constitutional provision or by an act of the legislature, cannot be admitted to exist unless it is given expressly, or unless it follows by an implication equally clear with express words.

There is nothing in the mere grant of power . . . to the directors of the company, to make needful rules and regulations touching the rates of toll and the manner of collecting the same, which can be properly interpreted as authorizing us to hold that the State parted with its general authority itself to regulate, at any time in the future when it might see fit to do so, the rates of toll to be collected by the company.

In *Stone v. Farmers' Loan and Trust Co.,* 116 U.S. 307, 325, the whole subject is fully considered, the authorities are cited, and the conclusion is arrived at, that the right of a State reasonably to limit the amount of charges by a railroad company for the transportation of persons and property within its jurisdiction cannot be granted away by its legislature unless by words of positive grant or words equivalent in law; and that a statute which grants to a railroad company the right "from time to time to fix, regulate and receive the tolls and charges by them to be received for transportation," does not deprive the State of its power, within the limits of its general authority, as controlled by the Constitution of the United States, to act upon the reasonableness of the tolls and charges so fixed and regulated. But, after reaching this conclusion, the court said "From what has thus been said, it is not to be inferred that this power of limitation or regulation is itself without limit. This power to regulate is not a power to destroy, and limitation is not the equivalent of confiscation. Under pretence of regulating fares and freights, the State cannot require a railroad corporation to carry persons or property without reward; neither can it do that which in law amounts to a taking of private property for public use without just compensation, or without due process of law. . . .

There being, therefore, no contract or chartered right in the railroad company which can prevent the legislature from regulating in some form the charges of the company for transportation, the question is whether the form adopted in the present case is valid.

The construction put upon the statute by the Supreme Court of Minnesota must be accepted by this court, for the purposes of the present case, as conclusive and not to be reexamined here as to its propriety or accuracy. The Supreme Court authoritatively declares that it is the expressed intention of the legislature of Minnesota, by the statute, that the rates recommended and published by the commission, if it proceeds in the manner pointed out by the act, are not simply advisory, nor merely *prima facie* equal and reasonable, but final and conclusive as to what are equal and reasonable charges; that the law neither contemplates nor allows any issue to be made or inquiry to be had as to their equality or reasonableness in fact; that, under the statute, the rates published by the commission are the only ones that are lawful, and, therefore, in contemplation of the law the only ones that are equal and reasonable; and that, in a proceeding for a mandamus under the statute, there is no fact to traverse except the violation of law in not complying with the recommendations of the commission. In other words, although the railroad company is forbidden to establish rates that are not equal and reasonable, there is no power in the courts to stay the hands of the commission, if it chooses to establish rates that are unequal and unreasonable.

This being the construction of the statute by which we are bound in considering the present case, we are of opinion that, so construed, it conflicts with the Constitution of the United States in the particulars complained of by the railroad company. It deprives the company of its right to a judicial investigation, by due process of law, under the forms and with the machinery provided by the wisdom of successive ages for the investigation judicially of the truth of a matter in controversy, and substitutes therefor, as an absolute finality, the action of a railroad commission which, in view of the powers conceded to it by the state court, cannot be regarded as clothed with judicial functions or possessing the machinery of a court of justice....

...The issuing of the peremptory writ of mandamus in this case was, therefore, unlawful, because in violation of the Constitution of the United States; and it is necessary that the relief administered in favor of the plaintiff in error should be a reversal of the judgment of the Supreme Court awarding that writ, and an instruction for further proceedings by it not inconsistent with the opinion of this court.

In view of the opinion delivered by that court, it may be impossible for any further proceedings to be taken other than to dismiss the proceeding for a mandamus, if the court should adhere to its opinion that, under the statute, it cannot investigate judicially the reasonableness of the rates fixed by the commission. Still, the question will be open for review; and The judgment of this court is, that the judgment of the Supreme Court of Minnesota, entered May 4, 1888, awarding a preemptory writ of mandamus in this case, be reversed, and the case be remanded to that court, with an instruction for further proceedings not inconsistent with the opinion of this court.

In Re Neagle
135 U.S. 1
1890

David Neagle, a deputy United States marshal, and the bodyguard of Supreme Court Justice Stephen J. Field, was arrested by local authorities in California for shooting and killing a man named David Terry, who had attacked Judge Field in a restaurant. Neagle was released by the federal Circuit Court on a writ of *habeus corpus* on the grounds that he was being held for "an act done or committed in pursuance of a law of the United States." The Supreme Court, by a vote of 6-2, validated the lower court's decision declaring that the Circuit Court had not excessively interfered with the state's jurisdiction, and that Neagle was merely "keeping the peace of the United States." Justice Lucius Quintus Cincinnatus Lamar joined by Chief Justice Melville Fuller dissented. The majority opinion delivered by Justice Samuel F. Miller, and Lamar's dissent follow.

. . . We are quite sure that if Neagle had been merely a brother or a friend of Judge Field, traveling with him, and aware of all the previous relations of Terry to the judge—as he was—of his bitter animosity, his declared purpose to have revenge even to the point of killing him, he would have been justified in what he did in defense of Mr. Justice Field's life, and possibly of his own.

But such a justification would be a proper subject for consideration on a trial of the case for murder in the courts of the State of California, and there exists no authority in the courts of the United States to discharge the prisoner while held in custody by the state authorities for this offense, unless there be found in aid of the defense of the prisoner some element of power and authority asserted under the government of the United States.

This element is said to be found in the facts that Mr. Justice Field, when attacked, was in the immediate discharge of his duty as judge of the circuit courts of the United States within California; that the assault upon him grew out of an animosity of Terry and wife, arising out of the previous discharge of his duty as circuit justice in the case for which they were committed for contempt of court; and that the deputy marshal of the United States, who killed Terry in defense of Field's life, was charged with a duty under the law of the United States to protect Field from the violence which Terry was inflicting, and which was intended to lead to Field's death. . . .

We have no doubt that Mr. Justice Field when attacked by Terry was engaged in the discharge of his duties as circuit justice of the ninth circuit, and was entitled to all the protection under those circumstances which the law could give him.

It is urged, however, that there exists no statute authorizing any such protection as that which Neagle was instructed to give Judge Field in the present case, and indeed no protection whatever against a vindictive or malicious assault growing out of the faithful discharge of his official duties; and that the language... of the Revised Statutes, that the party seeking the benefit of the writ of habeus corpus must in this connection show that he is "in custody for an act done or omitted in pursuance of a law of the United States," makes it necessary that upon this occasion it should be shown that the act for which Neagle is imprisoned was done by virtue of an act of Congress. It is not supposed that any special act of Congress exists which authorizes the marshals or deputy marshals of the United States in express terms to accompany the judges of the Supreme Court through their circuits, and act as a body-guard to them, to defend them against malicious assaults against their persons. But we are of opinion that this view of the statute is an unwarranted restriction of the meaning of a law designed to extend in a liberal manner the benefit of the writ of habeas corpus to persons imprisoned for the performance of their duty. And we are satisfied that if it was the duty of Neagle, under the circumstances, a duty which could only arise under the laws of the United States, to defend Mr. Justice Field from a murderous attack upon him, he brings himself within the meaning of the section we have recited. . . .

In the view we take of the Constitution of the United States, any obligation fairly and properly inferable from that instrument, or any duty of the marshal to be derived from the general scope of his duties under the laws of the United States, is "a law" within the meaning of this phrase. It would be a great reproach to the system of government of the United States, declared to be within its sphere sovereign and supreme, if there is to be found within the domain of its powers no means of protecting the judges. . . .

We cannot doubt the power of the President to take measures for the protection of a judge of one of the courts of the United States, who, while in the discharge of the duties of his office, is threatened with a personal attack which may probably result in his death, and we think it clear that where this protection is to be afforded through the civil power, the Department of Justice is the proper one to set in motion the necessary means of protection. The correspondence already recited in this opinion between the marshal of the northern district of California, and the Attorney General, and the district attorney of the United States for that district, although prescribing no very specific mode of affording this protection by the Attorney General, is sufficient, we think, to warrant the marshal in taking the steps which he did take, in making the provision which he did make, for the protection and defense of Mr. Justice Field. . . .

The result at which we have arrived upon this examination is that in the protection of the person and the life of Mr. Justice Field while in the discharge of his official duties, Neagle was authorized to resist the attack of Terry upon him; that Neagle was correct in the belief that without prompt action on his part the assault of Terry upon the judge would have ended in the death of the latter; that such being his well-founded belief, he was justified in taking the life of Terry, as the only means of preventing the death of the man who was intended to be his victim; that in taking the life of Terry, under the circumstances, he was acting under the authority of the law of the United States, and was justified in so doing; and that he is not liable to answer in the courts of California on account of his part in that transaction.

We therefore affirm the judgment of the circiut court authorizing his discharge from the custody of the sheriff of San Joaquin County.

Mr. Justice Lamar (with whom concurred Mr. Chief Justice Fuller) dissenting.

The Chief Justice and myself are unable to assent to the conclusion reached by the majority of the court.

Our dissent is not based on any conviction as to the guilt or innocence of the appellee. The view which we take renders that question immaterial to the inquiry presented by this appeal. That inquiry is, whether the appellee, Neagle, shall in this *ex parte* proceeding be discharged and delivered from any trial or further inquiry in any court, state or federal, for what he has been accused of in the forms prescribed by the constitution and laws of the State in which the act in question was committed. Upon that issue we hold to the principle announced by this court in the case of *Ex parte Crouch,* 112 U.S., 178, 180 in which Mr. Chief Justice [Thomas E.] Waite, delivering the opinion of the court, said: "It is elementary learning that, if a prisoner is in the custody of a state court of competent jurisdiction, not illegally asserted, he cannot be taken from that jurisdiction and discharged on *habeas corpus* issued by a court of the United States, simply because he is not guilty of the offence for which he is held. All questions which may arise in the orderly course of the proceeding against him are to be determined by the court to whose jurisdiction he has been subjected, and no other court is authorized to interfere to prevent it. Here the right of the prisoner to a discharge depends alone on the sufficiency of his defence to the information under which he is held. Whether his defence is sufficient or not is for the court which tries him to determine. If, in this determination, errors are committed, they can only be corrected in an appropriate form of proceeding for that purpose. The office of a writ of *habeas corpus* is neither to correct such errors, nor to take the prisoner away from the court which holds him for trial, for fear, if he remains, they may be committed. Authorities to this effect in our own reports are numerous. . . .

It is stated as the vital position in appellee's case, that it is not supposed that any special act of Congress exists which authorizes the marshals or deputy marshals of the United States in express terms to accompany the judges of the Supreme Court through their circuits and act as a body guard to them to defend them against malicious assaults against their persons; that in the view taken of the Constitution of the United States, any obligation fairly and properly inferrable from that instrument, or any duty of the marshal to be derived from the general scope of his duties under the laws of the United States, is "a law" within the meaning of this phrase; and that it would be a great reproach to the system of government of the United States, declared to be within its sphere sovereign and supreme, if there was to be found within the domain of its powers no means of protecting the judges, in the conscientious and faithful discharge of their duties, from the malice and hatred of those upon whom their judgments might operate unfavorably. In considering this position, it is indispensable to observe carefully the distinction between the individual man Neagle, and the same person in his official capacity as a deputy marshal of the United States; and also the individual man whose life he defended, and the same person in his official capacity of a Circuit Justice of the United States. . . .

Now, we agree, taking the facts of the case as they are shown by the record, that the personal protection of Mr. Justice Field, as a private citizen, even to the death of Terry, was not only the right, but was also the duty of Neagle and of any other bystander. And we maintain that for the exercise of that right or duty he is answerable to the courts of the State of California, and to them alone. But we deny that upon the facts of this record, he, as deputy marshal Neagle, or as private citizen Neagle, had any duty imposed on him by the laws of the United States growing out of the official character of Judge Field as a Circuit Justice. We deny that anywhere in this transaction, accepting throughout the appellee's version of the facts, he occupied in law any position other than what would have been occupied by any other person who should have interfered in the same manner, in any other assault of the same character, between any two other persons in that room. In short, we think that there was nothing whatever in fact of an official character in the transaction, whatever may have been the appellee's view of his alleged official duties and powers; and, therefore, we think that the courts of the United States have in the present state of our legislation no jurisdiction whatever in the premises, and that the appellee should have been remanded to the custody of the sheriff.

The contention of the appellee, however, is that it was his official duty as United States marshal to protect the justice; and that for so doing in discharge of this duty, "which could only arise under the laws of the United States," his detention by the state courts brings the case within . . . the Revised Statutes, as aforesaid.

We shall therefore address ourselves as briefly as is consistent with the gravity of the question involved, to a consideration of all justice of that claim. We must, however, call attention again to the formal and deliberate admission that it is not pretended that there is any *single* specific statute making it, in so many words, Neagle's duty to protect the justice. The position assumed is, and is wholly, that the authority and duty to protect the justice did arise directly and necessarily out of the Constitution and positive congressional enactments. . . .

Great as the crime of Terry was in his assault upon Mr. Justice Field, so far from its being a crime against the court, it was not even a contempt of court, and could not have received adequate punishment as such. The Revised Statutes limits contempt to cases of misbehavior in the presence of the court, or so near thereto as to obstruct the administration of justice. . . .

If the act of Terry had resulted in the death of Mr. Justice Field, would the murder of him have been a crime against the United States? Would the government of the United States, with all the supreme powers of which we have heard so much in this discussion, have been competent, in the present condition of its statutes, to prosecute in its own tribunals the murder of its own Supreme Court justice, or even to inquire into the heinous offence through its own tribunals? If yes, then the slaying of Terry by the appellee, in the necessary prevention of such act, was authorized by the law of the United States, and he should be discharged; and that, independently of any official character, the situation being the same in the case of any citizen. But if no, how stands the matter then? The killing of Terry was not by authority of the United States, no matter by whom done; and the only authority relied on for vindication must be that of the State, and the slayer should be remanded to the state courts to be tried. The question then recurs, Would it have been a crime against the United States? There can be but one answer. Murder is not an offence against the United States, except when committed on the high seas or in some port or harbor without the jursidiction of the State, or in the District of Columbia, or in the Territories, or at other places where the national government has exclusive jurisdiction. It is well settled that such crime must be defined by statute, and no such statute has yet been pointed out. The United States government being thus powerless to try and punish a man charged with murder, we are not prepared to affirm that it is omnipotent to discharge from trial and give immunity from any liability to trial where he is accused of murder, unless an express statute of Congress is produced permitting such discharge.

We are not unmindful of the fact that in the foregoing remarks we have not discussed the bearings of this decision upon the autonomy of the States, in divesting them of what was once regarded as their exclusive jurisdiction over crimes committed within their own territory, against their own laws, and in enabling a federal judge or court, by an order in a *habeas corpus* proceeding, to deprive a State of its power to maintain its own public order, or to protect the security of society and the lives of its own citizens, whenever the amenability to its courts of a federal officer or employee or agent is sought to be enforced. We have not entered upon that question, because, as arising here, its suggestion is sufficient, and its consideration might involve the extent to which legislation in that direction may constitutionally go, which could only be properly determined when directly presented, by the record in a case before the court of adjudication.

For these reasons, as briefly stated as possible, we think the judgment of the court below should be reversed and the prisoner remanded to the custody of the sheriff of San Joaquin County, California; and we are the less reluctant to express this conclusion, because we cannot permit outselves to doubt that the authorities of the State of California are competent and willing to do justice; and that even if the appellee had been indicted, and had gone to trial upon this record, God and his country would have given him a good deliverance. . . .

Leisy v. Hardin
135 U.S. 100
1890

This case introduced Chief Justice Melville Fuller's "unbroken package" concept. The Court ruled that a state cannot prohibit articles of commerce from being imported into a state, despite the lack of congressional legislation on the matter. In this case an Illinois brewer named Leisy sued to recover a quantity of beer that had been seized by state authorities in Iowa for violating the Iowa prohibition law prohibiting the sale of alcoholic beverages in that state. The beer had been shipped from Illinois in its original containers which, the Court declared, was an item in interstate commerce. It was exempt from the Iowa prohibition statute because the packages had remained unopened and the product was intact.

The power vested in Congress "to regulate commerce with foreign nations, and among the several States, and with the Indian tribes," is the power to prescribe the rule by which that commerce is to be governed, and is a power complete in itself, acknowledging no limitations other than those prescribed in the Constitution. It is co-extensive with the subject on which it acts and cannot be stopped at the external boundary of a state, but must enter its interior and must be capable of authorizing the disposition of those articles which it introduces, so that they may become mingled with the common mass of property. . . .

And while, by virtue of its jurisdiction over persons and property within its limits, a state may provide for the security of the lives, limbs, health and comfort of persons, and the protection of property so situated, yet a subject matter which has been confided exclusively to Congress by the Constitution is not within the jurisdiction of the police power of the state. . . .

The power to regulate commerce among the states is a unit, but if particular subjects within its operation do not require the application of a general or uniform system, the states may legislate in regard to them with a view to local needs and circumstances, until Congress otherwise directs; but the power thus exercised by the states is not identical in its extent with the power to regulate commerce among the states. The power to pass laws in respect to internal commerce, inspection laws, quarantine laws, health laws, and laws in relation to bridges, ferries, and highways, belongs to the class of powers pertaining to locality, essential to local intercommunication, to the progress and development of local prosperity, and to the protection, the safety, and welfare of society, originally necessarily belonging to, and upon the adoption of the Constitution reserved by, the states, except so far as falling within the scope of a power confided to the general government. Where the subject matter requires a uniform system as between the states, the power controlling it is vested exclusively in Congress, and cannot be encroached upon by the states; but where, in relation to the subject matter, different rules may be suitable for different localities, the states may exercise powers which, though they may be said to partake of the nature of the power granted to the general government, are strictly not such, but are simply local powers, which have full operation until or unless circumscribed by the action of Congress in effectuation of the general power. *Cooley v. Port Wardens of Philadelphia,* 12 Howard, 299. . . .

It was stated in the thirty-second number of the *Federalist* that the states might exercise concurrent and independent power in all cases but three: First, where the power was lodged exclusively in the federal Constitution; second, where it was given to the United States and prohibited to the states; third, where, from the nature and subjects of the power, it must be necessarily exercised by the national government exclusively. But it is easy to see that Congress may assert an authority under one of the granted powers, which would exclude the exercise by the states upon the same subject of a different but similar power, between which and that possessed by the general government no inherent repugnancy existed.

Whenever, however, a particular power of the general government is one which must necessarily be exercised by it, and Congress remains silent, this is not only not a concession that the powers reserved by the states may be exerted as if the specific power had not been elsewhere reposed, but, on the contrary, the only legitimate conclusion is that the general government intended that power should not be affirmatively exercised, and the action of the states cannot be permitted to effect that which would be incompatible with such intention. . . .

That ardent spirits, distilled liquors, ale, and beer, are subjects of exchange, barter and traffic, like any other commodity in which a right of traffic exists, and are so recognized by the usages of the commercial world, the laws of Congress and the decisions of courts, is not denied. Being thus articles of commerce, can a state, the absence of legislation on the part of Congress, prohibit importation from abroad or from a sister state? or when imported prohibit their sale by the importer? If the importation cannot be prohibited without the consent of Congress, when does property imported from abroad, or from a sister state, so become part of the common mass of property within a state as to be subject to its unimpeded control? . . .

The conclusion follows that, as the grant of the power to regulate commerce among the states, so far as one system is required, is exclusive, the states cannot exercise that power without the assent of Congress, and, in the absence of legislation, it is left for the courts to determine when state action does or does not amount to such exercise, or, in other words, what is or is not a regulation of such commerce. When that is determined, controversy is at an end. . . .

These decisions rest upon the undoubted right of the states of the Union to control their purely internal affairs, in doing which they exercise powers not surrendered to the national government; but whenever the law of the state amounts essentially to a regulation of commerce with foreign nations or among the states, as it does when it inhibits, directly or indirectly, the receipt of an imported commodity or its disposition before it has ceased to become an article of trade between one state and another or another country and this, it comes in conflict with a power which, in this particular, has been exclusively vested in the general government, and is therefore void. . . .

The plaintiffs in error are citizens of Illinois, are not pharmacists and have no permit, but import into Iowa beer, which they sell in original packages, as described. Under our decision in *Bowman v. Chicago etc. Railway Co.,* 125 U.S. 465, they had the right to import this beer into that state, and in the view which we have expressed they had the right to sell it, by which act alone it would become mingled in the common mass of property within the state. Up to that point of time, we hold that in the absence of congressional permission to do so, the state had no power to interfere by seizure, or any other action, in prohibition of importation and sale by the foreign or non-resident importer. Whatever our individual views may be as to the deleterious or dangerous qualities of particular articles, we cannot hold that any articles which Congress recognizes as subjects of interstate commerce are not such, or that whatever are thus recognized can be controlled by state laws amounting to regulations, while they retain that character; although, at the same time, if directly dangerous in themselves, the state may take appropriate measures to guard against injury before it obtains complete jurisdiction over them. To concede to a state the power to exclude, directly or indirectly, articles so situated, without congressional permission, is to concede to a majority of the people of a state, represented in the state legislature, the power to regulate commercial intercourse between the states, by determining what shall be its subjects, when that power was distinctly granted to be exercised by the people of the United States, represented in Congress, and its possession by the latter was considered essential to that more perfect union which the Constitution was adopted to create. . . .

The legislation in question is to the extent indicated repugnant to . . . article 1 of the Constitution of the United States, and therefore the judgment of the Supreme Court of Iowa is reversed and the cause remanded for further proceedings not inconsistent with this opinion. . . .

Late Corporation of the Church of Jesus Christ of the Latter-Day Saints v. United States (Mormon Church Case)

136 U.S. 1

1890

Known as the *Mormon Church* case, this decision concerned the disposition of Mormon Church property, including buildings and lands, after Congress enacted a statute which revoked the church's charter for failure to renounce the practice of polygamy. A unanimous Court ruled through Justice Joseph P. Bradley that these lands and buildings be used to establish and house the Utah Territory's common school districts. The Court refused to accept the plaintiff's petition that the property be equally divided among individual Mormons themselves. At the same time it validated Congress's right to repeal the church's charter under its constitutional authority to make all necessary rules and regulations respecting the territories or other property of the United States.

The principal questions raised are, first, as to the power of Congress to repeal the charter of the Church of Jesus Christ of Latter-Day Saints; and, secondly, as to the power of Congress and the courts to seize the property of said corporation and to hold the same for the purposes mentioned in the decree.

The power of Congress over the Territories of the United States is general and plenary, arising from and incidental to the right to acquire the Territory itself, and from the power given by the Constitution to make all needful rules and regulations respecting the Territory or other property belonging to the United States. It would be absurd to hold that the United States has power to acquire territory, and no power to govern it when acquired. The power to acquire territory, other than the territory northwest of the Ohio River (which belonged to the United States at the adoption of the Constitution,) is derived from the treaty-making power and the power to declare and carry on war. The incidents of these powers are those of national sovereignty, and belong to all independent governments. The power to make acquisitions of territory by conquest, by treaty and by cession is an incident of national sovereignty. The territory of Louisiana, when acquired from France, and the territories west of the Rocky Mountains, when acquired from Mexico, became the absolute property and domain of the United States, subject to such conditions as the government, in its diplomatic negotiations, had seen fit to accept relating to the rights of the people then inhabiting those territories. Having rightfully acquired said territories, the United States government was the only one which could impose laws upon them, and its sovereignty over them was complete. No State of the Union had any such right of sovereignty. . . .

The supreme power of Congress over the Territories and over the acts of the territorial legislatures established therein, is generally expressly reserved in the organic acts establishing governments in said Territories. This is true of the Territory of Utah. In the. . .section of the act establishing a territorial government in Utah, approved September 9, 1850, it is declared "that the legislative powers of said Territory shall extend to all rightful subjects of legislation, consistent with the Constitution of the United States and the provisions of this act. . . . All the laws passed by the legislative assembly and governor shall be submitted to the Congress of the United States, and if disapproved shall be null and of no effect. 9 Stat. 454.

This brings us directly to the question of the power of Congress to revoke the charter of the Church of Jesus Christ of Latter-Day Saints. That corporation, when the Territory of Utah was organized, was a corporation *de facto,* existing under an ordinance of the so-called State of Deseret, approved February 8, 1851. This ordinance had no validity except in the voluntary acquiescence of the people of Utah then residing there. Deseret, or Utah, had ceased to belong to the Mexican government by the treaty of Guadalupe Hidalgo, and in 1851, it belonged to the United States, and no government without authority from the United States, express or implied, had any legal right to exist there. The assembly of Deseret had no power to make any valid law. Congress had already passed the law for organizing the Territory of Utah into a government, and no other government was lawful within the bounds of that Territory. But after the organization of the territorial government of Utah under the act of Congress, the legislative assembly of the Territory passed the following resolution: *"Resolved, by the Legislative Assembly of the Territory of Utah,* That the laws heretofore passed by the provisional government of the State of Deseret, and which do not conflict with the organic act of said Territory, be and the same are hereby declared to be legal and in full force and virtue, and shall so remain until superseded by the action of the legislative assembly of the Territory of Utah." This resolution was approved October 4, 1851. The confirmation was repeated on the 19th of January, 1855, by the act of the legislative assembly entitled, "An act in relation to the compilation and revision of the laws and resolutions in force in Utah Territory, their publication and distribution." From the time of these confirmatory acts, therefore, the said corporation had a legal existence under its charter. But it is too plain for argument that this charter, or enactment, was subject to revocation and repeal by Congress whenever it should see fit to exercise its power for that purpose. Like any other act of the territorial legislature, it was subject to this condition. Not only so, but the power of Congress could be exercised in modifying or limiting the powers and privileges granted by such charter; for if it could repeal, it could modify; the greater includes the less. Hence there can be no question that the act of July 1, 1862, already recited, was a valid exercise of congressional power. Whatever may be the effect or true construction of this act, we have no doubt of its validity. As far as it went it was effective. If it did not absolutely repeal the charter of the corporation, it certainly took away all right or power which may have been claimed under it to establish, protect, or foster the practice of polygamy, under whatever disguise it might be carried on; and it also limited the amount of property which might be acquired by the Church of Jesus Christ of Latter-Day Saints; not interfering, however, with vested rights in real estate existing at that time. If the act of July 1, 1862, had but a partial effect, Congress had still the power to make the abrogation of its charter absolute and complete. This was done by the act of 1887. By. . . that act it is expressly declared that "the acts of the legislative assembly of the Territory of Utah, incorporating, continuing or providing for the corporation known as the Church of Jesus Christ of Latter-Day Saints, and the ordinance of the so-called general assembly of the State of Deseret, incorporating the said church, so far as the same may now have legal force and validity, are hereby disapproved and annulled, and the said corporation, so far as it may now have or pretend to have any legal existence, is hereby dissolved." This absolute annulment of the laws which gave the said corporation a legal existence has dissipated all doubt on the subject, and the said corporation has ceased to have any existence as a civil body, whether for the purpose of holding property or of doing any other corporate act. It was not necessary to resort to the condition imposed by the act of 1862, limiting the amount of real estate which any corporation or association for religious or charitable purposes was authorized to acquire or hold; although it is apparent from the findings of the court that this condition was violated by the corporation before the passage of the act of 1887. Congress, for good and sufficient reasons of its own, independent of that limitation, and of any violation of it, had a full and perfect right to repeal its charter and abrogate its corporate existence, which of course depended upon its charter.

The next question is, whether Congress or the court had the power to cause the property of the said corporation to be seized and taken possession of, as was done in this case. . . .

It is distinctly stated in the pleadings and findings of fact, that the property of the said corporation was held for the purpose of religious and charitable uses. But it is also stated in the findings of fact, and is a matter of public notoriety, that the religious and charitable uses intended to be subserved and promoted are the inculcation and spread of the doctrines and usages of the Mormon Church, or Church of Latter-Day Saints, one of the distinguishing features of which is the practice of polygamy—a crime against the laws, and abhorrent to the sentiments and feelings of the civilized world. Notwithstanding the stringent laws which have been passed by Congress—

notwithstanding all the efforts made to suppress this barbarous practice—the sect or community composing the Church of Jesus Christ of Latter-Day Saints perseveres, in defiance of law, in preaching, upholding, promoting and defending it. It is a matter of public notoriety that its emissaries are engaged in many countries in propagating this nefarious doctrine, and urging its converts to join the community in Utah. The existence of such a propaganda is a blot on our civilization. The organization of a community for the spread and practice of polygamy is, in a measure, a return to barbarism. It is contrary to the spirit of Christianity and of the civilization which Christianity has produced in the Western world. The question, therefore, is whether the promotion of such a nefarious system and practice, so repugnant to our laws and to the principles of our civilization, is to be allowed to continue by the sanction of the government itself; and whether the funds accumulated for that purpose shall be restored to the same unlawful uses as heretofore, to the detriment of the true interests of civil society.

It is unnecessary here to refer to the past history of the sect, to their defiance of the government authorities, to their attempt to establish an independent community, to their efforts to drive from the territory all who were not connected with them in communion and sympathy. The tale is one of patience on the part of the American government and people, and of contempt of authority and resistance to law on the part of the Mormons. Whatever persecutions they may have suffered in the early part of their history, in Missouri and Illinois, they have no excuse for their persistent defiance of law under the government of the United States.

One pretence for this obstinate course is, that their belief in the practice of polygamy, or in the right to indulge in it, is a religious belief, and, therefore, under the protection of the constitutional guaranty of religious freedom. This is altogether a sophistical plea. No doubt the Thugs of India imagined that their belief in the right of assassination was a religious belief; but their thinking so did not make it so. The practice of suttee by the Hindu widows may have sprung from a supposed religious conviction. The offering of human sacifices by our own ancestors in Britain was no doubt sanctioned by an equally conscientious impulse. But no one, on that account, would hesitate to brand these practices, now, as crimes against society, and obnoxious to condemnation and punishment by the civil authority.

The State has a perfect right to prohibit polygamy, and all other open offenses against the enlightened sentiment of mankind, notwithstanding the pretense of religious conviction by which they may be advocated and practised. *Davis v. Beason,* 133 U.S. 333. Any since polygamy has been forbidden by the laws of the United States, under severe penalties, and since the Church of Jesus Christ of Latter-Day Saints has persistently used and claimed the right to use, and the unincorporated community still claims the same right to use, the funds with which the late corporation was endowed for the purpose of promoting and propagating the unlawful practice as an integral part of their religious usages, the question arises, whether the government, finding these funds without legal ownership, has or has not, the right, through its courts, and in due course of administration, to cause them to be seized and devoted to objects of undoubted charity and usefulness—such for example as the maintenance of schools—for the benefit of the community whose leaders are now misusing them in the unlawful manner above described; setting apart, however, for the exclusive possession and use of the church, sufficient and suitable portions of the property for the purposes of public worship, parsonage buildings and burying grounds, as provided in the law.

The property in question has been dedicated to public and charitable uses. It matters not whether it is the product of private contributions, made during the course of half a century, or of taxes imposed upon the people, or of gains arising from fortunate operations in business, or appreciation in values; the charitable uses for which it is held are stamped upon it by charter, by ordinance, by regulation and by usage, in such an indelible manner that there can be no mistake as to their character, purpose or object.

The law respecting property held for charitable uses of course depends upon the legislation and jurisprudence of the country in which the property is situated and the uses are carried out; and when the positive law affords no specific provision for actual cases that arise, the subject must necessarily be governed by those principles of reason and public policy which prevail in all civilized and enlightened communities. . . .

The foregoing considerations place it beyond doubt that the general law of charities, as understood and administered in our Anglo-American system of laws, was and is applicable to the case now under consideration.

Then looking at the case as the finding of facts presents it, we have before us—Congress had before it—a contumacious organization, wielding by its resources an immense power in the Territory of Utah, and employing those resources and that power in constantly attempting to oppose, thwart and subvert the legislation of Congress and the will of the government of the United States. Under these circumstances we have no doubt of the power of Congress to do as it did. . . .

. . . The principal question discussed has been, whether the property of the church was in such a condition as to authorize the government and the court to take possession of it and hold it until it shall be seen what final disposition of it should be made; and we think it was in such a condition, and that it is properly held in the custody of the receiver. The rights of the church members will necessarily be taken into consideration in the final disposition of the case. There is no ground for granting their present application. The property is in the custody of the law, awaiting the judgment of the court as to its final disposition in view of the illegal uses to which it is subject in the hands of the Church of Latter-Day Saints, whether incorporated or unincorporated. The condition for claiming possession of it by the members of the sect or community under the act do not at present exist. . . .

McCall v. California
136 U.S. 104
1890

The Court, in a 6-3 decision read by Justice Lucius Quintus Cincinnatus Lamar, declared unconstitutional a license tax levied by the city of San Francisco upon a local office of a Chicago to New York railroad company on the ground that the tax was an unfair burden on interstate commerce. The Court reasoned that since the purpose of the local office was to solicit passengers for the railroad who were going to New York from California via Chicago, the local agency was therefore engaged in interstate commerce and thus was not subject to state and local taxation. This case established a precedent by severely limiting state or local taxation of agencies engaged in interstate commerce.

There are three assignments of error which are reducible to the single proposition that the order under which the plaintiff in error was convicted is repugnant to . . . article 1 of the Constitution of the United States, commonly known as the commerce clause of the Constitution, in that it imposes a tax upon interstate commerce, and that therefore the court below erred in not so deciding and in rendering judgment against the plaintiff in error.

This proposition presents the only question in the case, and if it appears from this record that the business in which the plaintiff in error was engaged was interstate commerce, it must follow that the license tax exacted of him as a condition precedent to his carrying on that business was a tax upon interstate commerce, and therefore violative of the commercial clause of the Constitution. . . .

Tested by these principles and definitions, what was the business or occupation carried on by the plaintiff in error on which the tax in question was imposed? It is agreed by both parties that his business was that of soliciting passengers to travel over the railroad which he represents as an agent. It is admitted that the travel which it was his business to solicit is not from one place to another within the State of California. His business, therefore, as a raiload agent had no connection, direct or indirect, with any domestic commerce between two or more places within the State. His employment was limited exclusively to inducing persons in the State of California to travel from that State into and through other States to the city of New York. To what, then, does his agency relate except to interstate transportation of persons? Is not that as much an agency of interstate commerce as if he were engaged in soliciting and securing the transportation of freight from San Francisco to New York City over that line of railroad? If the business of the New York, Lake Erie, and Western Railroad Company in carrying passengers by rail between Chicago and New York and intermediate points, in both directions, is interstate commerce, as much so as is the carrying of freight, it follows that the soliciting of passengers to travel over that route was a part of the business of securing the passenger traffic of the company. The object and effect of his soliciting agency were to swell the volume of the business of the road. It was one of the "means" by which the company sought to increase and doubtless did increase its interstate passenger traffic. It was not incidentally or remotely connected with the business of the road, but was a direct method of increasing that business. The tax upon it, therefore, was, according to the principles established by the decisions of this court, a tax upon a means or an occupation of carrying on interstate commerce, pure and simple. . . .

We might conclude our observations on the case with the above remarks, but we deem it proper to notice some of the points raised by the defendant in error and which were relied upon by the court below to control its decision sustaining the validity of the aforesaid order.

It is argued that the New York, Lake Erie, and Western Railroad Company is a foreign corporation operating between Chicago and New York City, wholly outside of and distinct from California; and it is very earnestly contended that the business of soliciting passengers in California for such a road cannot be interstate commerce, as it has not for its end the introduction of anything into the State. We do not think that fact, even as stated, is material in this case. The argument is based upon the assumption that the provision in the Constitution of the United States relating to commerce among the states applies as a limitation of power only to those States through which such commerce would pass, and that any other State can impose any tax it may deem proper upon such commerce. To state such a proposition is to refute it; for if the clause in question prohibits a State from taxing interstate commerce as it passes through its own territory, a fortiori, the prohibition will extend to such commerce when it does not pass through its territory. The argument entirely overlooks the fact that in this case the object was to send passenger traffic out of California into and through the other States traversed by the road for which the plaintiff in error was soliciting patronage.

It is further said that the soliciting of passengers in California for a railroad running from Chicago to New York, if connected with interstate commerce at all, is so very remotely connected with it that the hindrance to the business of the plaintiff in error caused by the tax could not directly affect the commerce of the road, because his business was not essential to such commerce. The reply to this proposition is, that the essentiality of the business of the plaintiff in error to the commerce of the road he represented is not the test as to whether that business was a part of interstate commerce. It may readily be admitted, without prejudicing his defence, that the road would continue to carry passengers between Chicago and New York even if the agent had been prohibited altogether from pursuing his business in California. The test is—Was this business a part of the commerce of the road? Did it assist, or was it carried on with the purpose to assist, in increasing the amount of passenger traffic on the road? If it did, the power to tax it involves the lessening of the commerce of the road to an extent commensurate with the amount of business done by the agent. . . .

Smith v. Alabama was a case in which an act of the state legislature imposing a license upon any locomotive engineer operating or running any engine or train of cars on any railroad in that State was resisted by an engineer of the Mobile and Ohio Railroad Company, who ran an engine drawing passenger coaches on that road from Mobile in that State to Corinth in Mississippi, on the ground that the statute of the State was an attempt to regulate interstate commerce, and was, therefore, repugnant to the commercial clause of the Constitution of the United States. We held, however, that the statute in question was not in its nature a regulation of commerce; that so far as it affected commercial transactions among the States, its effect was so indirect, incidental, and remote as not to burden or impede such commerce, and that it was not, therefore, in conflict with the Constitution of the United States or any law of Congress. It having been thus ascertained that the legislation of the State of Alabama did not impose any burden or tax upon interstate commerce, there is nothing to be found in the opinion in that case that is not in harmony with the doctrines we have asserted in this case. That opinion quoted at length from *Sherlock v. Alling,* 93 U.S. 99, 102, where it was expressly held that "the States cannot by legislation place burdens upon commerce with foreign nations or among the several States. The decisions go to that extent and their soundness is not questioned. But, upon an examination of the cases in which they were rendered, it will be found that the legislation adjudged invalid imposed a tax upon some *instrument* or subject of commerce, or *exacted a license fee from parties engaged in commercial pursuits,* or created an impediment to the free navigation of some public waters, or prescribed conditions in accordance with which commerce in particular articles or between particular places was required to be conducted. In all the cases the legislation condemned operated directly upon comerce, either by way of tax upon its business, license upon its pursuit in particular channels or conditions for carrying it on."

It results from what we have said that the judgment of the court below should be, and it hereby is, reversed, and the case is remanded to that court for further proceedings in conformity with this opinion.

Minnesota v. Barber

136 U.S. 313

1890

A unanimous Court speaking through Justice John Marshall Harlan, ruled unconstitutional a Minnesota act requiring state inspection of cattle brought into the state for slaughter within twenty-four hours of their arrival. The Court reasoned that the statute under review patently discriminated against meat products from other states and therefore placed an undue burden upon interstate commerce. This decision by the Fuller Court established an early precedent in opposition to state legislation which discriminated against interstate commerce under the guise of state police powers.

. . . It is our duty to inquire, in respect to the statute before us, not only whether there is a real or substantial relation between its avowed objects and the means devised for attaining those objects, but whether, by its necessary or natural operation, it impairs or destroys rights secured by the constitution of the United States.

Underlying the entire argument in behalf of the state is the proposition that it is impossible to tell, by an inspection of fresh beef, veal, mutton, lamb, or pork, designed for human food, whether or not it came from animals that were diseased when slaughtered; that inspection on the hoof, within a very short time before animals are slaughtered, is the only mode by which their condition can be ascertained.

. . . But we cannot assent to the suggestiion that the fact alleged in this case to exist is of that class. It may be the opinion of some that the presence of disease in animals at the time of their being slaughtered cannot be determined by inspection of the meat taken from them; but we are not aware that such is the view universally, or even generally, entertained. But if, as alleged, the inspection of fresh beef, veal, mutton, lamb, or pork will not necessarily show whether the animal from which it was taken was diseased when slaughtered, it would not follow that a statute like the one before us is within the constitutional power of the state to enact. On the contrary, the enactment of a similar statute by each one of the states composing the Union would result in the destruction of commerce among the several states, so far as such commerce is involved in the transportation from one part of the country to another of animal meats designed for human food, and entirely free from disease. A careful examination of the Minnesota act will place this construction of it beyond question.

The first section prohibits the sale of any fresh beef, veal, mutton, lamb, or pork for human food except as provided in that act. The second and third sections provide that all cattle, sheep, and swine to be slaughtered for human food within the respective jurisdictions of the inspectors shall be inspected, by the proper local inspector appointed in Minnesota, within 24 hours before the animals are slaughtered, and that a certificate shall be made by such inspector showing, if such be the fact, that the animals when slaughtered were found healthy and in suitable condition to be slaughtered for human food. The fourth section makes it a misdemeanor, punishable by fine or imprisonment, for any one to sell, expose or offer for sale, for human food in the state, any fresh beef, veal, mutton, lamb, or pork, not taken from an animal inspected and "certified before slaughter by the proper local inspector" appointed under that act. As the inspection must take place within the 24 hours immediately before the slaughtering, the act, by its necessary operation, excludes from the Minnesota market, practically, all fresh beef, veal, mutton, lamb, or pork—in whatever form, and although entirely sound, healthy, and fit for human food—taken from animals slaughtered in other states, and directly tends to restrict the slaughtering of animals whose meat is to be sold in Minnesota for human food to those engaged in such business in that state. . . . It will not do to say—certainly no judicial tribunal can with propriety assume—that the people of Minnesota may not, with due regard to their health, rely upon inspections in other states of animals there slaughtered for purposes of human food. If the object of the statute had been to deny altogether the citizens of other states the privilege of selling, within the limits of Minnesota, for human food, any fresh beef, veal, mutton, lamb, or pork from animals slaughtered outside of that state, and to compel the people of Minnesota wishing to buy such meats either to purchase those taken from animals inspected and slaughtered in the state, or to incur the cost of purchasing them, when desired for their own domestic use, at points beyond the state, that object is attained by the act in question. Our duty to maintain the constitution will not permit us to shut our eyes to these obvious and necessary results of the Minnesota statute. If this legislation does not make such discrimination against the products and business of other states in favor of the products and business of Minnesota as interferes with and burdens commerce among the several states, it would be difficult to enact legislation that would have that result.

The principals we have announced are fully supported by the decisioins of this court. In Woodruff v. Parham, 8 Wall. 123, 140, which involved the validity of an ordinance of the city of Mobile, Ala., relating to sales at auction, Mr. Justice [Samuel F.] Miller, speaking for this court, said: "There is no attempt to discriminate injuriously against the products of other states, or the rights of their citizens; and the case is not, therefore, an attempt to fetter commerce among the states, or to deprive the citizens of other states of any privilege or immunity possessed by citizens of Alabama. But a law having such operation would, in our opinion, be an infringement of the provisions of the constitution which relate to those subjects, and therefore void." So, in *Hinson v. Lott,* Id. 148, 151, decided at the same time, upon a writ of error from the supreme court of Alabama, it was said, in reference to the opinion of that court: "And it is also true, as conceded in that opinion, that congress has the same right to regulate commerce among the states that it has to regulate commerce with foreign nations, and that, whenever it exercises that power, all conflicting state laws must give way, and that, if Congress had made any regulation covering the matter in question, we need inquire no further. . . .

But a law providing for the inspection of animals whose meats are designed for human food cannot be regarded as a rightful exertion of the police powers of the state, if the inspection prescribed is of such a character, or is burdened with such conditions, as will prevent altogether the introduction into the state of sound meats, the product of animals slaughtered in other states. It is one thing for a state to exclude from its limits cattle, sheep, or swine actually diseased, or meats that, by reason of their condition, or the condition of the animals from which they are taken, are unfit for human food, and punish all sales of such animals or of such meats within its limits. It is quite a different thing for a state to declare, as does Minnesota, by the necessary operation of its statute, that fresh beef, veal, mutton, lamb, or pork—articles that are used in every part of this country to support human life—shall not be sold at all for human food within its limits unless the animal from which such meats are taken is inspected in that state, or, as is practically said, unless the animal is slaughtered in that state.

One other suggestion by the counsel for the state deserves to be examined. It is that, so far as this statute is concerned, the people of Minnesota can purchase in other states fresh beef, veal, mutton, lamb, and pork, and bring such meats into Minnesota for their own personal use. We do not perceive that this view strengthens the case of the state, for it ignores the right which the people of other states have in commerce between those states and the state of Minnesota, and it ignores the right of the people of Minnesota to bring into that state, for purposes of sale, sound and healthy meat, wherever such meat may have come into existence. But there is a consideration arising out of the suggestion just alluded to which militates somewhat against the theory that the statute in question is a legitimate exertion of the police powers of the state for the protection of the public health. If every hotel keeper, railroad, or mining corporation, or contractor in Minnesota furnishing subsistence to large numbers of persons, and every private family in that state that is so disposed, can, without violating the statute, bring into the state from other states, and use for their own purposes, fresh beef, veal, mutton, lamb, and pork taken from animals slaughtered outside of Minnesota which may not have been inspected at all, or not within 24 hours before being slaughtered, what becomes of the argument, pressed with so much earnestness, that the health of the people of that state requires that they be protected against the use of meats from animals not inspected in Minnesota within 24 hours before being slaughtered?. . . .

In the opinion of this court, the statute in question, so far as its provisions require, as a condition of sales in Minnesota, of fresh beef, veal, mutton, lamb, or pork, for human food, that the animals from which such meats are taken shall have been inspected in Minnesota before being slaughtered, is in violation of the constitution of the United States, and void.

Budd v. New York
143 U.S. 517
1891

In a 6-3 decision, the Supreme Court speaking through Justice Samuel Blatchford, reasserted the "public interest" doctrine of *Munn v. Illinois,* and stated that a "practical" as well as a legal monopoly could be endowed with that interest and thus be subject to regulation. This decision validated a New York State law regulating warehouse and grain elevator rates. Justices David J. Brewer, Henry B. Brown, and Stephen J. Field dissented, declaring that private enterprise was unduly restricted by this type of state regulatory measure.

The main question involved in these cases is whether this court will adhere to its decision in *Munn v. Illinois*. . . .

It is claimed, on behalf of Budd, that the statute of the State of New York is unconstitutional, because contrary to the provisions of. . . the Fourteenth Amendment to the Constitution of the United States, in depriving the citizen of his property without due process of law; that it is unconstitutional in fixing the maximum charge for elevating, receiving, weighing, and discharging grain by means of floating and stationary elevators and warehouses at five-eights of one cent a bushel and in forbidding the citizen to make any profit upon the use of his property or labor; and that the police power of the State extends only to property or business which is devoted by its owner to the public, by a grant to the public of the right to demand its use. It is claimed on behalf of Annan and Pinto that floating and stationary elevators in the port of New York are private property, not affected with any public interest, and not subject to the regulation of rates. . . .

The Court of Appeals, in its opinion in the Budd case, considered fully the question as to whether the legislature had power, under the constitution of the State of New York, to prescribe a maximum charge for elevating grain by stationary elevators, owned by individuals or corporations who had appropriated their property to that use and were engaged in that business; and it answered the inquiry in the affirmative. It also reviewed the case of *Munn v. Illinois,* . . . and arrived at the conclusion that this court there held that the legislation in question in that case was a lawful exercise of legislative power, and did not infringe that clause of the Fourteenth Amendment to the Constitution of the United States which provides that no State shall "deprive any person of life, liberty or property without due process of law"; and that the legislation in question in that case was similar to, and not distinguishable in principle from, the act of the State of New York....

The opinion further said that the criticism to which the case of *Munn v. Illinois* had been subjected proceeded mainly upon a limited and strict construction and definition of the police power; that there was little reason, under our system of government, for placing a close and narrow interpretation on the police power, or restricting its scope so as to hamper the legislative power in dealing with the varying necessities of society and the new circumstances as they arise calling for legislative intervention in the public interest; and that no serious invasion of constitutional guarantees by the legislature could withstand for a long time the searching influence of public opinion, which was sure to come sooner or later to the side of law, order and justice, however it might have been swayed for a time by passion or prejudice, or whatever aberrations might have marked its course.

We regard these views which we have referred to as announced by the Court of Appeals of New York, so far as they support the validity of the statute in question, as sound and just....

This court, in *Munn v. Illinois,* the opinion being delivered by Chief Justice [Morrison R.] Waite, and there being a published dissent by only two justices, considered carefully the question of the repugnancy of the Illinois statute to the Fourteenth Amendment. It said, that under the powers of government inherent in every sovereignty, "the government regulates the conduct of its citizens one toward another, and the manner in which each shall use his own property, when such regulation becomes necessary for the public good"; and that, "in their exercise it has been customary in England from time immemorial, and in this country from its first colonization, to regulate ferries, common carriers, hackmen, bakers, millers, wharfingers, innkeepers, etc., and in so doing to fix a maximum of charge to be made for services rendered, accommodations furnished, and articles sold." It was added: "To this day, statutes are to be found in many of the States upon some or all these subjects; and we think it has never yet been successfully contended that such legislation came within any of the constitutional prohibitions against interference with private property." It announced as its conclusions that, down to the time of the adoption of the Fourteenth Amendment, it was not supposed that statutes regulating the use, or even the price of the use, of private property necessarily deprived an owner of his property without due process of law; that, when private property was devoted to a public use, it was subject to public regulation; that Munn and Scott, in conducting the business of their warehouse, pursued a public employment and exercised a sort of public office, in the same sense as did a common carrier, miller, ferryman, inn-keeper, wharfinger, baker, cartman or hackney coachman; that they stood in the very gateway of commerce and took toll from all who passed; that their business tended "to a common charge," and had become a thing of public interest and use; that the toll on the grain was a common charge; and that, according to Lord Chief Justice Hale, every such warehouseman "ought to be under a public regulation, viz.": that he "take but reasonable toll."

This court further held in *Munn v. Illinois,* that the business in question was one in which the whole public had a direct and positive interest; that the statute of Illinois simply extended the law so as to meet a new development of commercial progress; that there was no attempt to compel the owners of the warehouses to grant the public an interest in their property, but to declare their obligations if they used it in that particular manner; that it mattered not that Munn and Scott had built their warehouses and established their business before the regulations complained of were adopted; that, the property being clothed with a public interest, what was a reasonable compensation for its use was not a judicial, but a legislative question; that, in countries where the common law prevailed, it had been customary from time immemorial for the legislature to declare what should be a reasonable compensation under such circumstances, or to fix a maximum beyond which any charge made would be unreasonable; that the warehouses of Munn and Scott were situated in Illinois and their business was carried on exclusively in that State; that the warehouses were no more necessarily a part of commerce itself than the dray or the cart by which, but for them, grain would be transferred from one railroad station to another; that their regulation was a thing of domestic concern; that, until Congress acted in reference to their interstate relations, the State might exercise all the powers of government over them, even though in so doing it might operate indirectly upon commerce outside its immediate jurisdiction; and that the provision of §9 of article 1 of the Constitution of the United States operated only as a limitation of the powers of Congress, and did not affect the States in the regulation of their domestic affairs. The final conclusion of the court was, that the act of Illinois was not repugnant to the Constitution of the United States; and the judgment was affirmed. . . .

In *Chicago &c. Railway Co. V. Minnesota,* 134 U.S. 418, 461, it was said by Mr. Justice [Joseph P.] Bradley, in his dissenting opinion, in which Mr. Justice [Horace] Gray and Mr. Justice [Lucius Quintus Cincinnatus] Lamar concurred, that the decision of the court in that case practically overruled *Munn v. Illinois;* but the opinion of the court did not say so, nor did it refer to *Munn v. Illinois;* and we are of opinion that the decision in the case in 134 U.S. is, as will be hereafter shown, quite distinguishable from the present cases.

It is thus apparent that this court has adhered to the decision in *Munn v. Illinois* and to the doctrines announced in the opinion of the court in that case; and those doctrines have since been repeatedly enforced in the decisions of the courts of the States. . . .

We must regard the principle maintained in *Munn v. Illinois* as firmly established; and we think it covers the present cases, in respect to the charge for elevating, receiving, weighing and discharging the grain, as well as in respect to the charge for trimming and shovelling to the leg of the elevator when loading, and trimming the cargo when loaded. If the shovellers or scoopers chose, they might do the shovelling by hand, or might use a steam-shovel. A steam-shovel is owned by the elevator owner, and the power for operating it is furnished by the engine of the elevator; and if the scooper uses the steam-shovel, he pays the elevator owner for the use of it.

The answer to the suggestion that by the statute the elevator owner is forbidden to make any profit from the business of shovelling to the leg of the elevator is that made by the Court of Appeals of New York in the case of Budd, that the words "actual cost," used in the statute, were intended to exclude any charge by the elevator owner, beyond the sum specified for the use of his machinery in shovelling and the ordinary expenses of operating it, and to confine the charge to the actual cost of the outside labor required for trimming and bringing the grain to the leg of the elevator; and that the purpose of the statute could be easily evaded and defeated if the elevator owner was permitted to separate the services, and to charge for the use of his steam-shovel any sum which might be agreed upon between himself and the shovellers' union, and thereby, under color of charging for the use of his steam-shovel, to exact of the carrier a sum for elevating beyond the rate fixed by the statute.

We are of opinion that the act of the legislature of New York is not contrary to the Fourteenth Amendment to the Constitution of the United States, and does not deprive the citizen of his property without due process of law; that the act, in fixing the maximum charges which it specifies, is not unconstitutional, nor is it so in limiting the charge for shovelling to the actual cost thereof; and that it is a proper exercise of the police power of the State. . . .

. . . The act is also constitutional as an exercise of the police power of the State.

So far as the statute in question is a regulation of commerce, it is a regulation of commerce only on the waters of the State of New York. It operates only within the limits of that State, and is no more obnoxious as a regulation of interstate commerce than was the statute of Illinois in respect to warehouses in *Munn v. Illinois.* It is of the same character with nagivation laws in respect to navigation within the State, and laws regulating wharfage rates within the State, and other kindred laws.

It is further contended that, under the decision of this court in *Chicago &c. Railway Company v. Minnesota,* . . . the fixing of elevator charges is a judicial question, as to whether they are reasonable or not; that the statute must permit and provide for a judicial settlement of the charges; and that, by the statute under consideration, an arbitrary rate is fixed and all inquiry is precluded as to whether that rate is reasonable or not. . . .

What was said in the opinion in 134 U.S. as to the question of the reasonableness of the rate of charge being one for judicial investigation, had no reference to a case where the rates are prescribed directly by the legislature. Not only was that the case in the statute of Illinois in *Munn v. Illinois,* but the doctrine was laid down by this court in *Wabash &c. Railway Co. v. Illinois,* . . . that it was the right of a State to establish limitations upon the power of railroad companies to fix the price at which they would carry passengers and freight, and that the question was of the same character as that involved in fixing the charges to be made by persons engaged in the warehousing business. So, too, in *Dow v. Beidelman,* 125 U.S. 680, 686, it was said that it was within the power of the legislature to declare what should be a reasonable compensation for the services of persons exercising a public employment, or to fix a maximum beyond which any charge made would be unreasonable. . . .

. . . The legislature may itself fix a maximum beyond which any charge would be unreasonable, in respect to services rendered in a public employment, or for the use of property in which the public has an interest, subject to the proviso that such power of limitation or regulation is not without limit, and is not a power to destroy, or a power to compel the doing of the services without reward, or to take private property for public use without just compensation or without due process of law, the court said that it had no means, "if it would under any circumstances have the power," of determining that the rate fixed by the legislature in that case was unreasonable, and that it did not appear that there had been any such confiscation of property as amounted to a taking of it without due process of law, or that there had been any denial of the equal protection of the laws.

In the cases before us, the records do not show that the charges fixed by the statute are unreasonable, or that property has been taken without due process of law, or that there has been any denial of the equal protection of the laws; even if under any circumstances we could determine that the maximum rate fixed by the legislature was unreasonable. . . .

Fong Yue Ting v. United States
149 U.S. 698
1893

The Court ruled against constitutional guarantees for Chinese aliens residing in the United States when it sustained the Chinese Immigration Act of 1892, one of whose provisions required all Chinese laborers legally residing in the United States, to obtain, within a year's time, residency certificates from the federal government. Several Chinese failed to secure the proper government documents and were arrested. For failing to comply with the act, they were to be deported. Fong Yue Ting, one of the petitioners, brought legal action to test the constitutionality of the statute. The opinion of the 6-3 Court, delivered by Justice Horace Gray, which validated the law was one of the clearest expressions of congressional sovereign authority with respect to international affairs, and formed the basis for United States immigration legislation not regulated by previous treaties.

The right to exclude or to expel all aliens, or any class of aliens, absolutely or upon certain conditions, in war or in peace, being an inherent and inalienable right of every sovereign and independent nation, essential to its safety, its independence, and its welfare, the question now before the court is whether the manner in which Congress has exercised this right in. . . the act of 1892, is consistent with the Constitution.

The United States are a sovereign and independent nation, and are vested by the Constitution with the entire control of international relations, and with all the powers of government necessary to maintain that control and to make it effective. The only government of this country, which other nations recognize or treat with, is the government of the Union; and the only American flag known throughout the world is the flag of the United States.

The Constitution of the United States speaks with no uncertain sound upon this subject. That instrument, established by the people of the United States as the fundamental law of the land, has conferred upon the President the executive power; has made him the commander-in-chief of the army and navy; has authorized him, by and with the consent of the Senate, to make treaties, and to appoint ambassadors, public ministers, and consuls; and has made it his duty to take care that the laws be faithfully executed. The Constitution has granted to Congress the power to regulate commerce with foreign nations, including the entrance of ships, the importation of goods, and the bringing of persons into the ports of the United States; to establish a uniform rule of naturalization, to define and punish piracies and felonies committed on the high seas and offenses against the law of nations; to declare war, grant letters of marque and reprisal, and make rules concerning captures on land and water; to raise and support armies, to provide and maintain a navy, and to make rules for the government and regulation of the land and naval forces; and to make all laws necessary and proper for carrying into execution these powers, and all other powers vested by the Constitution in the government of the United States, or in any department or officer thereof. And the several states are expressly forbidden to enter into any treaty, alliance, or confederation; to grant letters of marque and reprisal, to enter into any agreement or compact with another state, or with a foreign power; or to engage in war, unless actually invaded, or in such imminent danger as will not admit of delay....

The power to exclude or to expel aliens, being a power affecting international relations, is vested in the political departments of the government, and is to be regulated by treaty or by act of Congress, and to be executed by the executive authority according to the regulations so established....

The power to exclude aliens and the power to expel them rest upon one foundation, are derived from one source, are supported by the same reasons, and are in truth but parts of one and the same power.

The power of Congress, therefore, to expel, like the power to exclude aliens, or any specified class of aliens, from the country may be exercised entirely through executive officers; or Congress may call in the aid of the judiciary to ascertain any contested facts on which an alien's right to be in the country has been made by Congress to depend....

In our jurisprudence, it is well settled that the provisions of an act of Congress, passed in the exercise of its constitutional authority, on this, as on any other subject, if clear and explicit, must be upheld by the courts, even in contravention of express stipulations in an earlier treaty....

Chinese laborers, therefore, like all other aliens residing in the United States for a shorter or longer time, are entitled, so long as they are permitted by the government of the United States to remain in the country, to the safeguards of the Constitution, and to the protection of the laws, in regard to their rights of person and of property, and to their civil and criminal responsibility. But they continue to be aliens, having taken no steps towards becoming citizens, and incapable of becoming such under the naturalization laws; and therefore remain subject to the power of Congress to expel them, or to order them to be removed and deported from the country, whenever in its judgment their removal is necessary of expedient....

Upon careful consideration of the subject, the only conclusion which appears to us to be consistent with the principles of international law, with the Constitution and laws of the United States, and with the previous decisions of this court, is that in each of these cases the judgment of the circuit court, dismissing the writ of habeus corpus, is right and must be affirmed.

Justice David J. Brewer: On the Independence of the Court

1893

Justice David Josiah Brewer was the Court's ultraconservative from 1889, when he was appointed by President Benjamin Harrison, until his sudden death in 1910. In all, he served for twenty years on the nation's highest bench, and with his uncle constituted the Court's most formidable conservative combination. Brewer was a Social Darwinist, a racist, and a strict advocate of immigration restriction. He wrote and lectured widely on a variety of legal topics, and was regarded an expert on international law. Widely sought after as an after-dinner speaker, the selection that follows is an example of his talent, wit, and ideas concerning the Court and the law. Proceedings of the New York State Bar Association, 16th Annual Meeting (1893), pp. 37-47.

. . . It is the unvarying law, that the wealth of a community will be in the hands of a few; and the greater the general wealth, the greater the individual accumulations. The large majority of men are unwilling to endure that long self-denial and saving which makes accumulation possible; they have not the business tact and sagacity which brings about large combinations and great financial results; and hence it always has been, and until human nature is remodeled always will be true, that the wealth of the nation is in the hands of a few, while the many subsist upon the proceeds of their daily toll. But security is the chief end of government; and other things being equal, that government is best which protects to the fullest extent each individual, rich or poor, high or low, in the possession of his property and the pursuit of his business. It was the boast of our ancestors in the old country, that they were able to wrest from the power of the king so much security for life, liberty and property. Indeed, English history is the long story of a struggle therefor. The greatest of English orators opposing a bill which seemed to give power to the government to enter the homes of the individual, broke forth in his most eloquent eulogy of that protection and security which surrounded an English home, even against the king: "The poorest man in his cottage may bid defiance to all the forces of the crown. It may be frail; its roof may shake; the wind may blow through it; the storm may enter it, but the king of England cannot enter it. All his power dares not cross the threshold of that ruined tenement!"

Here, there is no monarch threatening trespass upon the individual. The danger is from the multitudes—the majority, with whom is the power; and if the passage quoted is the grandest tribute to the liberty which existed in England, I would thus paraphrase it to describe that which should prevail under this government by the people: The property of a great railroad corporation stretches far away from the domicile of its owner, through State after State, from ocean to ocean; the rain and the snow may cover it; the winds and the storms may wreck it; but no man or multitude dare touch a car or move a rail. It stands as secure in the eye and in the custody of the law, as the purposes of justice in the thought of God.

This movement expresses itself in two ways: First, in the improper use of labor organizations to destroy the freedom of the laborer, and control the uses of capital. I do not care to stop to discuss such wrongs as these—preventing one from becoming a skilled laborer, by forbidding employers to take more than a named number of apprentices, compelling equal wages for unequal skill and labor; forbidding extra hours of labor to one who would accumulate more than the regular stipend. That which I particularly notice, is the assumption of control over the employer's property, and blocking the access of laborers to it. The common rule as to strikes is this: Not merely do the employees quit the employment, and thus handicap the employer in the use of his property, and perhaps in the discharge of duties which he owes to the public; but they also forcibly prevent others from taking their places. It is useless to say that they only advise—no man is misled. When a thousand laborers gather around a railroad track, and say to those who seek employment that they had better not, and when that advice is supplemented every little while by a terrible assault on one who disregards it, every one knows that something more than advice is attended. It is coercion, force; it is the effort of the many, by the mere weight of numbers, to compel the one to do their bidding. It is a proceeding outside of the law, in defiance of the law; and in spirit and effect an attempt to strip from one that has, that which of right belongs to him—the full and undisturbed use and enjoyment of his own. It is not to be wondered at, that deeds of violence and cruelty attend such demonstrations as these; nor will it do to pretend that the wrong-doers are not the striking laborers, but lawless strangers who gather to look on. Were they strangers who made the history of the "Homestead" strike one of awful horror? Were they women from afar who so maltreated the surrendered guards; or were they the very ones who sought to compel the owners of that property to do their bidding? Even if it be true that at such places the lawless with gather,—who is responsible for their gathering? Weihe, the head of a reputable labor organization may only open the door to lawlessness; but Beekman, the anarchist and assassin, will be the first to pass through; and thus it will be always and everywhere. . . .

The other form of this movement assumes the guise of a regulation of the charges for the use of property subjected, or supposed to be, to a public use. This acts in two directions: One by extending the list of those things, charges for whose use the government may prescribe; until now we hear it affirmed that whenever property is devoted to a use in which the public has an interest, charges for that use may be fixed by law. And if there be any property in the use of which the public or some portion of it has no interest, I hardly know what it is or where to find it. And second, in so reducing charges for the use of property, which in fact is subject to a public use, that no compensation or income is received by those who have so invested their property. By the one it subjects all property and its uses to the will of the majority; by the other it robs property of its value. Statutes and decisions both disclose that this movement, with just these results, has a present and alarming existence. A switching company in Minneapolis had for eight years been operating under charges of $1.50 a car. With such charges it had not during that time paid off a floating debt incurred in construction, nor a dollar of interest or dividend to those who had invested in its stocks or bonds. Without a hearing before any tribunal, the State of Minnesota, through its railroad commission, reduced these charges to $1 a car. Of what value would the ownership of that property be to its owners; and how soon would all semblance of title be swept away under foreclosure by the unpaid bondholders? Sometimes there is an appeal from a majority, and that effort at confiscation failed. And yet that the effort was made and that it did receive some judicial sanction is but a revelation of the spirit which lies behind and prompts the movement, and of the extent to which it has taken hold of the public mind.

There are today ten thousand million of dollars invested in railroad property, whose owners in this country number less than two million persons. Can it be that whether that immense sum shall earn a dollar, or bring the slightest recompense to those who have invested perhaps their all in that business, and are thus aiding in the development of the country, depends wholly upon the whim and greed of that great majority of sixty millions who do not own a dollar. It may be said that that majority will not be so foolish, selfish and cruel as to strip that property of its earning capacity. I say that so long as constitutional guarantees lift on American soil their buttresses and bulwarks against wrong, and so long as the American judiciary breathes the free air of courage, it cannot. . . .

And so it is, that because of the growth of this movement, of its development in many directions and the activity of those who are in it, and especially because of the further fact that, carrying votes in its hand, it ever appeals to the trimming politician and time-serving demagogue and thus enters into so much of legislation, arises the urgent need of giving to the judiciary the utmost vigor and efficiency. Now, if ever in the history of this country, must there be somewhere and somehow a controlling force which speaks for justice and for justice only. Let this movement sweep on with obvious right and conceded wrong, the triumph of the former would be sure and speedy. Labor organizations are the needed and proper complement of capital organizations. They often work wholesome restraints on the greed, the unscrupulous rapacity which dominates much of capital; and the fact that they bring together a multitude of tiny forces, each helpless in a solitary struggle with capital, enables labor to secure its just rights. So also, in regulating the charges of property which is appropriated to a public use, the public is but exercising a legitimate function, and one which is often necessary to prevent extortion in respect to public uses. Within limits of law and justice labor organizations and State regulation of charges for the use of property which is in fact devoted to public uses are commendable. But with respect to the proposition that the public may rightfuly regulate the charges for the use of any property in whose use it has an interest, I am like the lawyer who, when declared guilty of contempt, responded promptly that he had shown no contempt, but on the contrary had carefully concealed his feelings. . . .

What, then, ought to be done? My reply is, strengthen the judiciary. How? Permanent tenure of office accomplishes this. If a judge is to go out of office in a few months the litigant will be more willing to disobey and take the chances of finally escaping punishment by delaying the proceedings until a new judge shall take the place—one whom his vote may select and from whom, therefore, he will expect slight if any punishment; while if the incumbent holds office for life, the duration of that life being uncertain, whether one or thirty years, no litigant wants to take the risk of disobedience with a strong probability that a punishment, though it may be delayed, will come and come with a severity equal to the wrong of the disobedience. . . .

. . . So if you would give the most force and effect to the decisions of your courts, you must give to the judges a permanent tenure of office.

Again, it will give greater independence of action. Judges are but human. If one must soon go before the people for re-election, how loath to rule squarely against public sentiment! There is no need of imputing conscious dishonesty; but the inevitable shrinking from antagonizing popular feeling or the wishes or interests of some prominent leader or leaders tends to delay or modify the due decision, while the judge who knows nothing can disturb his position does not hesitate promptly and clearly to "lay judgment to the line and righteousness to the plummet." "Let the jury determine," is the motto of one tribunal; "The court must decide," is the rule of the other. Cases at law and a jury are favored in the one; equity and its singleness of responsibility is the delight of the other. Far be it from me to intimate aught against the character or ability of that larger number of elective judges in this country who secure continuation in office only through the well-earned confidence of the people. The bulk of my judicial life has been spent in such tribunals and under such experiences, and I know the worth and prize of friendship of these men. I am simply comparing system with system. It is a significant fact that some of the older States which have the elective system are lengthening the terms of judicial office. The judges of your highest court hold office for fourteen years. And this is almost equivalent to a life tenure, for it will be found that the term of office of a justice of the supreme court of the United States (taking all who have held that office, including the present incumbents), averages less than fifteen years....

It may be said that this is practically substituting government by the judges for government by the people, and thus turning back the currents of history. The world has seen government by chiefs, by kings and emperors, by priests and by nobles. All have failed, and now government by the people is on trial. Shall we abandon that and try government by judges? But this involves a total misunderstanding of the relations of judges to government. There is nothing in this power of the judiciary detracting in the least from the idea of government of and by the people. The courts hold neither purse nor sword; they cannot corrupt nor arbitrarily control. They make no laws; they establish no policy; they never enter into the domain of popular action. They do not govern. Their functions in relation to the State are limited to seeing that popular action does not trespass upon right and justice as it exists in written constitutions and natural law. So it is that the utmost power of the courts and judges works no interference with true liberty, no trespass on the fullest and highest development of government of and by the people, it only means security to personal rights—the inalienable rights, life, liberty, and the pursuit of happiness; it simply nails the Declaraction of Independence, like Luther's theses against indulgences upon the doors of the Wittenburg church of human rights and dares the anarchist, the socialist and every other assassin of liberty to blot out a single word....

To that end the courts exist, and for that let all the judges be put beyond the reach of political office and all fear of losing position or compensation during good behavior. It may be that this is not popular doctrine today and that the drift is found in such declarations as these—that the employee has a right to remain on his employer's property and be paid wages, whether the employer wishes him or no; that the rights of the one who uses are more sacred than of him who owns property; and that the Dartmouth College case, though once believed to be good in morals and sound in law, is today an anachronism and a political outrage. The black flag of anarchism, flaunting destruction to property, and therefore relapse of society to barbarism; the red flag of socialism, inviting a redistribution of property which, in order to secure the vaunted equality, must be repeated again and again at constantly decreasing intervals, and that colorless piece of baby-cloth, which suggests that the State take all property and direct all the life and work of individuals as if they were little children, may seem to fill the air with their flutter. But as against these schemes, or any other plot or vagary of fiend, fool or fanatic, the eager and earnest protest and cry of the Anglo-Saxon is for individual freedom and absolute protection of all his rights of person and property; and it is the cry which, reverberating over this country from ocean to ocean, thank God, will not go unheeded. That personal independence which is the lofty characteristic of our race will assert itself, and no matter what may stand in the way or who may oppose, or how much of temporary miscarriage or disappointment there may be, it will finally so assert itself in this land that no man or masses shall dare to say to a laborer he must or must not work, or for whom or for how much he shall toil; and that no honest possessor of property shall live in fear of the slightest trespass upon his possessions. And to help and strengthen that good time, we shall yet see in every State an independent judiciary, made as independent of all outside influences as is possible, and to that end given a permanent tenure of office and an unchangeable salary; and above them that court, created by the fathers, supreme in fact as in name, holding all, individuals and masses, corporations and States—even the great Nation itself—unswervingly true to the mandates of justice. . . .

Brass v. North Dakota, Ex Rel. Stoeser
153 U.S. 391
1894

This was another case concerning the relationship between monopoly and "public interest." By a 5-4 decision, the Court speaking through Justice George Shiras, Jr., accepted as constitutional, regulation of a business where no "practical" or legal monopoly existed, thereby strengthening the state's police powers. It sustained a North Dakota statute which had established maximum rates for grain elevator operators in the state. The decisions in *Munn v. Illinois* (1877) and *Budd. v. New York* (1892) were affirmed, but the dissenters argued that once the legislature was given the power to regulate the grain elevator business, its enactments in this respect would no longer be subject to judicial review.

In the cases thus brought to this court from the States of Illinois and New York, we were asked to declare void statutes regulating the affairs of grain warehouses and elevators within those States, and held valid by their highest courts, because it was claimed that such legislation was repugnant to that clause. . . of article 1 of the Constitution of the United States, which confers upon Congress power to regulate commerce with foreign nations and among the several States, and to the Fourteenth Amendment, which ordains that no State shall deprive any person of life, liberty, or property without due process of law, nor deny to any person within its jurisdiction the equal protection of the laws.

In the case now before us the same contentions are made, but we are not asked to review our decisions made in the previous cases. Indeed, their soundness is tacitly admitted in the briefs and argument of the counsel of the plaintiff in error. But it is said that those cases arose out of facts so peculiar and exceptional, and so different from those of the present case, as to render the reasoning there used, and the conclusions reached, now inapplicable.

The concession, then, is that, upon the facts found to exist by the legislatures of Illinois and New York, their enactments were by the courts property declared valid, and the contention is that the facts upon which the legislature of North Dakota proceeded, and of which we can take notice in the present case, are so different as to call for the application of other principles, and to render an opposite conclusion necessary.

The differences in the facts of the respective cases, to which we are pointed, are mainly as follows: In the first place, what may be called a geographical difference is suggested, in that the operation of the Illinois and New York statutes is said to be restricted to the city of Chicago in the one case, and to the cities of Buffalo, New York, and Brooklyn in the other, while the North Dakota statute is applicable to the territory of the entire State.

It is, indeed, true what while the terms of the Illinois and New York statutes embrace in both cases the entire State, yet their behests are restricted to cities having not less than a prescribed number of inhabitants, and that there is no such restriction in the North Dakota law.

Upon this it is argued that the statutes of Illinois and New York arc intended to operate in great trade centres, where, on account of the business being localized in the hands of a few persons in close proximity to each other, great opportunities for combinations to raise and control elevating and storage charges are afforded, while the wide extent of the State of North Dakota and the small population of its country towns and villages are said to present no such opportunities.

The considerations mentioned are obviously addressed to the legislative discretion. It can scarcely be meant to contend that the statutes of Illinois and New York, valid in their present form, would become illegal if the law makers thought fit to repeal the clauses limiting their operation to cities of a certain size, or that the statute of North Dakota would at once be validated if one or more of her towns were to reach a population of one hundred thousand and her legislature were to restrict the operation of the statute to such cities.

Again, it is said that the modes of carrying on the business of elevating and storing grain in North Dakota are not similar to those pursued in the Eastern cities; that the great elevators used in transshipping grain from the Lakes to the railroads are essential; and that those who own them, if uncontrolled by law, could extort such charges as they pleased; and great stress is laid upon expressions used in our previous opinions, in which this business, as carried on at Chicago and Buffalo, is spoken of as a practical monopoly, to which shippers and owners of grain are compelled to resort. The surroundings in an agricultural State, where land is cheap in price and limitless in quantity, are thought to be widely different, and to demand different regulations.

These arguments are disposed of, as we think by the simple observation, already made, that the facts rehearsed are matters for those who make, not for those who interpret, the laws. When it is once admitted, as it is admitted here, that it is competent for the legislative power to control the business of elevating and storing grain, whether carried on by individuals or associations, in cities of one size and in some circumstances, it follows that such power may be legally exerted over the same business when carried on in smaller cities and in other circumstances. It may be conceded that that would not be wise legislation which provided the same regulations in every case, and overlooked differences in the facts that called for regulations. But, as we have no right to revise the wisdom or expediency of the law in question, so we would not be justified in imputing an improper exercise of discretion to the legislature of North Dakota....

The plaintiff in error, in his answer to the writ of mandamus, based his defence wholly upon grounds arising under the constitution of the State and of the United States. We are limited by this record to the questions whether the legislature of North Dakota, in regulating by a general law the business and charges of public warehousemen engaged in elevating and storing grain for profit, denies to the plaintiff in error the equal protection of the laws or deprives him of his property without due process of law, and whether such statutory regulations amount to a regulation of commerce between the States. The allegations and arguments of the plaintiff in error have failed to satisfy us that any solid distinction can be found between the cases in which those questions have been heretofore determined by this court and the present one. The judgment of the court below is accordingly affirmed.

Regan v. Farmers' Loan and Trust Company

154 U.S. 362

1894

The development of substantive due process under the Fourteenth Amendment was completed in this case when the Supreme Court speaking through Justice David J. Brewer unanimously ruled that a state rate-setting commission's decisions were subject to judicial scrutiny. The *Munn v. Illinois* precedents received their death blows from this decision. The majority opinion stated that unless the courts possessed the power to judge the "reasonableness" of the rates fixed by state commissions, due process under the Fourteenth amendment was being denied.

. . . There can be no doubt of the general power of a State to regulate the fares and freights which may be charged and received by railroads or other carriers, and that this regulation may be carried on by means of a commission. Such a commission is merely an administrative board created by the State for carrying into effect the will of the State, as expressed by its legislation. No valid objection, therefore, can be made on account of the general features of this act. . . .

It appears from the bill that, in pursuance of the powers given to it by this act, the state commission has made a body of rates for fares and freights. This body of rates, as a whole, is challenged by the plaintiff as unreasonable, unjust, and working a destruction of its rights of property. The defendant denies the power of the court to entertain an inquiry into that matter, insisting that the fixing of rates for carriage by a public carrier is a matter wholly within the power of the legislative department of the government and beyond examination by the courts.

It is doubtless true, as a general proposition, that the formation of a tariff of charges for the transportation by a common carrier of persons or property is a legislative or administrative rather than a judicial function. Yet it has always been recognized that, if a carrier attempted to charge a shipper an unreasonable sum, the courts had jurisdiction to inquire into that matter and to award to the shipper any amount exacted from him in excess of a reasonable rate; and also in a reverse case to render judgment in favor of the carrier for the amount found to be a reasonable charge. The province of the courts is not changed, nor the limit of judicial inquiry altered, because the legislature instead of the carrier prescribes the rates. The courts are not authorized to revise or change the body of rates imposed by a legislature or a commission; they do not determine whether one rate is preferable to another, or what under all circumstances would be fair and reasonable as between the carriers and the shippers; they do not engage in any mere administrative work; but still there can be no doubt of their power and duty to inquire whether a body of rates prescribed by a legislature or a commission is injust and unreasonable, and such as to work a practical destruction to rights of property, and, if found to be so, to restrain its operation. . . .

. . . That while it is not the province of the courts to enter upon the merely administrative duty of framing a tariff of rates for carriage, it is within the scope of judicial power and a part of judicial duty to restrain anything which, in the form of a regulation of rates, operates to deny to the owners of property invested in the business of transportation that equal protection which is the constitutional right of all owners of other property. There is nothing new or strange in this. It has always been a part of the judicial function to determine whether the act of one party (whether that party be a single individual, an organized body, or the public as a whole) operates to divest the other party of any rights of person or property. . . . It was, therefore, within the competency of the circuit court of the United States for the Western District of Texas, at the instance of the plaintiff, a citizen of another State, to enter upon an inquiry as to the reasonableness and justice of the rates. . . .

United States v. E.C. Knight Company (Sugar Trust Case)

156 U.S. 1

1895

Popularly known as the *Sugar Trust* case, the Court, speaking through Chief Justice Melville W. Fuller, by an 8 to 1 vote, narrowly interpreted the meaning of the Sherman Anti-Trust Act, when it declared that the E.C. Knight Company's attempt to monopolize the manufacture and sale of ninety-five percent of the sugar refining business in the United States was not an illegal combination in restraint of interstate commerce. The Court's interpretation declared that the manufacture of sugar was not, in the strict sense, "commerce." The decision in this case severely restricted the application of the Sherman Act to transportation as distinguished from manufacturing, and limited the effectiveness of the statute for the next ten years. Justice John Marshall Harlan vigorously dissented.

. . . The fundamental question is, whether conceding that the existence of a monopoly in manufacture is established by the evidence, that monopoly can be directly suppressed under the act of Congress in the mode attempted by this bill.

It cannot be denied that the power of a State to protect the lives, health, and property of its citizens, and to preserve good order and the public morals, "the power to govern men and things within the limits of its dominion," is a power originally and always belonging to the States, not surrendered by them to the general government, nor directly restrained by the Constitution of the United States, and essentially exclusive. The relief of the citizens of each State from the burden of monopoly and the evils resulting from the restraint of trade among such citizens was left with the States to deal with. . . .

The argument is that the power to control the manufacture of refined sugar is a monopoly over a necessary of life, to the enjoyment of which by a large part of the population of the United States interstate commerce is indispensable, and that, therefore, the general government in the exercise of the power to regulate commerce may suppress such monopoly directly and set aside the instruments which have created it. But this argument cannot be confined to necessaries of life merely, and must include all articles of general consumption. Doubtless the power to control the manufacture of a given thing involves in a certain sense the control of its disposition, but this is a secondary and not the primary sense; and although the exercise of that power may result in bringing the operation of commerce into play, it does not control it, and affects it only incidentally and indirectly. Commerce succeeds to manufacure, and is not a part of it. The power to regulate commerce is the power to prescribe the rule by which commerce shall be governed, and is a power independent of the power to suppress monopoly. But it may operate in repression of monopoly whenever it comes within the rules by which commerce is governed or whenever the transaction is itself a monopoly of commerce.

It is vital that the independence of the commercial power and of the police power, and the delimitation between them, however sometimes perplexing, should always be recognized and observed, for while the one furnishes the strongest bond of union, the other is essential to the autonomy of the States as required by our dual form of government; and acknowledged evils, however grave and urgent they may appear to be, had better be borne, than the risk be run, in the effort to suppress them, of more serious consequences by resort to expedients of even doubtful constitutionality.

It will be perceived how far-reaching the proposition is that the power of dealing with a monopoly directly may be exercised by the general government whenever interstate or international commerce may be ultimately affected. The regulation of commerce applies to the subjects of commerce, and not to matters of internal police. Contracts to buy, sell, or exchange goods to be transported among the several States, the transportation and its instrumentalities, and articles bought, sold, or exchanged for the purpose of such transit among the States, or put in the way of transit, may be regulated, but this is because they form part of interstate trade or commerce. The fact that an article is manufactured for export to another State does not of itself make it an article of interstate commerce. . . .

And Mr. Justice [Lucius Quintus Cincinnatus] Lamar remarked: "A situation more paralyzing to the state governments, and more provocative of conflicts between the general government and the States, and less likely to have been what the framers of the Constitution intended, it would be difficult to imagine."

Contracts, combinations, or conspiracies to control domestic enterprise in manufacture, agriculture, mining production in all its forms, or to raise or lower prices or wages, might unquestionably tend to restrain external as well as domestic trade, but the restraint would be an indirect result, however inevitable and whatever its extent, and such result would not necessarily determine the object of the contract, combination, or conspiracy.

Again, all the authorities agree that in order to vitiate a contract or combination it is not essential that its result should be a complete monopoly; it is sufficient if it really tends to that end and to deprive the public of the advantages which flow from free competition. Slight reflection will show that if the national power extends to all contracts and combinations in manufacture, agriculture, mining, and other productive industries, whose ultimate result may affect external commerce, comparatively little of business operations and affairs would be left for state control.

It was in the light of well-settled principles that the act of July 2, 1890 was framed. Congress did not attempt thereby to assert the power to deal with monopoly directly as such; or to limit and restrict the rights of corporations created by the States or the citizens of the States in the acquisition, control, or disposition of property; or to regulate or prescribe the price or prices at which such property or the products thereof should be sold; or to make criminal the acts of persons in the acquisition and control of property which the States of their residence or creation sanctioned or permitted. Aside from the provisions applicable where Congress might exercise municipal power, what the law struck at was combinations, contracts, and conspiracies to monopolize trade and commerce among the several States or with foreign nations; but the contracts and acts of the defendants related exclusively to the acquisition of the Philadelphia refineries and the business of sugar refining in Pennsylvania, and bore no direct relation to commerce between the States or with foreign nations. The object was manifestly private gain the manufacture of the commodity, but not through the control of interstate or foreign commerce. . . .

. . . There was nothing in the proofs to indicate any intention to put a restraint upon trade or commerce. . . .

In Re Debs
158 U.S. 564
1895

In 1895, Eugene V. Debs, president of the American Railway Union, led his members in a strike against the Pullman Company of Chicago, paralyzing all rail traffic west of the Mississippi River. In doing this, the union stopped interstate commerce and interfered with mail delivery. The Pullman Company secured an injunction from a federal court ordering Debs and the union to cease and desist from interference with interstate commerce. When Debs and the other officers of the union refused to obey the injunction, they were arrested, tried, and convicted for contempt of a federal court injunction and sentenced to prison. The case was appealed, and the Supreme Court, in a unanimous decision, denied Debs and the others a petition of habeus corpus on the ground that the federal government has the power to prevent forcible obstruction of interstate commerce and the mails. While many quarters throughout the nation applauded the opinion of Justice David J. Brewer, it became the most severely criticized of his decisions. It was the first time that an injunction had been applied to a labor union and was a precedent-setting decision.

The case presented by the bill is this: The United States, finding that the interstate transportation of persons and property, as well as the carriage of the mails, is forcibly obstructed, and that a combination and conspiracy exist to subject the control of such transportation to the will of the conspirators, applied to one of their courts, sitting as a court of equity, for an injunction to restrain such obstruction and prevent carrying into effect such conspiracy. Two questions of importance are presented: First. Are the relations of the general government to interstate commerce and the transportation of the mails such as authorize a direct interference to prevent a forcible obstruction thereof? Second. If authority exists, as authority in governmental affairs implies both power and duty, has a court of equity jurisdiction to issue an injunction in aid of the performance of such duty.

First. What are the relations of the general government to interstate commerce and the transportation of the mails? They are those of direct supervision, control, and management. While under the dual system which prevails with us the powers of government are distributed between the State and the Nation, and while the latter is properly styled a government of enumerated powers, yet within the limits of such enumeration it has all the attributes of sovereignty, and, in the exercise of those enumerated powers, acts directly upon the citizen, and not through the intermediate agency of the State....

Under the power vested in Congress to establish post offices and post roads, Congress has, by a mass of legislation, established the great post office system of the country, with all its detail of organization, its machinery for the transaction of business, defining what shall be carried and what not, and the prices of carriage, and also prescribing penalties for all offences against it.

Obviously these powers given to the national government over interstate commerce and in respect to the transportation of the mails were not dormant and unused. Congress had taken hold of these two matters, and by various and specific acts had assumed and exercised the powers given to it, and was in the full discharge of its duty to regulate interstate commerce and carry the mails. The validity of such exercise and the exclusiveness of its control had been again and again presented to this court for consideration. It is curious to note the fact that in a large proportion of the cases in respect to interstate commerce brought to this court the question presented was of the validity of state legislation in its bearings upon interstate commerce, and the uniform course of decision has been to declare that it is not within the competency of a State to legislate in such a manner as to obstruct interstate commerce. If a State with its recognized powers of sovereignty is impotent to obstruct interstate commerce, can it be that any mere voluntary association of individuals within the limits of that State has a power which the State itself does not possess?...

But there is no such impotency in the national government. The entire strength of the nation may be used to enforce in any part of the land the full and free exercise of all national powers and the security of all rights entrusted by the Constitution to its care. The strong arm of the national government may be put forth to brush away all obstructions to the freedom of interstate commerce or the transportation of the mails. If the emergency arises, the army of the Nation, and all its militia, are at the service of the Nation to compel obedience to its laws.

But passing to the second question, is there no other alternative than the use of force on the part of the executive authorities whenever obstructions arise to the freedom of interstate commerce or the transportation of the mails? Is the army the only instrument by which rights of the public can be enforced and the peace of the nation preserved? Grant that any public nuisance may be forcibly abated either at the instance of the authorities, or by any individual suffering private damage therefrom, the existence of this right of forcible abatement is not inconsistent with nor does it destroy the right of appeal in an orderly way to the courts for a judicial determination, and an exercise of their powers by writ of injunction and otherwise to accomplish the same....

When the choice is between redress or prevention of injury by force and by peaceful process, the law is well pleased if the individual will consent to waive his right to the use of force and await its action. Therefore, as between force and the extraordinary writ of injunction, the rule will permit the latter.

So, in the case before us, the right to use force does not exclude the right of appeal to the courts for a judicial determination and for the exercise of all their powers of prevention. Indeed, it is more to the praise than to the blame of the government, that, instead of determining for itself questions of right and wrong on the part of these petitioners and their associates and enforcing that determination by the club of the policeman and the bayonet of the soldier, it submitted all those questions to the peaceful determination of judicial tribunals, and invoked their consideration and judgment as to their measure of its rights and powers and the correlative obligations of those against whom it made complaint. And it is equally to the credit of the latter that the judgment of those tribunals was by the great body of them respected, and the troubles which threatened so much disaster terminated.

Neither can it be doubted that the government has such an interest in the subject matter as enables it to appear as party plaintiff in this suit. It is said that equity only interferes for the protection of property, and that the government has no property interest. A sufficient reply is that the United States have a property in the mails, the protection of which was one of the purposes of this bill. . . .

". . . We think that a carriage, whenever it is carrying the mail, is laden with the property of the United States within the true meaning of the compact."

We do not care to place our decision upon this ground alone. Every government, entrusted, by the very terms of its being, with powers and duties to be exercised and discharged for the general welfare, has a right to apply to its own courts for any proper assistance in the exercise of the one and the discharge of the other, and it is no sufficient answer to its appeal to one of those courts that it has no pecuniary interest in the matter. The obligations which it is under to promote the interest of all, and to prevent the wrongdoing of one resulting in injury to the general welfare, is often of itself sufficient to give it a standing in court. This proposition in some of its relations has heretofore received the sanction of this court. . . .

It is obvious from these decisions that while it is not the province of the government to interfere in any mere matter of private controversy between individuals, or to use its great powers to enforce the rights of one against another, yet, whenever the wrongs complained of are such as affect the public at large, and are in respect of matters which by the Constitution are entrusted to the care of the Nation, and concerning which the Nation owes the duty to all the citizens of securing to them their common rights, then the mere fact that the government has no pecuniary interest in the controversy is not sufficient to exclude it from the courts, or prevent it from taking measures therein to fully discharge those constitutional duties. . . .

Up to a recent date commerce, both interstate and international, was mainly by water, and it is not strange that both the legislation of Congress and the cases in the courts have been principally concerned therewith. The fact that in recent years interstate commerce has come mainly to be carried on by railroads and over artificial highways has in no manner narrowed the scope of the constitutional provision, or abridged the power of Congress over such commerce. On the contrary, the same fulness of control exists in the one case as in the other, and the same power to remove obstructions from the one as from the other.

Constitutional provisions do not change, but their operation extends to new matters as the modes of business and the habits of life of the people vary with each succeeding generation. The law of the common carrier is the same today as when transportation on land was by coach and wagon, and on water by canal boat and sailing vessel, yet in its actual operation it touches and regulates transportation by modes then unknown, the railroad train and the steamship. Just so is it with the grant to the national government of power over interstate commerce. The Constitution has not changed. The power is the same. But it operates to-day upon modes of interstate commerce unknown to the fathers, and it will operate with equal force upon any new modes of such commerce which the future may develop. . . .

The law is full of instances in which the same act may give rise to a civil action and a criminal prosecution. An assault with intent to kill may be punished criminally, under an indictment therefore, or will support a civil action for damages, and the same is true of all other offences which cause injury to person or property. In such cases the jurisdiction of the civil court is invoked, not to enforce the criminal law and punish the wrongdoer, but to compensate the injured party for the damages which he or his property has suffered, and it is no defence to the civil action that the same act by the defendant exposes him also to indictment and punishment in a court of criminal jurisdiction. So here, the acts of the defendants may or may not have been violations of the criminal law. If they were, that matter is for inquiry in other proceedings. The complaint made against them in this is of disobedience to an order of a civil court, made for the protection of property and the security of rights. If any criminal prosecution be brought against them for the criminal offenses alleged in the bill of complaint, of derailing and wrecking engines and trains, assaulting and disabling employees of the railroad companies, it will be no defense to such prosecution that they disobeyed the orders of injunction served upon them and have been punished for such disobedience.

Nor is there in this any invasion of the constitutional right of trial by jury. We fully agree with counsel that "it matters not what form the attempt to deny constitutional right may take. It is vain and ineffectual, and must be so declared by the courts," and we reaffirm the declaration made for the court by Mr. Justice [Joseph P.] Bradley in *Boyd v. United States,* 116 U.S. 616,635, that "it is the duty of courts to be watchful for the constitutional rights of the citizen, and against any stealthy encroachments thereon. Their motto should be *obsta principiis."* But the power of a court to make an order carries with it the equal power to punish for a disobedience of that order, and the inquiry as to the question of disobedience has been, from time immemorial, the special function of the court. And this is no technical rule. In order that a court may compel obedience to its orders it must have the right to inquire whether there has been any disobedience. . . .

In brief, a court, enforcing obedience to its orders by proceedings for contempt, is not executing the criminal laws of the land, but only securing to suitors the rights which it has adjudged them entitled to.

Further, it is said by counsel in their brief:

"No case can be cited where such a bill in behalf of the sovereign has been entertained against riot and mob violence, though occurring on the highway. It is not such fitful and temporary obstruction that constitutes a nuisance. The strong hand of executive power is required to deal with such lawless demonstrations.

"The courts should stand aloof from them and not invade executive prerogative, nor even at the behest or request of the executive travel out of the beaten path of well-settled judicial authority. A mob cannot be suppressed by injunction; nor can its leaders be tried, convicted, and sentenced in equity.

"It is too great a strain upon the judicial branch of the government to impose this essentially executive and military power upon courts of chancery."

We do not perceive that this argument questions the jurisdiction of the court, but only the expediency of the action of the government in applying for its process. It surely cannot be seriously contended that the court has jurisdiction to enjoin the obstruction of a highway by one person, but that its jurisdiction ceases when the obstruction is by a hundred persons. It may be true, as suggested, that in the excitement of passion a mob will pay little heed to processes issued from the courts, and it may be, as said by counsel in argument, that it would savor somewhat of the puerile and ridiculous to have read a writ of injunction to Lee's army during the late civil war. It is doubtless true that *inter arma leges silent,* and in the throes of rebellion or revolution the processes of civil courts are of little avail, for the power of the courts rests on the general support of the people and their recognition of the fact that peaceful remedies are the true resort for the correction of wrongs. But does not counsel's argument imply too much? Is it to be assumed that these defendants were conducting a rebellion or inaugurating a revolution, and that they and their associates were thus placing themselves beyond the reach of the civil process of the courts?. . .

Whatever any single individual may have thought or planned, the great body of those who were engaged in these transactions contemplated neither rebellion nor revolution, and when in the due order of legal proceedings the question of right and wrong was submitted to the courts, and by them decided, they unhesitatingly yielded to their decisions. The outcome, by the very testimony of the defendants, attests the wisdom of the course pursued by the government, and that it was well not to oppose force simply by force, but to invoke the jurisdiction and judgment of those tribunals to whom by the Constitution and in accordance with the settled conviction of all citizens is committed the determination of questions of right and wrong between individuals, masses, and States.

It must be borne in mind that this bill was not simply to enjoin a mob and mob violence. It was not a bill to command a keeping of the peace; much less was its purport to restrain the defendants from abandoning whatever employment they were engaged in. The right of any laborer, or any number of laborers, to quit work as not challenged. The scope and purpose of the bill was only to restrain forcible obstructions of the highways along which interstate commerce travels and the mails are carried. And the facts set forth at length are only those facts which tended to show that the defendants were engaged in such obstructions.

A most earnest and eloquent appeal was made to us in eulogy of the heroic spirit of those who threw up their employment, and gave up their means of earning a livelihood, not in defence of their own rights, but in sympathy for and to assist others whom they believed to be wronged. We yield to none in our admiration of any act of heroism or self-sacrifice, but we may be permitted to add that it is a lesson which cannot be learned too soon or too thoroughly that under this government of and by the people the means of redress of all wrongs are through the courts and at the ballot-box, and that no wrong, real or fancied, carries with it legal warrant to invite as a means of redress the cooperation of a mob, with its accompanying acts of violence.

We have given to this case the most careful and anxious attention, for we realize that it touches closely questions of supreme importance to the people of this country. Summing up our conclusions, we hold that the government of the United States is one having jurisdiction over every foot of soil within its territory, and acting directly upon each citizen; that while it is a government of enumerated powers, it has within the limitations of those powers, all the attributes of sovereignty; that to it is committed power over interstate commerce and the transmission of the mail; that the powers thus conferred upon the national government are not dormant, but have been assumed and put into practical exercise by the legislation of Congress; that in the exercise of those powers it is competent for the nation to remove all obstructions upon highways, natural or artificial, to the passage of interstate commerce or of carrying the mail; that while it may be competent for the government (through the executive branch and in the use of the entire executive power of the nation) to forcibly remove all such obstructions, it is equally within its competency to appeal to the civil courts for an inquiry and determination as to the existence and character of any alleged obstructions, and if such are found to exist, or threaten to occur, to invoke the powers of those courts to remove or restrain such obstructions; that the jurisdiction of courts to interfere in such matters by injunction is one recognized from ancient times and by indubitable authority. . . .

We enter into no examination of the act of July 2, 1890, . . . upon which the Circuit Court relied mainly to sustain its jurisdiction. It must not be understood from this that we dissent from the conclusions of that court in reference to the scope of the act, but simply that we prefer to rest our judgment on the broader ground which has been discussed in this opinion, believing it of importance that the principles underlying it should be fully stated and affirmed.

The petition for a writ of habeas corpus is denied.

Pollock v. Farmers' Loan and Trust Company (Income Tax Case)

158 U.S. 601

1895

Probably the most celebrated case of the Fuller Court was the *Income Tax* case. The case arose as a result of a clause within the Wilson-Gorman Tariff Act (1894), whereby a two-percent tax was levied on incomes in excess of $4,000 a year. Income derived from real estate and municipal bonds was also subject to the tax. In the first hearing of the case, *Pollock v. Farmers' Loan and Trust Company,* 157 U.S. 429, the Court, by a vote of 6 to 2, struck down that part of the tax clause that applied to real estate and municipal bonds, but divided 4 to 4 on the constitutionality of the income tax itself. (Justice Howell E. Jackson was absent from the first hearing due to illness.) In the rehearing of the case, a month later, the Court, by a 5 to 4 majority, held the income tax law unconstitutional on the ground that the income tax was a direct tax, and that any partial unconstitutionality of the income tax statute invalidated the entire measure. Justices John Marshall Harlan, Howell E. Jackson, Henry B. Brown, and Edward D. White all delivered ringing dissents, the first three of which follow Chief Justice Melville W. Fuller's opinion in this selection.

Whenever this court is required to pass upon the validity of an act of Congress as tested by the fundamental law enacted by the people, the duty imposed demands in its discharge the utmost deliberation and care, and invokes the deepest sense of responsibility. And this is especially so when the question involves the exercise of a great governmental power, and brings into consideration, as vitally affected by the decision, that complex system of government, so sagaciously framed to secure and perpetuate "an indestructible Union, composed of indestructible States."

We have, therefore, with an anxious desire to omit nothing which might in any degree tend to elucidate the questions submitted, and aided by further able arguments embodying the fruits of elaborate research, carefully reexamined these cases, with the result that, while our former conclusions remain unchanged, their scope must be enlarged by the acceptance of their logical consequences.

The very nature of the Constitution, as observed by Chief Justice [John] Marshall, in one of his greatest judgments, "requires that only its great outlines should be marked, its important objects designated, and the minor ingredients which compose those objects be deduced from the nature of the objects themselves." "In considering this question, then, we must never forget, that it is a *Constitution* that we are expounding," *McCulloch v. Maryland,* 4 Wheat. 316, 407.

As heretofore stated, the Constitution divided Federal taxation into two great classes, the class of direct taxes, and the class of duties, imposts, and excises; and prescribed two rules which qualified the grant of power as to each class.

The power to lay direct taxes apportioned among the several States in proportion to their representation in the popular branch of Congress, a representation based on population as ascertained by the census, was plenary and absolute; but to lay direct taxes without apportionment was forbidden. The power to lay duties, imposts, and excises was subject to the qualification that the imposition must be uniform throughout the United States. . . .

We know of no reason for holding otherwise than that the words "direct taxes," on the one hand, and "duties, imposts and excises," on the other, were used in the Constitution in their natural and obvious sense. Nor, in arriving at what those terms embrace, do we perceive any ground for enlarging them beyond, or harrowing them within, their natural and obvious import at the time the Constitution was framed and ratified.

And, passing from the text, we regard the conclusion reached as inevitable, when the circumstances which surrounded the convention and controlled its action and the views of those who framed and those who adopted the Constitution are considered.

Moreover, whatever the reasons for the constitutional provisions, there they are, and they appear to us to speak in plain language.

It is said that a tax on the whole income of property is not a direct tax in the meaning of the Constitution, but a duty, and, as a duty, leviable without apportionment, whether direct or indirect. We do not think so. Direct taxation was not restricted in one breath, and the restriction blown to the winds in another. . . .

Nor are we impressed with the contention that, because in the four instances in which the power of direct taxation has been exercised, Congress did not see fit, for reasons of expedience, to levy a tax upon personalty, this amounts to such a practical construction of the Constitution that the power did not exist, that we must regard ourselves bound by it. We should regret to be compelled to hold the powers of the general government thus restricted, and certainly cannot accede to the idea that the Constitution has become weakened by a particular course of inaction under it.

The stress of the argument is thrown, however, on the assertion that an income tax is not a property tax at all; that it is not a real estate tax, or a crop tax, or a bond tax; that it is an assessment upon the taxpayer on account of his money-spending power as shown by his revenue for the year preceding the assessment; that rents received, crops harvested, interest collected, have lost all connection with their origin, and although once not taxable have become transmuted in their new form into taxable subject-matter; in other words, that income is taxable irrespective of the source from whence it is derived. . . .

Admitting that this act taxes the income of property irrespective of its source, still we cannot doubt that such a tax is necessarily a direct tax in the meaning of the Constitution. . . .

What was decided in the *Hylton case* was, then, that a tax on carriages was an excise, and, therefore, an indirect tax. The contention of Mr. Madison in the House was only so far disturbed by it, that the court classified it where he himself would have held it constitutional, and he subsequently as President approved a similar act. . . . The contention of Mr. Hamilton in the Federalist was not disturbed by it in the least. In our judgment, the construction given to the Constitution by the authors of the Federalist (the five numbers contributed by Chief Justice Jay related to the danger from foreign force and influence, and to the treaty-making power) should not and cannot be disregarded.

The Constitution prohibits any direct tax, unless in proportion to numbers as ascertained by the census; and, in the light of the circumstances to which we have referred, is it not an evasion of that prohibition to hold that a general unapportioned tax, imposed upon all property owners as a body for or in respect of their property, is not direct, in the meaning of the Constitution, because confined to the income therefrom?

Whatever the speculative views of political economists or revenue reformers may be, can it be properly held that the Constitution, taken in its plain and obvious sense, and with due regard to the circumstances attending the formation of the government, authorizes a general unapportioned tax on the products of the farm and the rents of real estate, although imposed merely because of ownership and with no possible means of escape from payment, as belonging to a totally different class from that which includes the property from whence the income proceeds?

There can be but one answer, unless the constitutional restriction is to be treated as utterly illusory and futile, and the object of hold that a fundamental requisition, deemed so important as to be enforced by two provisions, one affirmative and one negative, can be refined away by forced distinctions between that which gives value to property, and the property itself.

Nor can we perceive any ground why the same reasoning does not apply to capital in personalty held for the purpose of income or ordinarily yielding income, and to the income therefrom. All the real estate of the country, and all its invested personal property, are open to the direct operation of the taxing power if an apportionment be made according to the Constitution. The Constitution does not say that no direct tax shall be laid by apportionment on any other property than land; on the contrary, it forbids all unapportioned direct taxes; and we know of no warrant for excepting personal property from the exercise of the power, or any reason why an apportioned direct tax cannot be laid and assessed, as Mr. Gallatin said in his report when Secretary of the Treasury in 1812, "upon the same objects of taxation on which the direct taxes levied under the authority of the State are laid and assessed."

Personal property of some kind is of general distribution; and so are incomes, though the taxable range thereof might be narrowed through large exemptions. . . .

In the disposition of the inquiry whether a general unapportioned tax on the income of real and personal property can be sustained, under the Constitution, it is apparent that the suggestion that the result of compliance with the fundamental law would lead to the abandonment of that method of taxation altogether, because of inequalities alleged to necessarily accompany its pursuit, could not be allowed to influence the conclusion; but the suggestion not unnaturally invites attention to the contention of appelants' counsel, that the want of uniformity and equality in this act is such as to invalidate it. Figures drawn from the census are given, showing that enormous assets of mutual insurance companies; of building associations; of mutual savings banks; large productive property of ecclesiastical organizations; are exempted, and it is claimed that the exemptions reach so many hundred millions that the rate of taxation would perhaps have been reduced one-half, if they had not been made. We are not dealing with the act from that point of view; but, assuming the data to be substantially reliable, if the sum desired to be raised had been apportioned, it may be doubted whether any State, which paid its quota and collected the amount by its own methods, would, or could under its constitution, have allowed a large part of the property alluded to to escape taxation. If so, a better measure of equality would have been attained than would be otherwise possible, since, according to the argument for the government, the rule of equality is not prescribed by the Constitution as to Federal taxation, and the observance of such a rule as inherent in all just taxation is purely a matter of legislative discretion.

Elaborate argument is made as to the efficacy and merits of an income tax in general, as on the one hand, equal and just, and on the other, elastic and certain; not that it is not open to abuse by such deductions and exemptions as might make taxation under it so wanting in uniformity and equality as in substance to amount to deprivation of property without due process of law; not that it is not open to fraud and evasion and is inquisitorial in its methods; but because it is preeminently a tax upon the rich, and enables the burden of taxes on consumption and of duties on imports to be sensibly diminished. And it is said that the United States as "the representative of an indivisible nationality, as a political sovereign equal in authority to any other on the face of the globe, adequate to all emergencies, foreign or domestic, and having at its command for offence and defence and for all governmental purposes all the resources of the nation," would be "but a maimed and crippled creation after all," unless it possesses the power to lay a tax on the income of real and personal property throughout the United States without apportionment.

The power to tax real and personal property and the income from both, there being an apportionment, is conceded; that such a tax is a direct tax in the meaning of the Constitution has not been, and, in our judgment, cannot be successfully denied; and yet we are thus invited to hesitate in the enforcement of the mandate of the Constitution, which prohibits Congress from laying a direct tax on the revenue from property of the citizen without regard to state lines, and in such manner that the States cannot intervene by payment in regulation of their own resources, lest a government of delegated powers should be found to be, not less powerful, but less absolute, than the imagination of the advocate has supposed.

We are not here concerned with the question whether an income tax be or be not desirable, nor whether such a tax would enable the government to diminish taxes on consumption and duties on imports, and to enter upon what may be believed to be a reform of its fiscal and commercial system. Questions of that character belong to the controversies of political parties, and cannot be settled by judicial decision. In these cases our province is to determine whether this income tax on the revenue from property does or does not belong to the class of direct taxes. If it does, it is, being unapportioned, in violation of the Constitution, and we must so declare.

Differences have often occurred in this court—differences exist now—but there has never been a time in its history when there has been a difference of opinion as to its duty to announce its deliberate conclusions unaffected by considerations not pertaining to the case in hand.

If it be true that the Constitution should have been so framed that a tax of this kind could be laid, the instrument defines the way for its amendment. In no part of it was greater sagacity displayed. Except that no State, without its consent, can be deprived of its equal suffrage in the Senate, the Constitution may be amended upon the concurrence of two-thirds of both houses, and the ratification of the legislatures or conventions of the several States, or through a Federal convention when applied for by the legislatures of two-thirds of the States, and upon like ratification. The ultimate sovereignty may be thus called into play by a slow and deliberate process, which gives time for mere hypothesis and opinion to exhaust themselves, and for the sober second thought of every part of the country to be asserted. . . .

Our conclusions may, therefore, be summed up as follows:

First. We adhere to the opinion already announced, that, taxes on real estate being indisputably direct taxes, taxes on the rents or income of real estate are equally direct taxes.

Second. We are of opinion that taxes on personal property, or on the income of personal property, are likewise direct taxes.

Third. The tax imposed by . . . the act of 1894, so far as it falls on the income of real estate and of personal property, being a direct tax within the meaning of the Constitution, and, therefore, unconstitutional and void because not apportioned according to representation, all those sections, constituting one entire scheme of taxation, are necessarily invalid....

Mr. Justice Jackson dissenting.

I am unable to yield by assent to the judgment of the court in these cases. My strength has not been equal to the task of preparing a formal dissenting opinion since the decision was agreed upon. I concur fully in the dissents expressed by Mr. Justice White on the former hearing and by the Justices who will dissent now, and will only add a brief outline of my views upon the main questions presented and decided.

It is not and cannot be denied that, under the broad and comprehensive taxing power conferred by the Constitution on the national government, Congress has the authority to tax incomes from whatsoever source arising, whether from real estate or personal property or otherwise. It is equally clear that Congress, in the exercise of this authority, has the discretion to impose the tax upon incomes above a designated amount. The underlying and controlling question now presented is, whether a tax on incomes received from land and personalty is a "direct tax," and subject to the rule of apportionment.

The decision of the court, holding the income tax law of August, 1894, void, is based upon the following propositions:

First. That a tax upon real and personal property is a direct tax within the meaning of the Constitution, and, as such, in order to be valid, must be apportioned among the several States according to their respective populations. Second. That the incomes derived or realized from such property are an inseparable incident thereof, and so far partake of the nature of the property out of which they arise as to stand upon the same footing as the property itself. From these premises the conclusion is reached that a tax on incomes arising from both real and personal property is a "direct tax," and subject to the same rule of apportionment as a tax laid directly on the property itself, and not being so imposed by the act of 1894, according to the rule of numbers, is unconstitutional and void. Third. That the invalidity of the tax on incomes from real and personal property being established, the remaining portions of the income tax law are also void, notwithstanding the fact that such remaining portions clearly come within the class of taxes designated as duties or excises in respect to which the rule of apportionment has no application, but which are controlled and regulated by the rule of uniformity.

It is not found, and could not be properly found by the court, that there is in the other provisions of the law any such lack of uniformity as would be sufficient to render these remaining provisions void for that reason. There is, therefore, no essential connection between the class of incomes which the court holds to be within the rule of apportionment and the other class falling within the rule of uniformity, and I cannot understand the principle upon which the court reaches the conclusion that, because one branch of the law is invalid for the reason that the tax is not laid by the rule of apportionment, it thereby defeats and invalidates another branch resting upon the rule of uniformity, and in respect to which there is no valid objection. If the conclusion of the court on this third proposition is sound, the principle upon which it rests could with equal propriety be extended to the entire revenue act of August 1894.

I shall not dwell upon these considerations. They have been fully elaborated by Mr. Justice Harlan. There is just as much room for the assumption that Congress would not have passed the customs branches of the law without the provision taxing incomes from real and personal estate, as that they would not have passed the provision relating to incomes resting upon the rule of uniformity. Unconstitutional provisions of an act will, no doubt, sometimes defeat constitutional provisions where they are so essentially and inseparably connected in substance as to prevent the enforcement of the valid part without giving effect to the invalid portion. But when the valid and the invalid portions of the act are not mutually dependent upon each other as considerations, conditions, or compensation for each other, and the valid portions are capable of separate enforcement, the latter are never, especially in revenue laws, declared void because of invalid portions of the law. . . .

In my judgment the principle announced in the decision practically destroys the power of the government to reach incomes from real and personal estate. There is to my mind little or no real difference between denying the existence of the power to tax incomes from real and personal estate, and attaching such conditions and requirements to its exercise as will render it impossible or incapable of any practical operation. You might just as well in this case strike at the power to reach incomes from the sources indicated as to attach these conditions of apportionment which no legislature can ever undertake to adopt, and which, if adopted, cannot be enforced with any degree of equality or fairness between the common citizens of a common country.

The decision disregards the well-established canon of construction to which I have referred, that an act passed by a coordinate branch of the government has every presumption in its favor, and should never be declared invalid by the courts unless its repugnancy to the Constitution is clear beyond all reasonable doubt. It is not a matter of conjecture; it is the established principle that it must be clear beyond a reasonable doubt. I cannot see, in view of the past, how this case can be said to be free of doubt.

Again, the decision not only takes from Congress its rightful power of fixing the rate of taxation, but substitutes a rule incapable of application without producing the most monstrous inequality and injustice between citizens residing in different sections of their common country, such as the framers of the Constitution never could have contemplated, such as no free and enlightened people can ever possibly sanction or approve.

The practical operation of the decision is not only to disregard the great principles of equality in taxation, but the further principle that in the imposition of taxes for the benefit of the government the burdens thereof should be imposed upon those having most *ability* to bear them. This decision, in effect, works out a directly opposite result, in relieving the citizens having the greater *ability,* while the burdens of taxation are made to fall most heavily and oppressively upon those having the least ability. It lightens the burdens upon the larger number, in some States subject to the tax, and places it most unequally and disproportionately on the smaller number in other States. Considered in all its bearings, this decision is, in my judgment, the most disastrous blow ever struck at the constitutional power of Congress. It strikes down an important portion of the most vital and essential power of the government in practically excluding any recourse to incomes from real and personal estate for the purpose of raising needed revenue to meet the government's wants and necessities under any circumstances.

I am therefore compelled to enter my dissent to the judgment of the court.

Mr. Justice Brown dissenting.

If the question what is, and what is not, a direct tax, were now, for the first time, presented, I should entertain a grave doubt whether, in view of the definitions of a direct tax given by the courts and writers upon political economy, during the present century, it ought not to be held to apply not only to an income tax, but to every tax, the burden of which is borne, both immediately and ultimately, by the person paying it. It does not, however, follow that this is the definition had in mind by the framers of the Constitution. The clause that direct taxes shall be apportioned according to the population was adopted, as was said by Mr. Justice Paterson, in *Hylton v. United States,* to meet a demand on the part of the Southern States, that representatives and direct taxes should be apportioned among the States according to their respective numbers. . . .

That the rule of apportionment was adopted for a special and temporary purpose, that passed away with the existence of slavery, and that it should be narrowly construed, is also evident from the opinion of Mr. Justice Paterson, wherein he says that "the Constitution has been considered as an accommodating system; it was the effect of mutual sacrifices and concessions; it was the work of compromise. The rule of apportionment is of this nature; it is radically wrong; it cannot be supported by any solid reasoning. Why should slaves, who are a species of property, be represented more than any other property? The rule ought not, therefore, to be extended by construction. Again, numbers do not afford a just estimate or rule of wealth. It is, indeed, a very uncertain and incompetent sign of opulence. There is another reason against the extension of the principle, laid down in the Constitution."

Irrespective, however, of the Constitution, a tax which is wanting in uniformity among members of the same class is, or may be, invalid. But this does not deprive the legislature of the power to make exemptions, provided such exemptions rest upon some principle, and are not purely arbitrary, or created solely for the purpose of favoring some person or body of persons. Thus in every civilized country there is an exemption of small incomes, which it would be manifest cruelty to tax, and the power to make such exemptions once granted, the amount is within the discretion of the legislature, and so long as that power is not wantonly abused, the courts are bound to respect it. In this law there is an exemption of $4,000, which indicates a purpose on the part of Congress that the burden of this tax should fall on the wealthy, or at least upon the well-to-do. If men who have an income or property beyond their pressing needs are not the ones to pay taxes, it is difficult to say who are; in other words, enlightened taxation is imposed upon property and not upon persons. Poll taxes, formerly a considerable source of revenue, are now practically obsolete. The exemption of $4,000 is designed, undoubtedly, to cover the actual living expenses of the large majority of families, and the fact that it is not applied to corporations have no corresponding expenses. The expenses of earning their profits are, of course, deducted in the same manner as the corresponding expenses of a private individual are deductible from the earnings of his business. The moment the profits of a corporation are paid over to the stockholders, the exemption of $4,000 attaches to them in the hands of each stockholder.

The fact that savings banks and mutual insurance companies, whose profits are paid to policy holders, are exempted, is explicable on the theory, (whether a sound one or not, I need not stop to inquire), that these institutions are not, in their original conception, intended as schemes for the accumulation of money; and if this exemption operates as an abuse in certain cases, and with respect to certain very wealthy corporations, it is probably that the recognition of such abuses was necessary to the exemption of the whole class.

It is difficult to overestimate the importance of these cases. I certainly cannot overstate the regret I feel at the disposition made of them by the court. It is never a light thing to set aside the deliberate will of the legislature, and in my opinion it should never be done, except upon the clearest proof of its conflict with the fundamental law. Respect for the Constitution will not be inspired by a narrow and technical construction which shall limit or impair the necessary powers of Congress. Did the reversal of these cases involve merely the striking down of the inequitable features of this law, or even the whole law, for its want of uniformity, the consequences would be less serious; but as it implies a declaration that every income tax must be laid according to the rule of apportionment, the decision involves nothing less than a surrender of the taxing power to the moneyed class. By resuscitating an argument that was exploded in the *Hylton case,* and has lain practically dormant for a hundred years, it is made to do duty in nullifying, not this law alone, but every similar law that is not based upon an impossible theory of apportionment. Even the spectre of socialism is conjured up to frighten Congress from laying taxes upon the people in proportion to their ability to pay them. It is certainly a strange commentary upon the Constitution of the United States and upon a democratic government that Congress has no power to lay a tax which is one of the main sources of revenue of nearly every civilized State. It is a confession of feebleness in which I find myself wholly unable to join. . . .

Mr. Justice Harlan dissenting.

At the former hearing of these causes it was adjudged that, within the meaning of the Constitution, a duty on incomes arising from rents was a direct tax on the lands from which such rents were derived, and, therefore, must be apportioned among the several States on the basis of population, and not by the rule of uniformity throughout the United States, as prescribed in the case of duties, imposts, and excises. And the court, eight of its members being present, was equally divided upon the question whether *all* the other provisions of the statute relating to incomes would fall in consequence of that judgment. . . .

It seems to me that the cases do not justify the conclusion that *all* the income tax sections of the statute must fall because some of them are declared to be invalid. Those sections embrace a large number of taxable subjects that do not depend upon, and have no necessary connection whatever with, the sections or clauses relating to income from rents of land and from personal property. As the statute in question states that its principal object was to reduce taxation and provide revenue, it must be assumed that such revenue is needed for the support of the government, and, therefore, its sections, so far as they are valid, should remain, while those that are invalid should be disregarded. The rule referred to in the cases above cited should not be applied with strictness where the law in question is a general law providing a revenue for the government. Parts of the statute being adjudged to be void, the injustice done to those whose incomes may be reached by those provisions of the statute that are not declared to be, in themselves, valid, could, in some way, be compensated by subsequent legislation.

If the sections of the statute relating to a tax upon incomes derived from other sources than rents and invested personal property are to fall because and only because those relating to rents and to income from invested personal property are invalid, let us see to what result such a rule may logically lead. There is no distinct, separate *statute* providing for a tax upon incomes. The income tax is prescribed by certain sections of a general statute known as the Wilson Tariff act. The judgment just rendered defeats the purpose of Congress by taking out of the revenue not less than thirty millions, and possibly fifty millions of dollars, expected to be raised by the duty on incomes. We know from the official journals of both Houses of Congress that taxation on imports would not have been reduced to the extent it was by the

Wilson act, except for the belief that that could be safely done if the country had the benefit of revenue derived from a tax on incomes. We know, from official sources, that each House of Congress distinctly refused to strike out the provisions imposing a tax on incomes. The two Houses indicated in every possible way that it *must* be a part of any scheme for the reduction of taxation and for raising revenue for the support of the government, that (with certain specified exceptions) incomes arising from every kind of property and from every trade and calling should bear some of the burdens of the taxation imposed. If the court knows, or is justified in believing an income tax that did not include a tax on incomes from real estate and personal property, we are more justified in believing that no part of the Wilson act would have become a law, without provision being made in it for an income tax. If, therefore, all the income tax sections of the Wilson act must fall because some of them are invalid, does not the judgment this day rendered furnish ground for the contention that the entire act falls when the court strikes from it all of the income tax provisions, without which, as every one knows, the act would never have been passed?

But the court takes care to say that there is no question as to the validity of any part of the Wilson act, except those sections providing for a tax on incomes. Thus something is saved for the support and maintenance of the government. It, nevertheless, results that those parts of the Wilson act that survive the new theory of the Constitution evolved by these cases, are those imposing burdens upon the great body of the American people who derive no rents from real estate, and who are not so fortunate as to own invested personal property, such as the bonds or stocks of corporations, that hold within their control almost the entire business of the country.

Such a result is one to be deeply deplored. It cannot be regarded otherwise than as a disaster to the contrary. The decree now passed dislocates—principally, for reasons of an economic nature—a sovereign power expressly granted to the general government and long recognized and fully established by judicial decisions and legislative actions. It so interprets constitutional provisions, originally designed to protect the slave property against oppressive taxation, as to give privileges and immunities never contemplated by the founders of the government.

If the decision of the majority had stricken down all the income tax sections, either because of unauthorized exemptions, or because of defects that could have been remedied by subsequent legislation, the result would not have been one to cause anxiety or regret; for, in such a case, Congress could have enacted a new statute that would not have been liable to constitutional objections. But the serious aspect of the present decision is that by a new interpretation of the Constitution, it so ties the hands of the legislative branch of the government, that without an amendment of that instrument, or unless this court, at some future time, should return to the old theory of the Constitution, Congress cannot subject to taxation—however great the needs or pressing the necessities of the government—either the invested personal property of the country, bonds, stocks, and investments of all kinds, or the income arising from the renting of real estate, or from the yield of personal property, except by the grossly unequal and unjust rule of apportionment among the States. Thus, undue and disproportioned burdens are placed upon the many, while the few, safely entrenched behind the rule of apportionment among the States on the basis of numbers, are permitted to evade their share of responsibility for the support of the government ordained for the protection of the rights of all.

I cannot assent to an interpretation of the Constitution that impairs and cripples the just powers of the National Government in the essential matter of taxation, and at the same time discriminates against the greater part of the people of our country. . . .

Justice John Marshall Harlan: In Defense of the Court

1896

One of the two "great dissenters" of the Fuller Court was John Marshall Harlan of Kentucky (the other was Oliver Wendell Holmes). Harlan came to the Court in 1877, and served a total of thirty-four years on the bench, the second longest tenure of any Supreme Court Justice. Harlan today would be considered a progressive liberal; many of his dissents were classics and of more importance than the majority opinion in the same cases. Some of them became precedents upon which future Courts based their decisions. This selection represents Harlan's retort to a toast made at a dinner hosted by the Cincinnati Bar Association in 1896. Harlan's judicial philosophy rings clear in these remarks. 30 *American Law Review.* 900 (1896).

The toast just read relates to the court of which I have the honor to be a member. It has not escaped observation that that tribunal is now the subject of frequent mention, both in the public prints and on the hustings. Some have expressed the belief that there is a purpose to have the Supreme Court reconstructed so as to accomplish certain objects of a political character. Whether any such purpose exists, I do not at this time affirm or deny. I could not do either without seeming to enter the field of political discussion. But this I may say, that the Supreme Court of the United States is safe in the hands of the People of the United States. That tribunal will, as heretofore, go forward in the path marked out by its own sense of duty. And the People will see to it that nothing is done that will impair its usefulness or cripple its just authority. When Washington invited John Jay to become the Chief Justice of the United States he said that the Judicial Department of the National Government was the keystone of our political fabric. If that seemed to be true at the organization of the General Government, before the Federal judicial system had been tried, how much more is it true, at this day, after the experience of more than a century. The American judicial system is now the wonder and admiration of enlightened statesmen throughout the world. When our government was organized, some Europeans ridiculed the idea that any government could be safely administered under a written constitution that established judicial tribunals and invested them with authority to enforce its sanctions and provisions against all. But wise statesmen in other lands are beginning to see and to admit that such tribunals must exist, if the exercise of arbitrary power is to be checked, and if the rights of life, liberty, and property are to be adequately protected, as well against illegal action by government as against the lawlessness of mere majorities. . . .

The Supreme Court of the United States has, now and then, been compelled to pass upon questions more or less connected with political matters. It has sometimes given a construction to the Constitution or to acts of Congress, or to State enactments alleged to be in violation of the supreme law of the land, that was displeasing to those who had reached different conclusions. But to the honor of the American People, its decisions have been respected, so far, at least, that no attempt has been made to overturn them by indirection, or in any mode not authorized by the Constitution.

Here I may be permitted to say that there is a tendency in some quarters to look to the Supreme Court of the United States for relief against legislation which is admittedly free from constitutional objection, and which therefore is not liable to criticism except upon grounds of public policy. But that court has itself said that the judiciary has nothing to do with the expediency of legislation, and cannot, with safety to our institutions, entrench upon the domain of another Department of the Government. The remedy for evils arising from impolitic and unjust legislation, not in conflict with the fundamental law, is with the people at the ballot-box. If we should ever come to that condition of things when the courts, acting simply upon their own view as to the wisdom of legislation, habitually interfere with the due course of public affairs, as ordained by the representatives of the people, we may look for the downfall of our Government, and the substitution of a government of men in the place of a government of laws. No more imperative or sacred duty rests upon the Judiciary than to sustain in its integrity the fundamental law of the land. An act of legislation inconsistent with that law cannot be regarded as binding; otherwise, as Chief Justice [John] Marshall has declared, written constitutions are absurd attempts, on the part of the people, to limit a power in its nature illimitable. But equally imperative and equally sacred is its duty to respect legislative enactments, except where their incompatibility with the Constitution is so manifest that a contrary view cannot for a moment be entertained. If an act of legislation, whether of Congress or of the States, be of doubtful constitutionality, let the will of the people, as expressed by their legislative department, have full operation until the people themselves, in the designated mode, shall otherwise ordain. No line of public policy can be long maintained in this country against the will of those who established, and who can change, the Constitution.

Wong Wing v. United States (Chinese Exclusion Act Case)

163 U.S. 228

1896

In another *Chinese Exclusion Act* case concerning procedural due process, the Court voted unanimously to invalidate a section of the 1892 statute which gave federal judges and commissioners the power to not only imprison illegal Chinese aliens residing in the United States, but also to sentence them to hard labor while they were awaiting deportation. Under the provisions of the act, these actions could be taken without the benefit of a traditional jury trial. The Court, speaking through Justice George Shiras, Jr., ruled that although these Chinese were not American citizens, this section of the act constituted "infamous punishment," and was a violation of due process under the Constitution's Fifth and Sixth Amendments.

On May 5, 1892, by an act of that date,... Congress enacted that all laws then in force, prohibiting and regulating the coming into this country of Chinese persons and persons of Chinese descent, should be continued in force for a period of ten years from the passage of the act.... in the following terms: "And it shall be the duty of all Chinese laborers within the limits of the United States, at the time of the passage of this act, and who are entitled to remain in the United States, to apply to the collector of internal revenue of their respective districts, within one year after the passage of this act, for a certificate of residence, and any Chinese laborer, within the limits of the United States, who shall neglect, fail or refuse to comply with the provisions of this act, or who, after one year from the passage hereof, shall be found within the jurisdiction of the United States without such certificate of residence, shall be deemed and adjudged to be unlawfully within the United States, and may be arrested by the United States customs official, collector of internal revenue or his deputies, United States marshal or his deputies, and taken before a United States judge, whose duty it shall be to order that he be deported from the United States as hereinbefore provided."

As against the validity of this section, it was contended that, whatever might be true as to the power of the United States to exclude aliens, yet there was no power to banish such aliens who had been permitted to become residents, and that, if such power did exist, it was in the nature of a punishment, and could only be lawfully exercised after a judicial trial.

But this court held, in the case of *Fong Yue Ting v. United States,*... that the right to exclude or to expel aliens, or any class of aliens, absolutely or upon certain conditions, in war or in peace, is an inherent and inalienable right of every sovereign and independent nation; that the power of Congress to expel, like the power to exclude, aliens or any class of aliens from the country may be exercised entirely through executive offices; and that the said . . . section of the act of May 5, 1892, was constitutional and valid. . . .

The present appeal presents a different question from those heretofore determined. It is claimed that, even if it be competent for Congress to prevent aliens from coming into the country, or to provide for the deportation of those unlawfully within its borders, and to submit the enforcement of the provisions of such laws to executive officers, yet the . . . section of the act of 1892, which provides that "any such Chinese person, or person of Chinese descent, convicted and adjudged to be not lawfully entitled to be or remain in the United States, shall be imprisoned at hard labor for a period not exceeding one year, and thereafter removed from the United States," inflicts an infamous punishment, and hence conflicts with the Fifth and Sixth Amendments of the Constitution, which declare that no person shall be held to answer for a capital or otherwise infamous crime unless on a presentment or indictment of a grand jury, and that in all criminal prosecutions the accused shall enjoy the right to a speedy and public trial, by an impartial jury of the State and district wherein the crime shall have been committed. . . .

On the other hand, it is contended on behalf of the Government that it has never been decided by this court that in all cases where the punishment may be confinement at hard labor the crime is infamous, and many cases are cited from the reports of the state Supreme Courts, where the constitutionality of statutes providing for summary proceedings without a jury trial, for the punishment by imprisonment at hard labor of vagrants and disorderly persons has been upheld. These courts have held that the constitutional guarantees refer to such crimes and misdemeanors as have, by the regular course of the law and the established modes of procedure, been the subject of trial by jury, and that they do not embrace every species of accusation involving penal consequences. It is urged that the offence of being and remaining unlawfully within the limits of the United States by an alien is a political offence, and is not within the common law cases triable only by a jury, and that the Constitution does not apply to such a case.

The Chinese exclusion acts operate upon two classes—one consisting of those who came into the country with its consent, the other of those who have come into the United States without their consent and in disregard of the law. Our previous decisions have settled that it is within the constitutional power of Congress to deport both of these classes, and to commit the enforcement of the law to executive officers.

The question now presented is whether Congress can promote its policy in respect to Chinese persons by adding to its provisions for their exclusion and explulsion punishment by imprisonment at hard labor, to be inflicted by the judgment of any justice, judge, or commissioner of the United States, without a trial by jury. In other words, we have to consider the meaning and validity of the. . . section of the act of May 5, 1892, in the following words: "That any such Chinese person, or person of Chinese descent, convicted and adjudged to be not lawfully entitled to be and remain in the United States, shall be imprisoned at hard labor for a period of not exceeding one year, and thereafter removed from the United States, as hereinbefore provided."

We think it clear that detention, or temporary confinement, as part of the means necessary to give effect to the provisions for the exclusion or expulsion of aliens would be valid. Proceedings to exclude or expel would be vain if those accused could not be held in custody pending the inquiry into their true character and while arrangements were being made for their deportation. Detention is a usual feature of every case of arrest on a criminal charge, even when an innocent person is wrongfully accused; but it is not imprisonment in a legal sense.

So, too, we think it would be plainly competent for Congress to declare the act of an alien in remaining unlawfully within the United States to be an offence, punishable by fine or imprisonment, if such offence were to be established by a judicial trial.

But the evident meaning of the section in question, and no other is claimed for it by the counsel for the Government, is that the detention provided for is an imprisonment at hard labor, which is to be undergone before the sentence of deportation is to be carried into effect, and that such imprisonment is to be adjudged against the accused by a justice, judge, or commissioner, upon a summary hearing. Thus construed, the. . . section comes before this court for the first time for consideration as to its validity. . . .

Our views, upon the question thus specifically pressed upon our attention, may be briefly expressed thus: We regard it as settled by our previous decisions that the United States can, as a matter of public policy, by Congressional enactment, forbid aliens or classes of aliens from coming within their borders, and expel aliens or classes of aliens from their territory, and can, in order to make effectual such decree of exclusion or expulsion, devolve the power and duty of identifying and arresting the persons included in such decree, and causing their deportation, upon executive or subordinate officials.

But when Congress sees fit to further promote such a policy by subjecting the persons of such aliens to infamous punishment at hard labor, or by confiscating their property, we think such legislation to be valid, must provide for a judicial trial to establish the guilt of the accused.

No limits can be put by the courts upon the power of Congress to protect, by summary methods, the country from the advent of aliens whose race or habits render them undesirable as citizens, or to expel such if they have already found their way into our land and unlawfully remain therein. But to declare unlawful residence within the country to be an infamous crime, punishable by deprivation of liberty and property, would be to pass out of the sphere of constitutional legislation, unless provision were made that the fact of guilt should first be established by a judicial trial. It is not consistent with the theory of our government that the legislature should, after having defined an offence as an infamous crime, find the fact of guilt and adjudge the punishment by one of its own agents. . . .

And in the case of *Yick Wo v. Hopkins,* 118 U.S. 356, 369, it was said: "The Fourteenth Amendment to the Constitution is not confined to the protection of citizens. It says: 'Nor shall any State deprive any person of life, liberty, or property without due process of law; nor deny to any person within its jurisdiction the equal protection of the law.' These provisions are universal in their application to all persons within the territorial jurisdiction, without regard to any differences of race, of color, or nationality; and the equal protection of the laws is a pledge of the protection of equal laws." Applying this reasoning to the Fifth and Sixth Amendments, it must be concluded that all persons within the territory of the United States are entitled to the protection guaranteed by those amendments, and that even aliens shall not be held to answer for a capital or other infamous crime, unless on a presentment or indictment of a grand jury, nor be deprived of life, liberty, or property without due process of law.

Our conclusion is that the commissioner, in sentencing the appellants to imprisonment at hard labor at and in the Detroit house of correction, acted without jurisdiction, and that the Circuit Court erred in not discharging the prisoners from such imprisonment, without prejudice to their detention according to law for deportation.

The judgment of the Circuit Court is reversed and the cause remanded to that court with directions to proceed therein in accordance with this opinion.

Plessy v. Ferguson
163 U.S. 537
1896

With Justice Henry B. Brown delivering the majority opinion, the Court, by a vote of 7 to 1, wrote into law the "separate but equal" doctrine in this case. The decision sustained a Louisiana statute which segregated accommodations for black and white passengers on railroad cars travelling within the state. The Louisiana law had been challenged by Homer A. Plessy, a Louisiana resident with one-eighth negroid blood. Plessy had been arrested and fined for violating the state law four years earlier. The Supreme Court, in its opinion, reasoned that "separate but equal" facilities did not violate the Thirteenth and Fourteenth Amendments to the Constitution. Justice John Marshall Harlan, in a brilliant dissent, made his legendary remark, "Our Constitution is color-blind." A portion of that dissent follows the majority opinion in this selection.

The information filed in the criminal District Court charged in substance that Plessy, being a passenger between two stations within the State of Louisiana, was assigned by officers of the company to the coach used for the race to which he belonged, but he insisted upon going into a coach used by the race to which he did not belong. Neither in the information nor plea was his particular race or color averred.

The petition for the writ of prohibition averred that petitioner was seven eights Caucasian and one eighth African blood; that the mixture of colored blood was not discernible in him, and that he was entitled to every right, privilege and immunity secured to citizens of the United States of the white race; and that, upon such theory, he took possession of a vacant seat in a coach where passengers of the white race were accommodated, and was ordered by the conductor to vacate said coach and take a seat in another assigned to persons of the colored race, and having refused to comply with such demand he was forcibly ejected with the aid of a police officer, and imprisoned in the parish jail to answer a charge of having violated the above act.

The constitutionality of this act is attacked upon the ground that it conflicts both with the Thirteenth Amendment of the Constitution, abolishing slavery, and the Fourteenth Amendment, which prohibits certain restrictive legislation on the part of the States.

1. That it does not conflict with the Thirteenth Amendment, which abolished slavery and involuntary servitude, except as a punishment for

crime, is too clear for argument. Slavery implies involuntary servitude—a state of bondage; the ownership of mankind as a chattel, or at least the control of the labor and services of one man for the benefit of another, and the absence of a legal right to the disposal of his own person, property and services. This amendment was said in the *Slaughter House cases,* 16 Wall. 36, to have been intended primarily to abolish slavery, as it had been previously known in this country, and that it equally forbade Mexican peonage or the Chinese coolie trade, when they amounted to slavery or involuntary servitude, and that the use of the word "servitude" was intended to prohibit the use of all forms of involuntary slavery, of whatever class or name. It was intimated, however, in that case that this amendment was regarded by the statesmen of that day as insufficient to protect the colored race from certain laws which had been enacted in the Southern States, imposing upon the colored race onerous disabilities and burdens, and curtailing their rights in the pursuit of life, liberty, and property to such an extent that their freedom was of little value; and that the Fourteenth Amendment was devised to meet this exigency.

So, too, in the *Civil Rights cases,* 109 U.S. 3, 24, it was said that the act of a mere individual, the owner of an inn, a public conveyance or place of amusement, refusing accommodations to colored people, cannot be justly regarded as imposing any badge of slavery or servitude upon the applicant, but only as involving an ordinary civil injury, properly cognizable by the laws of the State, and presumably subject to redress by those laws until the contrary appeals. "It would be running the slavery argument into the ground," said Mr. Justice Bradley, "to make it apply to every act of discrimination which a person may see fit to make as to the guests he will entertain, or as to the people he will take into his coach or cab or car, or admit to his concert or theatre, or deal with in other matters of intercourse or business."

A statute which implies merely a legal distinction between the white and colored races—a distinction which is founded in the color of the two races, and which must always exist so long as white men are distinguished from the other race by color—has no tendency to destroy the legal equality of the two races, or reestablish a state of involuntary servitude. Indeed, we do not understand that the Thirteenth Amendment is strenuously relied upon by the plaintiff in error in this connection.

2. By the Fourteenth Amendment, all persons born or naturalized in the United States, and subject to the jurisdiction thereof, are made citizens of the United States and of the State wherein they reside; and the States are forbidden from making or enforcing any law which shall abridge the privileges or immunities of citizens of the United States, or shall deprive any person of life, liberty or property without due process of law, or deny to any person within their jurisdiction the equal protection of the laws.

The proper construction of this amendment was first called to the attention of this court in the *Slaughter House cases,* . . . which involved, however, not a question of race, but one of exclusive privileges. The case did not call for any expression of opinion as to the exact rights it was intended to secure to the colored race, but it was said generally that its main purpose was to establish the citizenship of the negro; to give definitions of citizenship of the United States and of the States, and to protect from the hostile legislation of the States the privileges and immunities of citizens of the United States, as distinguished from those of citizens of the States.

The object of the amendment was undoubtedly to enforce the absolute equality of the two races before the law, but in the nature of things it could not have been intended to abolish distinctions based upon color, or to enforce social, as distinguished from political equality, or a comingling of the two races upon terms unsatisfactory to either. Laws permitting, and even requiring, their separation in places where they are liable to be brought into contact do not necessarily imply the inferiority of either race to the other, and have been generally, if not universally, recognized as within the competency of the state legislatures in the exercise of their police power. The most common instance of this is connected with the establishment of separate schools for white and colored children, which has been held to be a valid exercise of the legislative power even by courts of States where the political rights of the colored race have been longest and most earnestly enforced. . . .

While we think the enforced separation of the races, as applied to the internal commerce of the State, neither abridges the privileges or immunities of the colored man, deprives him of his property without due process of law, nor denies him the equal protection of the laws, within the meaning of the Fourteenth Amendment, we are not prepared to say that the conductor, in assigning passengers to the coaches according to their race, does not act at his peril, or that the provision of the second section of the act, that denies to the passenger compensation in damages for a refusal to receive him into the coach in which he properly belongs, is a valid exercise of the legislative power. Indeed, we understand it to be conceded by the State's attorney, that such part of the act as exempts from liability the railway company and its officers is unconstitutional. The power to assign to a particular coach obviously implies the power to determine to which race the passenger belongs, as well as the power to determine who, under the laws of the particular State, is to be deemed a white, and who a colored person. This question, though indicated in the brief of the plaintiff in error, does not properly arise upon the record in this case, since the only issue made is as to the unconstitutionality of the act, so far as it requires the railway to provide separate accommodations, and the conductor to assign passengers according to their race.

It is claimed by the plaintiff in error that, in any mixed community, the reputation of belonging to the dominant race, in this instance the white race, is *property,* in the same sense that a right of action, or of inheritance, is property. Conceding this to be so, for the purposes of this case, we are unable to see how this statute deprives him of, or in any way affects his right to, such property. If he be a white man and assigned to a colored coach, he may have his action for damages against the company for being deprived of his so called property. Upon the other hand, if he be a colored man and be so assigned, he has been deprived of no property, since he is not lawfully entitled to the reputation of being a white man.

In this connection, it is also suggested by the learned counsel for the plaintiff in error that the same argument that will justify the state legislature in requiring railways to provide separate accommodations for the two races will also authorize them to require separate cars to be provided for people whose hair is of a certain color, or who are aliens, or who belong to certain nationalities, or to enact laws requiring colored people to walk upon one side of the street, and white people upon the other, or requiring white men's houses to be painted white, and colored men's black, or their vehicles or business signs to be of different colors, upon the theory that one side of the street is as good as the other, or that a house or vehicle of one color is as good as one of another color. The reply to all this is that every exercise of police power must be reasonable, and extend only to such laws as are enacted in good faith for the promotion for the public good, and not for the annoyance or repression of a particular class. . . .

So far, then, as a conflict with the Fourteenth Amendment is concerned, the case reduces itself to the question whether the statute of Louisiana is a reasonable regulation, and with respect to this there must necessarily be a large discretion on the part of the legislature. In determining the question of reasonableness it is at liberty to act with reference to the established usages, customs and traditions of the people, and with a view to the promotion of their comfort, and the preservation of the public peace and good order. Gauged by this standard, we cannot say that a law which authorizes or even requires the separation of the two races in public conveyances is unreasonable, or more obnoxious to the Fourteenth Amendment than the acts of Congress requiring separate schools for colored children in the District of Columbia, the constitutionality of which does not seem to have been questioned, or the corresponding acts of state legislatures.

We consider the underlying fallacy of the plaintiff's argument to consist in the assumption that the enforced separation of the two races stamps the colored race with a badge of inferiority. If this be so, it is not by reason of anything found in the act, but solely because the colored race chooses to put that construction upon it. The argument necessarily assumes that if, as has been more than once the case, and is not unlikely to be so again, the colored race should become the dominant power in the state legislature, and should enact a law in precisely similar terms, it would thereby relegate the white race to an inferior position. We imagine that the white race, at least, would not acquiesce in this assumption. The argument also assumes that social prejudices may be overcome by legislation, and that equal rights cannot be secured to the negro except by an enforced comingling of the two races. We cannot accept this proposition. If the two races are to meet upon terms of social equality, it must be the result of natural affinities, a mutual appreciation of each other's merits and a voluntary consent of individuals. As was said by the Court of Appeals of New York in *People v. Gallagher,* 93 N.Y. 438, 448, "this end can neither be accomplished nor promoted by laws which conflict with the general sentiment of the community upon whom they are designed to operate. When the government, therefore, has secured to each of its citizens equal rights before the law and equal opportunities for improvement and progress, it has accomplished the end for which it was organized and performed all of the functions respecting social advantages with which it is endowed." Legislation is powerless to eradicate racial instincts or to abolish distinctions based upon physical differences, and the attempt to do so can only result in accentuating the difficulties of the present situation. If the civil and political rights of both races be equal one cannot be inferior to the other civilly or politically. If one race be inferior to the other socially, the Constitution of the United States cannot put them upon the same plane. . . .

Mr. Justice Harlan dissenting.

By the Louisiana statute, the validity of which is here involved, all railway companies (other than street railroad companies) carrying passengers in that State are required to have separate but equal accommodations for white and colored persons, "by providing two or more passenger coaches for each passenger train, *or* by dividing the passenger coaches by a *partition* so as to secure separate accommodations." Under this statute, no colored person is permitted to occupy a seat in a coach assigned to white persons; nor any white person, to occupy a seat in a coach assigned to colored persons. The managers of the railroad are not allowed to exercise any discretion in the premises, but are required to assign each passenger to some coach or compartment set apart for the exclusive use of his race. If a passenger insists upon going into a coach or compartment not set apart for persons of his race, he is subject to be fined, or to be imprisoned in the parish jail. Penalties are prescribed for the refusal or neglect of the officers, directors, conductors and employees of railroad companies to comply with the provisions of the act.

Only "nurses attending children of the other race" are excepted from the operation of the statute. No exception is made of colored attendants travelling with adults. A white man is not permitted to have his colored servant with him in the same coach, even if his condition of health requires the constant, personal assistance of such servant. If a colored maid insists upon riding in the same coach with a white woman whom she has been employed to serve, and who may need her personal attention while traveling, she is subject to be fined or imprisoned for such an exhibition of zeal in the discharge of duty.

While there may be in Louisiana persons of different races who are not citizens of the United States, the words in the act, "white and colored races," necessarily include all citizens of the United States of both races residing in that State. So that we have before us a state enactment that compels, under penalties, the separation of the two races in railroad passenger coaches, and makes it a crime for a citizen of either race to enter a coach that has been assigned to citizens of the other race.

Thus the State regulates the use of a public highway by citizens of the United States solely upon the basis of race.

However apparent the injustice of such legislation may be, we have only to consider whether it is consistent with the Constitution of the United States. . . .

In respect of civil rights, common to all citizens, the Constitution of the United States does not, I think, permit any public authority to know the race of those entitled to be protected in the enjoyment of such rights. Every true man has pride of race, and under appropriate circumstances when the rights of others, his equals before the law, are not to be affected, it is his privilege to express such pride and to take such action based upon it as to him seems proper. But I deny that any legislative body or judicial tribunal may have regard to the race of citizens when the civil rights of those citizens are involved. Indeed, such legislation, as that here in question, is inconsistent not only with that equality of rights which pertains to citizenship, National and State, but with the personal liberty enjoyed by every one within the United States.

The Thirteenth Amendment does not permit the withholding or the deprivation of any right necessarily inhering in freedom. It not only struck down the institution of slavery as previously existing in the United States, but it prevents the imposition of any burdens or disabilities that constitute badges of slavery or servitude. It decreed universal civil freedom in this country. This court has so adjudged. But that amendment having been found inadequate to the protection of the rights of those who had been in slavery, it was followed by the Fourteenth Amendment, which added greatly to the dignity and glory of American citizenship, and to the security of personal liberty, by declaring that "all persons born or naturalized in the United States, and subject to the jurisdiction thereof, are citizens of the United States and of the State wherein they reside," and that "no State shall make or enforce any law which shall abridge the privileges or immunities of citizens of the United States; nor shall any State deprive any person of life, liberty or property without due process of law, nor deny to any person within its jurisdiction the equal protection of the laws." These two amendments, if enforced according to their true intent and meaning, will protect all the civil rights that pertain to freedom and citizenship. Finally, and to the end that no citizen should be denied, on account of his race, the privilege of participating in the political control of his country, it was declared by the Fifteenth Amendment that "the right of citizens of the United States to vote shall not be denied or abridged by the United States or by any State on account of race, color or previous condition of servitude."

These notable additions to the fundamental law were welcomed by the friends of liberty throughout the world. They removed the race line from our governmental systems. They had, as this court has said, a common purpose, namely, to secure "to a race recently emancipated, a race that through many generations have been held in slavery, all the civil rights that the superior race enjoy." They declared, in legal effect, this court has further said, "that the law in the States shall be the same for the black as for the white; that all persons, whether colored or white, shall stand equal before the laws of the States, and, in regard to the colored race, for whose protection the amendment was primarily designed, that no discrimination shall be made against them by law because of their color." We also said: "The words of the amendment, it is true, are prohibitory, but they contain a necessary implication of a positive immunity, or right, most valuable to the colored race—the right to exemption from unfriendly legislation against them distinctively as colored—exemption from legal discriminations, implying inferiority in civil society, lessening the security of their enjoyment of the rights which others enjoy, and discriminations which are steps towards reducing them to the condition of a subject race." It was, consequently, adjudged that a state law that excluded citizens of the colored race from juries, because of their race and however well qualified in other respects to discharge the duties of jurymen, was repugnant to the Fourteenth Amendment....

The decisions referred to show the scope of the recent amendments of the Constitution. They also show that it is not within the power of a State to prohibit colored citizens, because of their race, from participating as jurors in the administration of justice.

It was said in argument that the statute of Louisiana does not discriminate against either race, but prescribes a rule applicable alike to white and colored citizens. But this argument does not meet the difficulty. Everyone knows that the statute in question had its origin in the purpose, not so much to exclude white persons from railroad cars occupied by blacks, as to exclude colored people from coaches occupied by or assigned to white persons. Railroad corporations of Louisiana did not make discrimination among whites in the matter of accommodation for travellers. The thing to accomplish was, under the guise of giving equal accommodation for whites and blacks, to compel the latter to keep to themselves while travelling in railroad passenger coaches. No one would be so wanting in candor as to assert the contrary. The fundamental objection, therefore, to the statute is that it interferes with the personal freedom of citizens. "Personal liberty," it has been well said, "consists in the power of locomotion, of changing situation, or removing one's person to whatsoever places one's own inclination may direct, without imprisonment or restraint, unless by due course of law.". . . If a white man and a black man choose to occupy the same public conveyance on a public highway, it is their right to do so, and no government, proceeding alone on grounds of race, can prevent it without infringing the personal liberty of each.

It is one thing for railroad carriers to furnish, or to be required by law to furnish, equal accommodations for all whom they are under a legal duty to carry. It is quite another thing for government to forbid citizens of the white and black races from travelling in the same public conveyance, and to punish officers of railroad companies for permitting persons of the two races to occupy the same passenger coach. If a State can prescribe, as a rule of civil conduct, that whites and blacks shall not travel as passengers in the same railroad coach, why may it not so regulate the use of the streets of its cities and towns as to compel white citizens to keep on one side of a street and black citizens to keep on the other? Why may it not, upon like grounds, punish whites and blacks who ride together in street cars or in open vehicles on a public road or street? Why may it not require sheriffs to assign whites to one side of a court-room and blacks to the other? And why may it not also prohibit the comingling of the two races in the galleries of legislative halls or in public assemblages convened for the consideration of the political questions of the day? Further, if this statute of Louisiana is consistent with the personal liberty of citizens, why may not the State require the separation in railroad coaches of native and naturalized citizens of the United States, or of Protestants and Roman Catholics?. . .

The white race deems itself to be the dominant race in this country. And so it is, in prestige, in achievements, in education, in wealth and in power. So, I doubt not, it will continue to be for all time, if it remains true to its great heritage and holds fast to the principles of constitutional liberty. But in view of the Constitution, in the eye of the law, there is in this country no superior, dominant, ruling class of citizens. There is no caste here. Our Constitution is color-blind, and neither knows nor tolerates classes among citizens. In respect of civil rights, all citizens are equal before the law. The humblest is the peer of the most powerful. The law regards man as man, and takes no account of his surroundings or of his color when his civil rights as guaranteed by the supreme law of the land are involved. It is, therefore, to be regretted that this high tribunal, the final expositor of the fundamental law of the land, has reached the conclusion that it is competent for a State to regulate the enjoyment by citizens of their civil rights solely upon the basis of race.

In my opinion, the judgment this day rendered will, in time, prove to be quite as pernicious as the decision made by this tribunal in the *Dred Scott case*. It was adjudged in that case that the descendants of Africans who were imported into this country and sold as slaves were not included nor intended to be included under the word "citizens" in the Constitution, and could not claim any of the rights and privileges which that instrument provided for and secured to citizens of the United States; that at the time of the adoption of the

Constitution they were "considered as a subordinate and inferior class of beings, who had been subjugated by the dominant race, and, whether emancipated or not, yet remained subject to their authority, and had no rights or privileges but such as those who held the power and the government might choose to grant them." 19 How. 393, 404. The recent amendments of the Constitution, it was supposed, had eradicated these principles from our institutions. But it seems that we have yet, in some of the States, a dominant race—a superior class of citizens, which assumes to regulate the enjoyment of civil rights, common to all citizens, upon the basis of race. The present decision, it may well be apprehended, will not only stimulate aggressions, more or less brutal and irritating, upon the admitted rights of colored citizens, but will encourage the belief that it is possibly, by means of state enactments, to defeat the beneficient purposes which the people of the United States had in view when they adopted the recent amendments of the Constitution, by one of which the blacks of this country were made citizens of the United States and of the States in which they respectively reside, and whose privileges and immunities, as citizens, the States are forbidden to abridge. Sixty millions of whites are in no danger from the presence here of eight millions of blacks. The destinies of the two races, in this country, are indissolubly linked together, and the interests of both require that the common government of all shall not permit the seeds of race rate to be planted under the sanction of law. What can more certainly arouse race hate, what more certainly create and perpetuate a feeling of distrust between these races, than state enactments, which, in fact, proceed on the ground that colored citizens are so inferior and degraded that they cannot be allowed to sit in public coaches occupied by white citizens? That, as all will admit, is the real meaning of such legislation as was enacted in Louisiana. . . .

The arbitrary separation of citizens, on the basis of race, while they are on a public highway, is a badge of servitude wholly inconsistent with the civil freedom and the equality before the law established by the Constitution. It cannot be justified upon any legal grounds.

If evils will result from the comingling of the two races upon public highways established for the benefit of all, they will be infinitely less than those that will surely come from state legislation regulating the enjoyment of civil rights upon the basis of race. We boast of the freedom enjoyed by our people above all other peoples. But it is difficult to reconcile that boast with a state of the law which, practically, puts the brand of servitude and degradation upon a large class of our fellow-citizens, our equals before the law. The thin disguise of "equal" accommodations for passengers in railroad coaches will not mislead any one, nor atone for the wrong this day done. . . .

I am of opinion that the statute of Louisiana is inconsistent with the personal liberty of citizens, white and black, in that State, and hostile to both the spirit and letter of the Constitution of the United States. If laws of like character should be enacted in the several States of the Union, the effect would be in the highest degree mischievous. Slavery, as an institution tolerated by law would, it is true, have disappeared from our country, but there would remain a power in the States, by sinister legislation, to interfere with the full enjoyment of the blessings of freedom; to regulate civil rights, common to all citizens, upon the basis of race; and to place in a condition of legal inferiority a large body of American citizens, now constituting a part of the political community called the People of the United States, for whom, and by whom through representatives, our government is administered. Such a system is inconsistent with the guarantee given by the Constitution to each State of a republican form of government, and may be stricken down by Congressional action, or by the courts in the discharge of their solemn duty to maintain the supreme law of the land, anything in the constitution or laws of any State to the contrary notwithstanding.

For the reasons stated, I am constrained to withhold my assent from the opinion and judgment of the majority.

Justice Stephen J. Field: On the Role of the Court

1897

Stephen J. Field was appointed to the Supreme Court by Abraham Lincoln in 1863, and served a little over thirty-four years on the bench, retiring at the end of the 1897 term. His was once the longest Supreme Court tenure in the history of the United States. Field was a politician as well as a judge and always harbored ambitions of someday rising to President of the United States or Chief Justice of the Supreme Court; neither desire ever materialized. An arch-conservative like his nephew Justice David Brewer, his puritanical background forged within him a narrow judicial philosophy which manifested itself in a very rigid interpretation of the Constitution. This selection captures some of the Field philosophy. 42 1. Ed. 1219, 1221 (1897).

This power of that court is sometimes characterized by foreign writers and jurists as a unique provision of a disturbing and dangerous character, tending to defeat the popular will as expressed by the legislature. In thus characterizing it they look at the power as one that may be exercised by way of supervision over the general legislation of Congress, determining the validity of an enactment in advance of its being contested. But a declaration of the unconstitutionality of an Act of Congress or of the State cannot be made in that way by the Judicial Department. The unconstitutionality of an Act cannot be pronounced except as required for the determination of contested litigation. No such authority as supposed would be tolerated in this country. It would make the Supreme Court a third house of Congress, and its conclusions would be subject to all the infirmities of general legislation.

The limitations upon legislative power, arising from the nature of the Constitution and its specific restraints in favor of private rights, cannot be disregarded without conceding that the legislature can change at will the form of our government from one of limited to one of unlimited powers. Whenever, therefore, any court, called upon to construe an enactment of Congress or of a State, the validity of which is assailed, finds its provisions inconsistent with the Constitution, it must give effect to the latter, because it is the fundamental law of the whole people, and, as such, superior to any law of Congress or any law of a State. Otherwise the limitations upon legislative power expressed in the Constitution or implied by it must be considered as vain attempts to control a power which is in its nature uncontrollable.

This unique power, as it is termed, is therefore not only a disturbing or dangerous force, but is a necessary consequence of our form of government, both of the United States and of the States, in all their branches, within the limits assigned to them by the Constitution of the United States, and thus secure justice to the people against the unrestrained legislative will of either—the reign of law against the sway of arbitrary power....

And so, in the great majority of cases in which the validity of an Act of Congress or of a State has been called in question, its decisions have been in the same direction, to uphold and carry out the provisions of the Constitution. In some instances the court, in the exercise of its powers in this respect, may have made mistakes. The judges would be more than human if this were not so. They have never claimed infalibility; they have often differed among themselves. All they have ever asserted is, that they have striven to the utmost of their abilities to be right, and to perform the functions with which they are clothed to the advancement of justice and the good of the country.

In respect to their liability to err in their conclusions this may be said—that in addition to the desire which must be ascribed to them to be just—the conditions under which they perform their duties, the publicity of their proceedings, the discussions before them, and the public attention which is drawn to all decisions of general interest, tend to prevent any grave departure from the purposes of the Constitution. And, further, there is this corrective of error in every such departure; it will not fit harmoniously with other rulings; it will collide with them, and thus compel explanations and qualifications until the error is eliminated....

Furthermore, I hardly need say that, to retain the respect and confidence conceded in the past, the court, whilst cautiously abstaining from assuming powers granted by the Constitution to other departments of the government, must unhesitatingly and to the best of its ability enforce, as heretofore, not only all the limitations of the Constitution upon the federal and state governments, but also all the guaranties it contains of the private rights of the citizen, both of person and of property. As population and wealth increase; as the inequalities in the conditions of men become more and more marked and disturbing; as the enormous aggregation of wealth possessed by power should become dominating in the legislation of the country, and thus encroach upon the rights or crush out the business of individuals of small means; as population in some quarters presses upon the means of subsistence, and angry menaces against order find vent in loud denunciations,—it becomes more and more the imperative duty of the court to enforce with a firm hand all the guaranties of the Constitution. Every decision weakening their restraining power is a blow to the peace of society and to its progress and improvement. It should never be forgotten that protection to property and to persons cannot be separated. Where property is insecure, the rights of persons are unsafe. Protection to the one goes with protection to the other; and there can be neither prosperity nor progress where either is uncertain.

That the Justices of the Supreme Court must possess the ability and learning required by the duties of their office, and a character for purity and integrity beyond reproach, need not be said. But it is not sufficient for the performance of his judicial duty that a judge should act honestly in all that he does. He must be ready to act in all cases presented for his judicial determination with absolute fearlessness. Timidity, hesitation and cowardice in any public officer excite and deserve only contempt, but infinitely more in a judge than in any other, because he is appointed to discharge a public trust of the most sacred character. To decide against his conviction of the law or judgment as to the evidence, whether moved by prejudice, or passion, or the clamor of the crowd, is to assent to a robbery as infamous in morals and as deserving of punishment as that of the highwayman or the burglar; and to hesitate or refuse to act when duty calls is hardly less the subject of just reproach. If he is influenced by apprehensions that his character will be attacked, or his motives impugned, or that his judgment will be attributed to the influence of particular classes, cliques, or associations, rather than to this own convictions of the law, he will fail lamentably in his high office....

Allgeyer v. Louisiana

165 U.S. 578

1897

A unanimous Court speaking through Justice Rufus Wheeler Peckham, declared unconstitutional a Louisiana act which refused to grant licenses to out-of-state insurance companies to carry on business within the state, if they failed to meet all the conditions required by the state insurance statutes. The Court ruled that this Louisiana law was a violation of the freedom of contract clause under the Fourteenth Amendment. This case was one of the first dealing with this relatively new principle, and as such, established the precedent that would be employed by the Court in subsequent cases concerned with the same concept.

There is no doubt of the power of the State to prohibit foreign insurance companies from doing business within its limits. The State can impose such conditions as it pleases upon the doing of any business by those companies within its borders, and unless the conditions be complied with the prohibition may be absolute. The cases upon this subject are cited in the opinion of the court in *Hooper v. California,* 155 U.S. 648.

We think the distinction between that case and the one at bar is plain and material. The State of California made it a misdemeanor for a person in that State to procure insurance for a resident of the State from an insurance company not incorporated under its laws, and which had not filed a bond required by those laws relative to insurance....

In the case before us the contract was made beyond the territory of the State of Louisiana, and the only thing the facts show was done within that State was the mailing of a letter of notification...which was done after the principal contract had been made....

We do not intend to throw any doubt upon or in the least to shake the authority of the *Hooper case,* but the facts of that case and the principle therein decided are totally different from the case before us. In this case the only act which it is claimed was a violation of the statute in question consisted in sending the letter through the mail notifying the company of the property to be covered by the policy already delivered. We have then a contract which it is conceded was made outside and beyond the limits of the jurisdiction of the State of Louisiana, being made and to be performed within the State of New York, where the premiums were to be paid and losses, if any, adjusted. The letter of notification did not constitute a contract made or entered into within the State of Louisiana. It was but the performance of an act rendered necessary by the provisions of the contract already made between the parties outside of the State.. It was a mere notification that the contract already in existence would attach to that particular property. In any event, the contract was made in New York, outside of the jurisdiction of Louisiana, even though the policy was not to attach to the particular property until the notification was sent.

It is natural that the state court should have remarked that there is in this "statute an apparent interference with the liberty of defendants in restricting their rights to place insurance on property of their own whenever and in what company they desired." Such interference is not only apparent, but it is real, and we do not think that it is justified for the purpose of upholding what the State says is its policy with regard to foreign insurance companies which had not complied with the laws of the State for doing business within its limits. In this case the company did no business within the State, and the contracts were not therein made.

The Supreme Court of Louisiana says that the act of writing within that State, the letter of notification, was an act therein done to effect an insurance on property then in the State, in a marine insurance company which had not complied with its laws, and such act was, therefore, prohibited by the statute. As so construed we think the statute is a violation of the Fourteenth Amendment of the Federal Constitution, in that it deprives the defendants of their liberty without due process of law. The statute which forbids such act does not become due process of law, because it is inconsistent with the provisions of the Constitution of the Union. The liberty mentioned in that amendment means not only the right of the citizen to be free from the mere physical restraint of his person, as by incarceration, but the term is deemed to embrace the right of the citizen to be free in the enjoyment of all his faculties; to be free to use them in all lawful ways; to live and work where he will; to earn his livelihood by any lawful calling; to pursue any livelihood or avocation, and for that purpose to enter into all contracts which may be proper, necessary and essential to his carrying out to a successful conclusion the purposes above mentioned....

Has not a citizen of a State, under the provisions of the Federal Constitution...a right to contract outside of the State for insurance on his property—a right of which state legislation cannot deprive him? We are not alluding to acts done within the State by an insurance company or its agents doing business therein, which are in violation of these statutes. Such acts come within the principle of the *Hooper case (supra),* and would be controlled by it. When we speak of the liberty to contract for insurance or to do an act to effectuate such a contract already existing, we refer to and have in mind the facts of this case, where the contract was made outside the State, and as such as a valid and proper contract. The act done within the limits of the State under the circumstances of this case and for the purpose therein mentioned, we hold a proper act, one which the defendants were at liberty to perform and which the state legislature had no right to prevent, at least w reference to the Federal Constitution. To deprive the citizen of such a right herein described without due process of law is illegal. Such a statute as this i. question is not due process of law, because it prohibits an act which under the Federal Constitution the defendants had a right to perform. This does not interfere in any way with the acknowledged right of the State to enact such legislation in the legitimate exercise of its police or other powers as to it may seem proper. In the exercise of such right, however, care must be taken not to infringe upon those other rights of the citizen which are protected by the Federal Constitution.

In the privilege of pursuing an ordinary calling or trade and of acquiring, holding and selling property must be embraced the right to make all proper contracts in relation thereto, and although it may be conceded that this right to contract in relation to persons or property or to do business within the jurisdiction of the State may be regulated and sometimes prohibited when the contracts or business conflict with the policy of the State as contained in its statutes, yet the power does not and cannot extend to prohibiting a citizen from making contracts of the nature involved in the case outside of the limits and jurisdiction of the State, and which are also to be performed outside of such jurisdiction; nor can the State legally prohibit its citizens from doing such an act as writing this letter of notification, even though the property which is the subject of the insurance may at the time when such insurance attaches be within the limits of the State. The mere fact that a citizen may be within the limits of a particular State does not prevent his making a contract outside its limits while he himself remains within it.

The Atlantic Mutual Insurance Company of New York has done no business of insurance within the State of Louisiana and has not subjected itself to any provisions of the statute in question. It had the right to enter into a contract in New York with citizens of Louisiana for the purpose of insuring the property of its citizens, even if that property were in the State of Louisiana, and correlatively the citizens of Louisiana had the right without the State of entering into contract with an insurance company for the same purpose. Any act of the state legislature which should prevent the entering into such a contract, or the mailing within the State of Louisiana of such a notification as is mentioned in this case, is an improper and illegal interference with the conduct of the citizen, although residing in Louisiana, in his right to contract and to carry out the terms of a contract validly entered into outside and beyond the jurisdiction of the State.

In such a case as the facts here present the policy of the State in forbidding insurance companies which had not complied with the laws of the State from doing business within its limits cannot be so carried out as to prevent the citizen from writing such a letter of notification as was written by the plaintiffs in error in the State of Louisiana, when it is written pursuant to a valid contract made outside the State and with reference to a company which

...t doing business within its limits.

...or these reasons we think the statute in question...of the Laws of ...ouisiana of 1894, was a violation of the Federal Constitution, and afforded ...o justification for the judgment awarded by that court against the plaintiffs in error. That judgment must, therefore, be reversed, and the case remanded to the Supreme Court of Louisiana for further proceedings not inconsistent with this opinion.

Interstate Commerce Commission v. Cincinnati, New Orleans and Texas Pacific Railway Company
167 U.S. 479
1897

The majority decision of the Court in this case, delivered by Justice David J. Brewer, emasculated, still further, the Interstate Commerce Act of 1887. The Court expressed the opinion that it could find nothing in the provisions of this federal statute which gave the Interstate Commerce Commission any implied authority to set new railroad rates after the Commission had decided that the carrier's rate schedules were unreasonable. As a result, the Court denied the Commission quasi-legislative power, and any positive rate-setting authority. This case completed the process of restricting the Interstate Commerce Commission's powers that the Court had begun in the *Wabash* case in 1886.

Before the passage of the [Interstate Commerce] act it was generally believed that there were great abuses in railroad management and railroad transportation, and the grave question which Congress had to consider was how those abuses should be corrected and what control should be taken of the business of such corporations. The present inquiry is limited to the question as to what it determined should be done with reference to the matter of rates. There were three obvious and dissimilar courses open for consideration. Congress might itself prescribe the rates; or it might commit to some subordinate tribunal this duty; or it might leave with the companies the right to fix rates, subject to regulations and restrictions, as well as to that rule which is as old as the existence of common carriers, to wit, that rates must be reasonable. There is nothing in the act fixing rates. Congress did not attempt to exercise that power, and if we examine the legislative and public history of the day it is apparent that there was no serious thought of doing so.

The question debated is whether it vested in the commission the power and the duty to fix rates; and the fact that this is a debatable question, and has been most strenuously and earnestly debated, is very persuasive that it did not. The grant of such a power is never to be implied....

It is one thing to inquire whether the rates which have been charged and collected are reasonable—that is a judicial act; but an entirely different thing to prescribe rates which shall be charged in the future—that is a legislative act....

. . . Now, nowhere in the interstate commerce act do we find words similar to those in the statutes referred to, giving to the commission power to "increase or reduce any of the rates"; "to establish rates of charges"; "to make and fix reasonable and just rates of freight and passenger tariffs"; "to make a schedule of reasonable maximum rates of charges"; "to fix tables of maximum charges"; to compel the carrier "to adopt such rate, charge, or classification as said commissioners shall declare to be equitable and reasonable." . . .

. . . Congress did not intend to give to the commission the power to prescribe any tariff and determine what for the future should be reasonable and just rates. The power given is the power to execute and enforce, not to legislate. . . .

We have, therefore, these considerations presented: First. The power to prescribe a tariff of rates for carriage by a common carrier is a legislative and not an administrative or judicial function, and, having respect to the large amount of property invested in railroads, the various companies engaged therein, the thousands of miles of road, and the millions of tons of freight carried, the varying and diverse conditions attaching to such carriage, is a power of supreme delicacy and importance. Second. That Congress has transferred such a power to any administrative body is not to be presumed or implied from any doubtful and uncertain language. The words and phrases efficacious to make such a delegation of power are well understood and have been frequently used, and if Congress had intended to grant such a power to the Interstate Commerce Commission it cannot be doubted that it would have used language open to no misconstruction, but clear and direct. Third. Incorporating into a statute the common law obligation resting upon the carrier to make all its charges reasonable and just, and directing the commission to execute and enforce the provisions of the act, does not by implication carry to the commissioner or invest it with the power to exercise the legislative function of prescribing rates which shall control in the future. Fourth. Beyond the inference which irresistibly follows from the omission to grant in express terms to the commission this power of fixing rates, is the clear language . . . recognizing the right of the carrier to establish rates, to increase or reduce them, and prescribing the conditions upon which such increase or reduction may be made, and requiring, as the only conditions of its action, first, publication, and, second, the filing of the tariff with the commission. The grant to the commission of the power to prescribe the form of the schedules, and to direct the place and manner of publication of joint rates, thus specifying the scope and limit of its functions in this respect, strengthens the conclusion that the power to prescribe rates or fix any tariff for the future is not among the powers granted to the commission. . . .

Smyth v. Ames
169 U.S. 466
1898

This case completed the evolution of substantive due process under the Fourteenth Amendment, when the Court by a 7-0 vote, struck down a Nebraska law fixing railroad rates, on the grounds that the rates established by the state did not provide the railroad companies with a "fair return on a fair value" of their properties. The Court speaking through Justice John Marshall Harlan, declared the rates unreasonable, and thereafter placed all rate-fixing by the states under Court scrutiny.

We are now to inquire whether the Nebraska statute is repugnant to the Constitution of the United States.

By the Fourteenth Amendment it is provided that no State shall deprive any person of property without due process of law, nor deny to any person within its jurisdiction the equal protection of the laws. That corporations are persons within the meaning of this Amendment is now settled. What amounts to deprivation of property without due process of law or what is a denial of the equal protection of the laws is often difficult to determine, especially where the question relates to the property of a *quasi* public corporation and the extent to which it may be subjected to public control. But this court, Speaking by Chief Justice [Morrison R.] Waite, has said that, while a State has power to fix the charges by railroad companies for the transportation of persons and property within its own jurisdiction, unless restrained by valid contract, or unless what is done amounts to a regulation of foreign or interstate commerce, such power is not without limit; and that, "under pretence of regulating fares and freights, the State cannot require a railroad corporation to carry persons or property without reward, neither can it do that which in law amounts to the taking of private property for public use without just compensation, or without due process of law."...

[T]hese principles must be regarded as settled:

1. A railroad corporation is a person within the meaning of the Fourteenth Amendment declaring that no State shall deprive any person of property without due process of law, nor deny to any person within its jurisdiction the equal protection of the laws.

2. A state enactment, or regulations made under the authority of a state enactment, establishing rates for the transportation of persons or property by railroad that will not admit of the carrier earning such compensation as under all the circumstances is just to it and to the public, would deprive such

…its property without due process of law and deny to it the equal …on of the laws, and would therefore be repugnant to the Fourteenth …ment of the Constitution of the United States.

…While rates for the transportation of persons and property within the …ts of a State are primarily for its determination, the question whether they …e so unreasonably low as to deprive the carrier of its property without such …ompensation as the Constitution secures, and therefore without due process of law, cannot be so conclusively determined by the legislature of the State or by regulations adopted under its authority, that the matter may not become the subject of judicial inquiry. . . .

[T]he plaintiffs contended that a railroad company is entitled to exact such charges for transportation as will enable it, at all times, not only to pay operating expenses, but also to meet the interest regularly accruing upon all its outstanding obligations, and justify a dividend upon all its stock; and that to prohibit it from maintaining rates or charges for transportation adequate to *all* those ends will deprive it of its property without due process of law, and deny to it the equal protection of the laws. This contention was the subject of elaborate discussion; and, as it bears upon each case in its important aspects, it should not be passed without examination.

In our opinion, the broad proposition advanced by counsel involves some misconception of the relations between the public and a railroad corporation. It is unsound in that it practically excludes from consideration the fair value of the property used, omits altogether any consideration of the right of the public to be exempt from unreasonable exactions, and makes the interests of the corporation maintaining a public highway the sole test in determining whether the rates established by or for it are such as may be rightfully prescribed as between it and the public. . . .

What was said in *Covington & Lexington Turnpike Road Co. v. Sandford,* 164 U.S. 578, 597-7, is pertinent to the question under consideration. It was there observed: "It cannot be said that a corporation is entitled, as of right, and without reference to the interests of the public, to realize a given per cent upon its capital stock. When the question arises whether the legislature has exceeded its constitutional power in prescribing rates to be charged by a corporation controlling a public highway, stockholders are not the only persons whose rights or interests are to be considered. The rights of the public are not to be ignored. . . .

. . . The legislature has the authority, in every case, where its power has not been restrained by contract, to proceed upon the ground that the public may not rightfully be required to submit to unreasonable exactions for the use of a public highway established and maintained under legislative authority. If a corporation can not maintain such a highway and earn dividends for stockholders, it is a misfortune for it and them which the Constitution does not require to be remedied by imposing unjust burdens upon the public."

We hold, however, that the basis of all calculations as to the reasonableness of rates to be charged by a corporation maintaining a highwa legislative sanction must be the fair value of the property being used b the convenience of the public. And in order to ascertain that valu original cost of construction, the amount expended in permanent impr ments, the amount and market value of its bonds and stock, the present compared with the original cost of construction, the probable earnin capacity of the property under particular rates prescribed by statute, and the sum required to meet operating expenses, are all matters for consideration, and are to be given such weight as may be just and right in each case. We did not say that there may not be other matters to be regarded in estimating the value of the property. What the company is entitled to ask is a fair return upon the value of that which it employs for the public convenience. On the other hand, what the public is entitled to demand is that no more be exacted from it for the use of a public highway than the services rendered by it are reasonable worth.

Decree of the Circuit Court affirmed.

United States v. Wong Kim Ark
169 U.S. 649
1898

By a 7-2 decisiion, the Court, speaking through Justice Horace Gray, declared that an American born child of Chinese citizens, living in the United States, was an American citizen by virtue of the citizenship clause of the Fourteenth Amendment. This case arose, when Wong Kim Ark, the plaintiff, who had been born in California, was denied reentry into the United States, under the Chinese Exclusion Acts, after returning to the country from a visit to China.

The question presented by the record is whether a child born in the United States, of parents of Chinese descent, who at the time of his birth are subjects of the emperor of China, but have a permanent domicile and residence in the United States, and are there carrying on business, and are not employed in any diplomatic or official capacity under the emperor of China, becomes at the time of his birth a citizen of the United States, by virtue of the first clause of the Fourteenth Amendment of the Constitution: "All persons born or naturalized in the United States, and subject to the jurisdiction thereof, are citizens of the United States and of the State wherein they reside."...

The Constitution nowhere defines the meaning of these words either by way of inclusion or of exclusion that "all persons born or naturalized in the United States, and subject to the jurisdiction thereof, are citizens of the United States."...

The fundamental principle of the common law with regard to English nationality was birth within the allegiance—also called "ligealty," "obedience," "faith," or "power"—of the king. The principle embraced all persons born within the king's allegiance and subject to his protection. Such allegiance and protection were mutual—as expressed in the maxim, "Protectio trahit subjectionem, et subjectio protectionem,"—and were not restricted to natural-born subjects and naturalized subjects, or to those who had taken an oath of allegiance; but were predicable of aliens in amity so long as they were within the kingdom. Children, born in England, of such aliens, were therefore natural-born subjects. But the children, born within the realm, of foreign ambassadors, or the children of alien enemies, born during and within their hostile occupation of part of the king's dominions, were not natural-born subjects....

It thus clearly appears that by the law of England for the last three centuries, beginning before the settlement of this country and continuing to the present day, aliens, while residing in the dominions poss crown of England, were within the allegiance, the obedience, t loyalty, the protection, the power, and the jurisdiction of th sovereign; and therefore every child born in England of alien paren natural-born subject, unless the child of an ambassador or other dipl agent of a foreign state, or of an alien enemy in hostile occupation of the p where the child was born.

The same rule was in force in all the English colonies upon this contine down to the time of the Declaration of Independence and in the United States afterwards. . . .

The first section of the Fourteenth Amendment of the Constitution begins with the words, "All persons born or naturalized in the United States, and subject to the jurisdiction thereof, are citizens of the United States and of the State wherein they reside." As appears upon the face of the amendment, as well as from the history of the times, this was not intended to impose any new restrictions upon citizenship, or to prevent any persons from becoming citizens by the fact of birth within the United States, who would thereby have become citizens according to the law existing before its adoption. It is declaratory in form, and enabling and extending in effect. Its main purpose doubtless was, as has been often recognized by this court, to establish the citizenship of free negroes, which had been denied in the opinion delivered by Chief Justice Taney in Dred Scott v. Sanford, 19 Howard 393 (1857). . . .

The real object of the Fourteenth Amendment of the Constitution, in qualifying the words "all persons born in the United States" by the addition "and subject to the jurisdiction thereof," would appear to have been to exclude, by the fewest and fittest words (besides children of members of the Indian tribes, standing in a peculiar relation to the national government, unknown to the common law), the two classes of cases—children born of alien enemies in hostile occupation, and children of diplomatic representatives of a foreign state. . . .

The foregoing considerations and authorities irresistibly lead us to these conclusions: The Fourteenth Amendment affirms the ancient and fundamental rule of citizenship by birth within the territory, in the allegiance and under the protection of the country, including all children here born of resident aliens, with the exceptions or qualifications (as old as the rule itself) of children of foreign sovereigns or their ministers, or born on foreign public ships, or of enemies within and during a hostile occupation of part of our territory, and with the single additional exception of children of members of the Indian tribes owing direct allegiance to their several tribes. The amendment, in clear words and in manifest intent, includes the children born within the territory of the United States of all other persons, of whatever race or color, domiciled within the United States. . . .

Downes v. Bidwell (Insular Case)

182 U.S. 244

1901

This case was the third in a series usually referred to as the *Insular* cases, which were heard by the Court following the Spanish-American War. In the first two, *DeLima v. Bidwell,* 182 U.S. 1 (1901), and *Dooley v. United States,* 182 U.S. 222 (1901), the Court ruled that Puerto Rico was a "territory appurtenant and belonging to the United States," and as such, exports to and imports from the island were not subject to the customs duties imposed upon foreign countries by the United States. In this case, however, a 5-4 majority ruled that the Constitution did not automatically extend to Puerto Rico, and that for revenue purposes Puerto Rico was not part of the United States. The result of this decision, coupled with the two earlier cases, was to give Congress exclusive jurisdiction over the territories of the United States. In other words, the Constitution of the United States did not necessarily follow the flag. Chief Justice Melville W. Fuller's dissent follows Justice Henry B. Brown's majority decision in this selection.

In the case of *De Lima v. Bidwell* just decided, we held that upon the ratification of the treaty of peace with Spain, Porto Rico ceased to be a foreign country, and became a territory of the United States, and that duties were no longer collectible upon merchandise brought from that island. We are now asked to hold that it became a part of the *United States* within that provision of the Constitution which declares that "all duties, imposts and excises shall be uniform throughout the United States."...

If Porto Rico be a part of the United States, the Foraker act imposing duties upon its products is unconstitutional, not only by reason of a violation of the uniformity clause, but because by section 9, "vessels bound to or from one State" cannot "be obliged to enter, clear or pay duties in another."

The case also involves the broader question whether the revenue clauses of the Constitution extend of their own force to our newly acquired territories. The Constitution itself does not answer the question. Its solution must be found in the nature of the government created by that instrument, in the opinion of its contemporaries, in the practical construction put upon it by Congress and in the decisions of this court....

Indeed, whatever may have been the fluctuations of opinion in other bodies, (and even this court has not been exempt from them), Congress has been consistent in recognizing the difference between the Sta territories under the Constitution.

The decisions of this court upon this subject have not been altog harmonious. Some of them are based upon the theory that the Constitu does not apply to the territories without legislation. Other cases, arising fr territories where such legislation has been had, contain language whic would justify the inference that such legislation was unnecessary, and that the Constitution took effect immediately upon the cession of the territory to the United States. It may be remarked, upon the threshold of an analysis of these cases, that too much weight must not be given to general expression found in several opinions that the power of Congress over territories is complete and supreme, because these words may be interpreted as meaning only supreme under the Constitution; nor upon the other hand, to general statements that the Constitution covers the territories as well as the States, since in such cases it will be found that acts of Congress had already extended the Constitution to such territories. . . .

To sustain the judgment in the case under consideration it by no means becomes necessary to show that none of the articles of the Constitution apply to the Island of Porto Rico. There is a clear distinction between such prohibitions as go to the very root of the power of Congress to act at all, irrespective of time or place, and such as are operative only "throughout the United States" or among the several States. . . .

Upon the other hand, when the Constitution declares that all duties shall be uniform "throughout the United States," it becomes necessary to inquire whether there be any territory over which Congress has jurisdiction which is not a part of the United States," by which term we understand the *States* whose people *united* to form the Constitution, and such as have since been admitted to the Union upon an equality with them. Not only did the people in adopting the Thirteenth Amendment thus recognize a distinction between the United States and "any place subject to their jurisdiction," but Congress itself, in the Act of March 27, 1804, . . . providing for the proof of public records, applied the provisions of the act, not only to "every court and office within the United States," but to the "courts and offices of the respective territories of the United States. . . .

We are also of opinion that the power to acquire territory by treaty implies, not only the power to govern such territory, but to prescribe upon what terms the United States will receive its inhabitants, and what their status shall be in what Chief Justice Marshall termed the "American empire." There seems to be no middle ground between this position and the doctrine that if their inhabitants do not become, immediately upon annexation, citizens of the United States, their children thereafter born, whether savages or civilized, are such, and entitled to all the rights, privileges and immunities of citizens. If such be their status, the consequences will be extremely serious. Indeed, it is doubtful if Congress would ever assent to the annexation of territory upon ɪtion that its inhabitants, however foreign they may be to our habits, ɒns, and modes of life, shall become at once citizens of the United ɔ. . . .

is obvious that in the annexation of out-lying and distant possessions ɩve questions will arise from differences of race, habits, laws and customs ɩ the people, and from differences of soil, climate and production, which may require action on the part of Congress that would be quite unnecessary in the annexation of contiguous territory inhabited only by people of the same race, or by scattered bodies of native Indians.

We suggest, without intending to decide, that there may be a distinction between certain natural rights enforced in the Constitution by prohibitions against interference with them, and what may be termed artificial or remedial rights which are peculiar to our own system of jurisprudence. Of the former class are the rights to one's own religious opinions and to a public expression of them, or, as sometimes said, to worship God according to the dictates of one's own conscience; the right to personal liberty and individual property; to freedom of speech and of the press; to free access to courts of justice, to due process of law, and to an equal protection of the laws; to immunities from unreasonable searches and seizures, as well as cruel and unusual punishments; and to such other immunities as are indispensible to a free government. . . .

Patriotic and intelligent men may differ widely as to the desirableness of this or that acquisition, but this is solely a political question. We can only consider this aspect of the case so far as to say that no construction of the Constitution should be adopted which would prevent Congress from considering each case upon its merits, unless the language of the instrument imperatively demand it. A false step at this time might be fatal to the development of what Chief Justice Marshall called the American empire. Choice in some cases, the natural gravitation of small bodies toward large ones in others, may bring about conditions which would render the annexation of distant possessions desirable. If those possessions are inhabited by alien races, differing from us in religion, customs, laws, methods of taxation and modes of thought, the administration of government and justice, acording to Anglo-Saxon principles may for a time be impossible; and the question at once arises whether large concessions ought not to be made for a time, that, ultimately, our own theories may be carried out, and the blessings of a free government under the Constitution extended to them. We decline to hold that there is anything in the Constitution to forbid such action.

We are therefore of opinion that the Island of Porto Rico is a territory appurtenant and belonging to the United States, but not a part of the United States within the revenue clauses of the Constitution; that the Foraker act is constitutional, so far as it imposes duties upon imports from such island, and that the plaintiff cannot recover back the duties exacted in this case.

The judgment of the Circuit Court is therefore affirmed.

Mr. Justice Fuller dissenting:
. . . The question is whether when Congress has created a civil gov for Porto Rico, has constituted its inhabitants a body politic, has gi governor and other officers, a legislative assembly, and courts, with rig appeal to this court, Congress can, in the same act and in the exercise of power conferred by the first clause of section eight, impose duties on t commerce between Porto Rico and the States and other territories in contravention of the rule of uniformity qualifying the power. If this can be done, it is because the power of Congress over commerce between the States and any of the territories is not restricted by the Constitution. This was the position taken by the Attorney General, with a candor and ability that did him great credit. . . .

Great stress is thrown upon the word "incorporation" as if possessed of some occult meaning, but I take it that the act under consideration made Porto Rico, whatever its situation before, an organized territory of the United States. Being such, and the act undertaking to impose duties . . . how is it that the rule which qualifies power does not apply to its exercise in respect of commerce with that territory? The power can only be exercised as prescribed, and even if the rule of uniformity could be treated as a mere regulation of the granted power—a suggestion as to which I do not assent—the validity of these duties comes up directly, and it is idle to discuss the distinction between a total want of power and a defective exercise of it.

The concurring opinion recognizes the fact that Congress, in dealing with the people of new territories or possessions, is bound to respect the fundamental guarantees of life, liberty, and property, but assumes that Congress is not bound in those territories or possessions, to follow the rule of taxation prescribed by the Constitution. And yet the power to tax involves the power to destroy, and the levy of duties touches all our people in all places under the jurisdiction of the government.

The logical result is that Congress may prohibit commerce altogether between the States and territories, and may prescribe one rule of taxation in one territory, and a different rule in another.

That theory assumes that the Constitution created a government empowered to acquire countries throughout the world, to be governed by different rules than those obtaining in the original States and territories, and substitutes for the present system of republican government a system of domination over distant provinces in the exercise of unrestricted power.

In our judgment, so much of the Porto Rican act as authorized the imposition of duties is invalid. . . .

·y Peter Dunne: Mr. Dooley on the Court
1901

Finley Peter Dunne, one of the most astute and humorous political writers of this period, began his journalistic career as a sports reporter in Chicago. During the latter part of the nineteenth century, he moved to New York where he joined the political desk of the *New York Times.* Through his creation, the Irish saloon-keeper, Mr. Dooley, Dunne acutely and critically analyzed a variety of topics in the contemporary American scene. In this selction, Mr. Dooley commented on the Court's performance and action in the so-called Insular cases. Finley Peter Dunne, *Mr. Dooley on the Choice of Law,* ed. E.J. Bander (Charlottesville, Va., 1963), pp. 47-52.

"I see," said Mr. Dooley, "Th' supreme coort has decided th' constitution don't follow th' flag."

"Who said it did?" asked Mr. Hennessy.

"Some wan," said Mr. Dooley. "It happened a long time ago an' I don't raymimber clearly how it come up, but some fellow said that ivrywhere th' constitution wint, th' flag was sure to go. 'I don't believe wan wurrud iv if,' says th' other fellow. 'Ye can't make me think th' constitution is goin' thrapezing' around iverywhere a young lifttnant in th' ar-rmy takes it into his head to stick a flag pole. It's too old. It's a home-staying constitution with a blue coat with brass buttons onto it, an' it walks with a goold-headed cane. It's old and' it's feeble, an' it prefers to set on th' front stoop an' amuse th' childher. It wudden't last a minyit in thim thropical climes. 'T wud get a pain in th' fourteenth amindmint an' die befure th' doctors cud get ar-round to cut it out. No, sir, we'll keep it with us, an' threat it tenderly without too much hard wurruk, an' whin it plays out entirely we'll give it dacint buryal an' incorp'rate oursilves under th' laws iv Noo Jarsay. That's what we'll do,' says he. 'But,' says th' other, 'if it wants to thravel, why not lave it?' 'But it don't want to.' 'I say it does.' 'How'll we find out?' 'We'll ask th' supreme coort. They'll know what's good f'r it.' "

"So it wint up to th' supreme coort. They'se wan thing about th' supreme coort, if ye lave annything to thim, ye lave it to thim. Ye don't get a check that entitles ye to call f'r it in a hour. The supreme coort iv th' United States ain't in anny hurry about catchin' th' mails. It don't have to make th' las' car. I'd back th' Aujitoroom again it anny day f'r a foot race. If ye're lookin' f'r a game iv quick decisions an' base hits, ye've got to hire another empire. It niver gives a decision till th' crowd has dispersed an' th' players have packed their bats in th' bags an' started f'r home.

"F'r awhile ivrybody watched to see what th' supreme coort kenw meself I felt I cudden't make another move in th' game till I h thim. Buildin' op'rations was suspinded and' we sthud wringin' our outside th' dure waitin' f'r information fr'm th' bedside. 'What're they now?' 'They just put th' argymints iv larned cousel in th' ice box an' th' c justice is in a corner writin' a pome. Brown j. an' Harlan J. is discussin' t condition iv th' Roman Empire befure th' fire. Th' rest iv th' coort is considherin' th' question iv whether they ought or ought not to wear ruchin' on their skirts an' hopin' crinoline won't come in again. No decision to-day?' An' so it wint f'r days, an' weeks an' months. Th' men that had argyied that th' constitution ought to shadow th' flag to all th' touch resorts on th' Passyfic coast an' th' men that argyied that th' flag was so lively that no constitution cud follow it an' survive, they died or lost their jobs or wint back to Salem an' were f'rgotten. Expansionists contracted an' anti-expansionists blew up an' little childher was born into th' wurruld an' grew to manhood an' niver heerd iv Porther Ricky except whin some wan get a job there. I'd about made up me mind to thry an' put th' thing out iv me thoughts an' go back to wurruk when I woke up wan mornin' an' see be th' pa-aper that th' Supreme Coort had warned th' constitution to lave th' flag alone an' tind to its own business.

"That's what th' pa-aper says, but I've r-read over th' decision an' I don't see annything iv th' kind there. They'se not a wurrud about th' flag an' not enough to tire ye about th' constitution. 'T is a matther iv limons, Hinnissy, that th' Supreme Coort has been settin' on f'r this gineration—a cargo iv limons sint fr'm Porther Ricky to some Eyetalian in Philydelphy. Th' decision was r-read be Brown J., him bein' th' las' justice to make up his mind, an' ex-officio, as Hogan says, th' first to speak, after a crool an' bitther contest. Says Brown J: 'Th' question here is wan iv such gr-reat importance that we've been sthrugglin' over it iver since ye see us las' an' on'y come to a decision (Fuller C.J., Gray J., Harlan J., Shiras J., McKenna J., White J., Brewer J., an' Peckham J. dissentin' fr'm me an' each other) because iv th' hot weather comin' on. Wash'n'ton is a dhreadful place in summer (Fuller C.J. dissentin'). Th' whole fabric iv our government is threatened, th' lives iv our people an' th' progress iv civilization put to th' bad. Men are excited. But why? We ar-re not. (Harlan J., "I am." Fuller C.J. dissentin', but not f'r th' same reason.) This thing must be settled wan way or th' other undher that deal ol' constitution be varchue iv which we are here an' ye ar-re there an' Congress is out West practicin' law. Now what does th' constitution say? We'll look it up thoroughoy whin we get through with this case (th' rest iv th' coort dissentin'). In th' manetime we must be governed be th' ordnances iv th' Khan iv Belloochistan, th' laws iv Hinnery th' Eighth, the opinyon if Justice iv th' Peace Oscar Sarson in th' case iv th' township iv Red Wing varsus Petersen, an' th' Dhred Scott decision. What do they say about limons? Nawthin' at all. Again we take th' Dhred Scott decision. This is wan iv th' worst I iver r-read. If I cudden't write a betther wan with blindhers on, I'd bench. This horrible fluke iv a decision throws a gr-reat, an almost ight on th' case. I will turn it off. (McKenna J. concurs, but thinks it o be blowed out.) But where was I? I must put on me specs. Oh, about ions. Well, th' decision iv th' Disthrict iv Columbya is a state; second, it is not; third, that New York is a state; fourth, that it is a crown colony; th, that all states ar-re states an' all territories ar-re territories in th' eyes iv of other powers, but Gawd knows what they ar-re at home In th' case iv Hogan varsus Mullins, th' decision is he must paper th' barn. (Hinnery VIII, sixteen, six, four, eleven). In Wiggins varsus et al. th' cow belonged (Louis XIV, 90 in rem.) In E.P. Vigore varsus Ad Lib., the custody iv th' childher. I'll now fall back a furlong or two in me chair, while me larned but misguided collagues r-read th' Histhry iv Iceland to show ye how wrong I am. But mind ye, what I've said goes. I let thim talk because it exercises their throats, but ye've heard all th' decision on this limon case that'll get into th' fourth reader.' A voice fr'm th' audjeence, 'Do I get my money back?' Brown J.: 'Who ar-re ye?' Th' Voice: 'Th' man that ownded th' limons.' Brown J.: 'I don't know.' (Gray Jr., White J., dissentin' an' th' r-rest iv th' birds concurrin' but f'r entirely diff'rent reasons.'

"An' there ye have th' decision, Hinnissy, that's shaken th' intellicts iv th' natins to their very foundations, or will if they thry to read it. 'Tis all r-right. Look it over some time. 'T is fine spoort if ye don't care f'r checkers. Some say it laves th' flag up in th' air an' some say that's where it laves th' constitution. Annyhow, somethin's in th' air. But there's wan thing I'm sure about."

"What's that?" asked Mr. Hennessy.

"That is," said Mr. Dooley, "no matther whether th' constitution follows th' flag or not, th' supreme coort follows th' illiction returns."

Champion v. Ames
(The Lottery Case)

188 U.S. 321

1903

Known as the *Lottery* case, the Court, speaking through Justice John Marshall Harlan, by a narrow 5-4 majority, sustained the constitutionality of an 1895 Congressional statute, which prohibited the distribution of lottery tickets through the mails. The Court ruled that Congress had not exceeded its authority under the commerce clause in passing this piece of legislation, and that through its power to regulate interstate commerce, possessed the authority to prohibit the passage of lottery tickets from state to state.

We come then to inquire whether there is any solid foundation upon which to rest the contention that Congress may not regulate the carrying of lottery tickets from one State to another, at least by corporations or companies whose business it is, for hire, to carry tangible property from one State to another.

It was said in argument that lottery tickets are not of any real or substantial value in themselves, and therefore are not subjects of commerce. If that were conceded to be the only legal test as to what are to be deemed subjects of commerce that may be regulated by Congress, we cannot accept as accurate the broad statement that such tickets are of no value. Upon their face they showed that the lottery company offered a large capital prize, to be paid to the holder of the ticket winning the prize at the drawing advertised to be held as Asuncion, Paraguay. Money was placed on deposit in different banks in the United States to be applied by the agents representing the lottery company to the prompt payment of prizes. . . .

We are of opinion that lottery tickets are subjects of traffic and therefore are subjects of commerce, and the regulation of the carriage of such tickets from State to State, at least by independent carriers, is a regulation of commerce among the several States.

But it is said that the statute in question does not regulate the carrying of lottery tickets from State to State, but by punishing those who cause them to be so carried Congress in effect prohibits such carrying; that in respect of the carrying from one State to another of articles or things that are, in face, or according to usage in business, the subjects of commerce, the authority given Congress was not to *prohibit,* but only to *regulate*. . . .

We have said that the carrying from State to State of lottery tickets s interstate commerce, and that the regulation of such commerce is ıe power of Congress under the Constitution. Are we prepared to say provision which is, in effect, a *prohibition* of the carriage of such .es from State to State is not a fit or appropriate mode for the *regulation* .hat particular kind of commerce? If lottery traffic, *carried on through .terstate commerce,* is a matter of which Congress may take cognizance and over which its powers may be exerted, can it be possible that it must tolerate the traffic, and simply regulate the manner in which it may be carried on? Or may not Congress, for the protection of the people of all the States, and under the power to regulate interstate commerce, devise such means, within the scope of the Constitution, and not prohibited by it, as will drive that traffic out of commerce among the States?...

It is said, however, that if, in order to suppress lotteries carried on through interstate commerce, Congress may exclude lottery tickets from such commerce, that principle leads necessarily to the conclusion that Congress may arbitrarily exclude from commerce among the States any article, commodity or thing, of whatever kind or nature, or however useful or valuable, which it may choose, no matter with what motive, to declare shall not be carried from one State to another. It will be time enough to conisder the constitutionality of such legislation when we must do so. The present case does not require the court to declare the full extent of the power that Congress may exercise in the regulation of commerce among the States. We may, however, repeat, in this connection, what the court has heretofore said, that the power of Congress to regulate commerce among the States, although plenary, cannot be deemed arbitrary, since it is subject to such limitations or restrictions as are prescribed by the Constitution. This power therefore, may not be exercised so as to infringe rights secured or protected by that instrument. It would not be difficult to imagine legislation that would be justly liable to such an objection as that stated, and be hostile to the objects for the accomplishment of which Congress was invested with the general power to regulate commerce among the several States. But, as often said, the possible abuse of a power is not an argument against its existence. There is probably no governmental power that may not be exerted to the injury of the public. If what is done by Congress is manifestly in excess of the powers granted to it, then upon the courts will rest the duty of adjudging that its action is neither legal nor binding upon the people. But if what Congress does is within the limits of its power, and is simply unwise or injurious, the remedy is that suggested by Chief Justice Marshall in *Gibbons v. Ogden,* when he said: “The wisdom and the discretion of Congress, their identity with the people, and the influence which their constituents possess at elections, are, in this, as in many other instances, as that, for example, of declaring war, the sole restraints on which they have relied, to secure them from its abuse. They are the restraints on which the people must often rely solely, in all representative governments.”

The whole subject is too important, and the questions sugges consideration are too difficult of solution, to justify any attempt to la a rule for determining in advance the validity of every statute that r enacted under the commerce clause.

We decide nothing more in the present case than that lottery tickets subjects of traffic among those who choose to sell or buy them; that tr carriage of such tickets by independent carriers from one State to another is therefore interstate commerce; that under its power to regulate commerce among the several States Congress—subject to the limitations imposed by the Constitution upon the exercise of the powers granted—has plenary authority over such commerce, and may prohibit the carriage of such tickets from State to State; and that legislation to that end, and of that character, is not inconsistent with any limitation or restriction imposed upon the exercise of the powers granted to Congress....

orthern Securities Company v. United States (The Merger Case)

193 U.S. 197

1904

In a sense, the decision in this case reversed the Court's opposition to the Sherman Anti-Trust Act when a 5-4 majority, led by Justice John Marshall Harlan, ruled that this giant railroad-holding company violated the statute. The Northern Pacific, Great Northern and Burlington Railroads had been combined into a massive corporation known as the Northern Securities Company. The government charged that the holding company was attempting to restrain trade under the Sherman Act, and the Court agreed.

The Government charges that if the combination was held not to be in violation of the act of Congress, then all efforts of the National Government to preserve to the people the benefits of free competition among carriers engaged in interstate commerce will be wholly unavailing, and all transcontinental lines, indeed the entire railway systems of the country, may be absorbed, merged and consolidated, thus placing the public at the absolute mercy of the holding corporation. . . .

We will not incumber this opinion by extended extracts from the former opinions of this court. It is sufficient to say that from the decisions . . . certain propositions are plainly deducible and embrace the present case. Those propositions are:

That although the act of Congress known as the Anti-Trust Act has no reference to the mere manufacture or production of articles or commodities within the limits of the several States, it does embrace and declare to be illegal every contract, combination or conspiracy, in whatever form, of whatever nature, and whoever may be parties to it, which directly or necessarily operates *in restraint* of trade or commerce *among the several States or with foreign nations;*

That the act is not limited to restraints of interstate and international trade or commerce that are unreasonable in their nature, but embraces *all* direct *restraints* imposed by any combination, conspiracy or monopoly upon such trade or commerce.

That railroad carriers engaged in interstate or international commerce are embraced by the act;

That combinations even among *private* manufacturers or dealers whereby interstate or international commerce is restrained are equally embraced by the act;

The Congress has the power to establish *rules* by which *interstate* *international* commerce shall be governed, and, by the Anti-Trust Act, prescribed the rule of free competition among those engaged in su commerce;

That *every* combination or conspiracy which would extinguish competition between otherwise competing railroads engaged in *interstate trade or commerce,* and which would *in that way* restrain such trade or commerce, is made illegal by the act;

That the natural effect of competition is to increase commerce, and an agreement whose direct effect is to prevent this play of competition restrains instead of promotes trade and commerce;

That to vitiate a combination, such as the act of Congress condemns, it need not be shown that the combination, in fact, results or will result in a total suppression of trade or in a complete monopoly, but it is only essential to show that by its necessary operation it tends to restrain interstate or international trade or commerce and to deprive the public of the advantages that flow from free competition;

That the constitutional guarantee of liberty of contract does not prevent Congress from prescribing the rule of free competition for those engaged in *interstate and international* commerce....

The means employed in respect of the combinations forbidden by the Anti-Trust Act, and which Congress deemed germane to the end to be accomplished, was to prescribe as *a rule* for *interstate and international* commerce (not for domestic commerce), that it should not be vexed by combinations, conspiracies or monopolies which restrain commerce by destroying or restricting competition. We say that Congress has prescribed such a rule, because in all the prior cases in this court the Anti-Trust Act has been construed as forbidding any combination which by its necessary operation destroys or restricts free competition among those engaged in interstate commerce; in other words, that to destroy or restrict free competition in interstate commerce was to restrain such commerce. Now, can this court say that such a rule is prohibited by the Constitution or is not one that Congress could appropriately prescribe when exerting its power under the commerce clause of the Constitution? Whether the free operation of the normal laws of competition is a wise and wholesome rule for trade and commerce is an economic question which this court need not consider or determine....

We cannot agree that Congress may strike down combinations among manufacturers and dealers in iron pipe, tiles, grates and mantels that restrain commerce among the States in such articles, but may not strike down combinations among stockholders of competing railroad carriers, which restrain commerce as involved in the transportation of passengers and property among the several States.... Indeed, if the contentions of the dants are sound why may not *all* the railway companies in the United es, that are engaged, under state charters, in interstate and international nmerce, enter into a combination such as the one here in question, and by e device of a holding corporation obtain the absolute control throughout he entire country of rates for passengers and freight, beyond the power of Congress to protect the public against their exactions? The argument in behalf of the defendants necessarily leads to such results, and places Congress, although invested by the people of the United States with full authority to regulate interstate and international commerce, in a condition of utter helplessness....

...There was no actual investment, in any substantial sense, by the Northern Securities Company in the stock of the two constituent companies. If it was, in form, such a transaction, it was not, in fact, one of that kind. However that company may have acquired for itself any stock in the Great Northern and Northern Pacific Railway companies, no matter how it obtained the means to do so, all the stock it held or acquired in the constituent companies was acquired and held to be used in suppressing competition between those companies....

Guided by these long-established rules of construction, it is manifest that if the Anti-Trust Act is held not to embrace a case such as is now before us, the plain intention of the legislative branch of the Government will be defeated. . . .

McCray v. United States
195 U.S. 27
1904

By a 6-3 decision, the Court, led by Justice Edward D. White, validated a federal police statute that utilized an excise tax as an instrument of social control. The Court reasoned that an excise tax placed upon artifically colored oleomargarine was not in conflict with the Constitution as an attempt to use the federal taxing power to regulate manufacturing, a matter reserved to the states. Justice White's opinion held that the Court had no power to inquire into the motive behind the law, as long as Congress possessed the power to levy the tax in question.

The summary which follows embodies the propositions contained in the assignments of error, and the substance of the elaborate argument by which those assignments are deemed to be sustained. Not denying the general power of Congress to impose excise taxes, and conceding that the acts in question, on their face, purport to levy taxes of that character, the propositions are these:

(a) That the power of internal taxation which the Constitution confers on Congress is given to that body for the purpose of raising revenue, and that the tax on artificially colored oleomargarine is void because it is of such an onerous character as to make it manifest that the purpose of Congress in levying it was not to raise revenue but to suppress the manufacture of the taxed article.

(b) The power to regulate the manufacture and sale of oleomargarine being solely reserved to the several States, it follows that the acts in question enacted by Congress for the purpose of suppressing the manufacture and sale of oleomargarine, when artificially colored, are void, because usurping the reserved power of the States, and therefore exerting an authority not delegated to Congress by the Constitution.

(c) Whilst it is true—so the argument proceeds—that Congress in exerting the taxing power conferred upon it may use all means appropriate to the exercise of such power, a tax which is fixed at such a high rate as to suppress the production of the article taxed, is not a legitimate means to the lawful end....

Whilst, as a result of our written constitution, it is axiomatic that the judicial department of the government is charged with the solemn duty of enforcing the Constitution, and therefore in cases properly presented, of determining whether a given manifestation of authority has exceeded the

:r conferred by that instrument, no instance is afforded from the ndation of the government where an act, which was within a power nferred, was declared to be repugnant to the Constitution, because it .ppeared to the judicial mind that the particular exertion of constitutional power was either unwise or unjust. To announce such a principle would amount to declaring that in our constitutional system the judiciary was not only charged with the duty of upholding the Constitution but also with the responsibility of correcting every possible abuse arising from the exercise by the other departments of their conceded authority. So to hold would be to overthrow the entire distinction between the legislative, judicial and executive departments of the government. . . .

It being thus demonstrated that the motive or purpose of Congress in adopting the acts in question may not be inquired into, we are brought to consider the contention relied upon to show that the acts assailed were beyond the power of Congress, putting entirely out of view all considerations based upon purpose or motive. . . . The right of Congress to tax within its delegated power being unrestrained, except as limited by the Constitution, it was within the authority conferred on Congress to select the objects upon which an excise should be laid. It therefore follows that, in exerting its power, no want of due process of law could possibly result, because that body chose to impose an excise on artifically colored oleomargarine and not upon natural butter artificially colored. The judicial power may not usurp the functions of the legislative in order to control that branch of the government. . . .

But it is urged that artifically colored oleomargarine and artificially colored natural butter are in substance and effect one and the same thing, and from this it is deduced that to lay an excise tax only on oleomargarine artificially colored and not on butter so colored is violative of the due process clause of the Fifth Amendment, because, as there is no possible distinction between the two, the act of Congress was a mere arbitrary imposition of an excise on the one article and not on the other, although essentially of the same class. Conceding merely for the sake of argument that the due process clause of the Fifth Amendment, would avoid an exertion of the taxing power which, without any basis for classification, arbitrarily taxed one article and excluded an article of the same class, such concession would be wholly inapposite to the case in hand. . . .

. . . As it has been thus decided that the distinction between the two products is so great as to justify the absolute prohibition of the manufacture of oleomargarine artificially colored, there is no foundation for the proposition that the difference between the two was not sufficient, under the extremist view, to justify a classification, distinguishing between them. . . .

Let us concede, for the sake of argument only, the premise of fact upon which the proposition is based. Moreover, concede for the sake of argument only, that even although a particular exertion of power by Congress was not restrained by any express limitation of the Constitution, if by the perverted exercise of such power so great an abuse was manifested as to destroy fundamental rights which no free government could consistently violate, that it would be the duty of the judiciary to hold such acts to be void upon the assumption that the Constitution by necessary implication forbade them.

Such concession, however, is not controlling in this case. This follows when the nature of oleomargarine, artificially colored to look like butter, is recalled. As we have said, it has been conclusively settled by this court that the tendency of that article to deceive the public into buying it for butter is such that the States may, in the exertion of their police powers, without violating the due process clause of the Fourteenth Amendment, absolutely prohibit the manufacture of the article. It hence results, that even although it be true that the effect of the tax in question is to repress the manufacture of artificially colored oleomargarine, it cannot be said that such repression destroys rights which no free government could destroy, and, therefore, no ground exists to sustain the proposition that the judiciary may invoke an implied prohibition, upon the theory that to do so is essential to save such rights from destruction. And the same considerations dispose of the contention based upon the due process clause of the Fifth Amendment. That provision, as we have previously said, does not withdraw or expressly limit the grant of power to tax conferred upon Congress by the Constitution. From this it follows, as we have also previously declared, that the judiciary is without authority to void an act of Congress exerting the taxing power, even in a case where to the judicial mind it seems that Congress had in putting such power in motion abused its lawful authority by levying a tax which was unwise or oppressive, or the result of the enforcement of which might be to indirectly affect subjects not within the powers delegated to Congress. . . .

Dorr v. United States (Insular Case)

195 U.S. 138

1904

This Supreme Court action was another of the so-called *Insular* cases where the Court once again ruled that the Constitution does not necessarily follow the flag. Dorr, the publisher of the *Manila Freedom,* a Philippine newspaper, was tried for libel in a federal court in the Philippines without the benefit of a traditional indictment and a twelve-man jury of his peers. By a vote of 8 to 1, the Court ruled that trial without the traditional jury system did not deprive the plaintiff of his rights under the Constitution since the Bill of Rights could be extended to acquired territory only by an act of Congress. Therefore, the Court reasoned that since Filipinos were not citizens of the United States and since Congress had shown no intention to extend citizenship to them, no constitutional rights had been violated. Justice William R. Day, who delivered the opinion of the Court, stated, "If the United States acquires territory where trial by jury is not known but where, due to customs and preference, the people have another method—are these considerations to be ignored and they coerced to accept a system of trial unknown to them and unsuited to their needs?

In every case where Congress undertakes to legislate in the exercise of the power conferred by the Constitution, the question may arise as to how far the exercise of the power is limited by the "prohibitions" of that instrument. The limitations which are to be applied in any given case involving territorial government must depend upon the relation of the particular territory to the United States concerning which Congress is exercising the power conferred by the Constitution. That the United States may have territory which is not incorporated in the United States as a body politic, we think was recognized by the framers of the Constitution in enacting the article already considered, giving power over the territories, and is sanctioned by the opinions of the justices concurring in the judgment in Downes v. Bidwell. . . .

Until Congress shall see fit to incorporate territory ceded by treaty into the United States, we regard it as settled by that decision that the territory is to be governed under the power existing in Congress to make laws for such territories and subject to such constitutional restrictions upon the powers of that body as are applicable to the situation.

For this case, the practical question is, must Congress, in establishing a system for trial of crimes and offenses committed in the Philippine Islands, carry to their people by proper affirmative legislation a system of trial by jury. . . .

The legislation upon the subject shows that not only has Congress hitherto refrained from incorporating the Philippines into the United States, but in the act of 1902, providing for temporary civil government, . . . there is express provision that . . . the Revised Statutes of 1878 shall not apply to the Philippine Islands. This is the section giving force and effect to the Constitution and laws of the United States, not locally inapplicable, within all the organized territories, and every territory thereafter organized, as elsewhere within the United States. . . .

As we have had occasion to see in the case of Kepner v. United States, 195 U.S. 100 (1904), the President, in his instructions to the Philippine Commission while impressing the necessity of carrying into the new government the guarantees of the bill of rights, securing those safeguards to life and liberty which are deemed essential to our government, was careful to reserve the right to trial by jury, which was doubtless due to the fact that the civilized portion of the island has a system of jurisprudence founded upon the civil law, and the uncivilized parts of the archipelago were wholly unfitted to exercise the right of trial by jury. The Spanish system in force in the Philippines, gave the right to the accused to be tried before judges who acted in effect as a court of inquiry and whose judgments were not final until passed in review before the audiencia or supreme court, with right of final review and power to grant a new trial for errors of law in the supreme court at Madrid. To this system the Philippine Commission, in executing the power conferred by the orders of the President and sanctioned by act of Congress, act of July 1, 1902, . . . has added a guaranty of the right of the accused to be heard by himself and counsel, to demand the nature and cause of the accusation against him, to have a speedy and public trial, to meet the witnesses against him face to face, and to have compulsory process to compel the attendance of witnesses in his behalf. And, further, that no person shall be held to answer for a criminal offense without due process of law, nor be put twice in jeopardy of punishment for the same offense, nor be compelled in any criminal case to be a witness against himself. As appears in the Kepner case, supra, the accused is given the right of appeal from the judgment of the court of first instance to the Supreme Court, and, in capital cases, the case goes to the latter court without appeal. It cannot be successfully maintained that this system does not give an adequate and efficient method of protecting the rights of the accused as well as executing the criminal law by judicial proceedings, which give full opportunity to be heard by competent tribunals before judgment can be pronounced. Of course, it is a complete answer to this suggestion to say, if such be the fact, that the constitutional requirements as to a jury trial, either of their own force or as limitations upon the power of Congress in setting up a government, must control in all the territory, whether incorporated or not, of the United States....

If the right to trial by jury were a fundamental right which goes wherever the jurisidction of the United States extends, or if Congress, in framing laws for outlying territory belonging to the United States, was obliged to establish that system by affirmative legislation, it would follow that no matter what the needs or capacities of the people, trial by jury, and in no other way, must be forthwith established, although the result may be to work injustice and provoke disturbance rather than to aid the orderly administration of justice. If the United States, impelled by its duty or advantage, shall acquire territory peopled by savages, and of which it may dispose or not hold for ultimate admission to statehood, if this doctrine is sound, it must establish there the trial by jury. To state such a proposition demonstrates the impossiblity of carrying it into practice. Again, if the United States shall acquire by treaty the cession of territory having an established system of jurisprudence, where jury trials are unknown, but a method of fair and orderly trial prevails under an acceptable and long-established code, the preference of the people must be disregarded, their established customs ignored and they themselves coerced to accept, in advance of incorporation into the United States, a system of trial unknown to them and unsuited to their needs. We do not think it was intended, in giving power to Congress to make regulations for the territories, to hamper its exercise with this condition.

We conclude that the power to govern territory, implied in the right to acquire it, and given to Congress in the Constitution in article 4...to whatever other limitations it may be subject, the extent of which must be decided as questions arise, does not require that body to enact for ceded territory, not made a part of the United States by congressional action, a system of laws which shall include the right of trial by jury, and that the Constitution does not, without legislation and of its own force, carry such right to territory so situated....

Swift and Company v. United States (Beef Trust Case)

196 U.S. 375

1905

The *Beef Trust* case saw a unanimous Court declare that the attempt by a number of meat packing companies to fix livestock prices in the stockyards of different states, and thus establish a total monopoly over the meat packing industry, was a violation of the Sherman Anti-Trust Act. It was in this case that Justice Oliver Wendell Holmes, who delivered the opinion of the Court, introduced his "current of commerce" doctrine stating that interstate commerce could recognize within its definition some "domestic transactions."

The scheme as a whole seems to us to be within reach of the law. The constituent elements, as we have stated them, are enough to give to the scheme a body and, for all that we can say, to accomplish it. Moreover, whatever we may think of them separately when we take them up as distinct charges, they are alleged sufficiently as elements of the scheme. It is suggested that the several acts charged are lawful and that intent can make no difference. But they are bound together as the parts of a single plan. The plan may make the parts unlawful. . . .

Intent is almost essential to such a combination and is essential to such an attempt. Where acts are not sufficient in themselves to produce a result which the law seeks to prevent—for instance, the monopoly—but require further acts in addition to the mere forces of nature to bring that result to pass, an intent to bring it to pass is necessary in order to produce a dangerous probability that it will happen. *Commonwealth v. Peaslee,* 177 Massachusetts 267, 272. But when that intent and the consequent dangerous probability exist, this statute, like many others and like the common law in some cases, directs itself against that dangerous probability. . . .

One further observation should be made. Although the combination alleged embraces restraint and monopoly of trade within a single State, its effect upon commerce among the States is not accidental, secondary, remote or merely probable. . . .

Moreover, it is a direct object, it is that for the sake of which the several specific acts and courses of conduct are done and adopted. Therefore the case is not like *United States v. E.C. Knight Co.,* . . . where the subject matter of the combination was manufacture and the direct object monopoly of manufacture within a State. However likely monopoly of commerce among the States in the article manufactured was to follow from the agreement it was not a necessary consequence nor a primary end. Here the subject matter is sales and the very point of the combination is to restrain and monopolize commerce among the States in respect of such sales. . . .

It is said that this charge is too vague and that it does not set forth a case of commerce among the States. Taking up the latter objection first, commerce among the States is not a technical legal conception, but a practical one, drawn from the course of business. When cattle are sent for sale from a place in one State, with the expectation that they will end their transit, after purchase, in another, and when in effect they do so, with only the interruption necessary to find a purchaser at the stock yards, and when this is a typical, constantly recurring course, the current thus existing is a current of commerce among the States, and the purchase of the cattle is a part and incident of such commerce. What we say is true at least of such a purchase by residents in another State from that of the seller and of the cattle. . . .

[W]e are of opinion that the carrying out of the scheme alleged, by the means set forth, properly may be enjoined, and that the bill cannot be dismissed. . . .

Lochner v. New York
198 U.S. 45
1905

This case, concerning the right of freedom of contract, was one of the most controversial dealt with by the Fuller Court. It involved the validity of a New York maximum working hours law, which had set a ten-hour day or a sixty-hour week for those employed in the baking and confectionary industry. By a slim 5 to 4 vote, the majority, led by Justice Rufus W. Peckham, declared the New York act unconstitutional on the grounds that it violated the freedom of contract clause of the Fourteenth Amendment. The Court held that the statute illegally interfered with the rights of individuals, both employers and employees, "for reasons entirely arbitrary." The decision declared that the act applied to an occupation that was neither dangerous nor injurious to health or morals. Justices John Marshall Harlan, Edward D. White, Rufus W. Day, and Oliver Wendell Holmes dissented. Following the decision, a portion of Justice Holmes's dissent is cited in this selection.

. . . The mandate of the statute that "no employee shall be required or permitted to work," is the substantial equivalent of an enactment that "no employee shall contract or agree to work," more than ten hours per day, and as there is no provision for special emergencies the statute is mandatory in all cases. It is not an act merely fixing the number of hours which shall constitute a legal day's work, but an absolute prohibition upon the employer, permitting, under any circumstances, more than ten hours work to be done in his establishment. The employee may desire to earn the extra money, which would arise from his working more than the prescribed time, but this statute forbids the employer from permitting the employee to earn it.

The statute necessarily interferes with the right of contract between the employer and employee, concerning the number of hours in which the latter may labor in the bakery of the employer. The general right to make a contract in relation to this business is part of the liberty of the individual protected by the Fourteenth Amendment of the Federal Constitution. . . .

The State, therefore, has power to prevent the individual from making certain kinds of contracts, and in regard to them the Federal Constitution offers no protection. If the contract be one which the State, in the legitimate exercise of its police power, has the right to prohibit, it is not prevented from prohibiting it by the Fourteenth Amendment. Contracts in violation of a statute, either of the Federal or state government, or a contract to let one's property for immoral purposes, or to do any other unlawful act, could obtain no protection from the Federal Constitution, as coming under the liberty of person or of free contract. Therefore, when the State, by its legislature, in the assumed exercise of its police powers, has passed an act which seriously limits the rights to labor or the right of contract in regard to their means of livelihood between persons who are *sui juris* (both employer and employee), it becomes of great importance to determine which shall prevail—the right of the individual to labor for such time as he may choose, or the right of the State to prevent the individual from laboring or from entering into any contract to labor, beyond a certain time prescribed by the State.

This court has recognized the existence and upheld the exercise of the police powers of the States in many cases which might fairly be considered as border ones, and it has, in the course of its determination of questions regarding the asserted invalidity of such statutes, on the ground of their violation of the rights secured by the Federal Constitution, been guided by rules of a very liberal nature, the application of which has resulted, in numerous instances, in upholding the validity of state statutes thus assailed. Among the later cases where the state law has been upheld by this court is that of *Holden v. Hardy,* . . . A provision in the act of the legislature of Utah was there under consideration, the act limiting the employment of workmen in all underground mines or workings, to eight hours per day, "except in cases of emergency, where life or property is in imminent danger." It also limited the hours of labor in smelting and other institutions for the reduction or refining of ores or metals to eight hours per day, except in like cases of emergency. . . .

It will be observed that, even with regard to that class of labor, the Utah statute provided for cases of emergency wherein the provisions of the statute would not apply. The statute now before this court has no emergency clause in it, and, if the statute is valid, there are no circumstances and no emergencies under which the slightest violation of the provision of the act would be innocent. There is nothing in *Holden v. Hardy* which covers the case now before us. . . .

It must, of course, be conceded that there is a limit to the valid exercise of the police power by the State. There is no dispute concerning this general proposition. Otherwise the Fourteenth Amendment would have no efficacy and the legislatures of the States would have unbounded power, and it would be enough to say that any piece of legislation was enacted to conserve the morals, the health or the safety of the people; such legislation would be valid, no matter how absolutely without foundation the claim might be. The claim of the police power would be a mere pretext—become another and delusive name for the supreme sovereignty of the State to be exercised free from constitutional restraint. This is not contended for. In every case that comes before this court, therefore, where legislation of this character is concerned and where the protection of the Federal Constitution is sought, the question necessarily arises: Is this a fair, reasonable and appropriate exercise of the police power of the State, or is it an unreasonable, unnecessary and arbitrary interference with the right of the individual to his personal liberty or to enter into those contracts in relation to labor which may seem to him appropriate or necessary for the support of himself and his family? Of course the liberty of contract relating to labor includes both parties to it. The one has as much right to purchase as the other to sell labor.

This is not a question of substituting the judgment of the court for that of the legislature. If the act be within the power of the State it is valid, although the judgment of the court might be totally opposed to the enactment of such a law. But the question would still remain: Is it within the police power of the State? and that question must be answered by the court.

The question whether this act is valid as a labor law, pure and simple, may be dismissed in a few words. There is no reasonable ground for interfering with the liberty of person or the right of free contract, by determining the hours of labor, in the occupation of a baker. There is no contention that bakers as a class are not equal in intelligence and capacity to men in other trades or manual occupations, or that they are not able to assert their rights and care for themselves without the protecting arm of the State, interfering with their independence of judgment and of action. They are in no sense wards of the State. Viewed in the light of a purely labor law, with no reference whatever to the question of health, we think that a law like the one before us involves neither the safety, the morals nor the welfare of the public, and that the interest of the public is not in the slightest degree affected by such an act. The law must be upheld, if at all, as a law pertaining to the health of the individual engaged in the occupation of a baker. It does not affect any other portion of the public than those who are engaged in that occupation. Clean and wholesome bread does not depend upon whether the baker works but ten hours per day or only sixty hours a week. The limitation of the hours of labor does not come within the police power on that ground.

It is a question of which of two powers or rights shall prevail—the power of the State to legislate or the right of the individual to liberty of person and freedom of contract. The mere assertion that the subject relates though but in a remote degree to the public health does not ncesssarily render the enactment valid. The act must have a more direct relation, as a means to an end, and the end itself must be appropriate and legitimate, before an act can be held to be valid which interferes with the general right of an individual to be free in his person and in his power to contract in relation to his own labor.

This case has caused much diversity of opinion in the state courts. In the Supreme Court two of the five judges composing the Appellate Division dissented from the judgment affirming the validity of the act. In the Court of Appeals three of the seven judges also dissented from the judgment upholding the statute. Although found in what is called a labor law of the State, the Court of Appeals has upheld the act as one relating to the public health—in other words, as a health law. One of the judges of the Court of

Appeals, in upholding the law, stated that, in his opinion, the regulation in question could not be sustained unless they were able to say, from common knowledge, that working in a bakery and candy factory was an unhealthy employment. The judge held that, while the evidence was not uniform, it still led him to the conclusion that the occupation of a baker or confectioner was unhealthy and tended to result in diseases of the respiratory organs. Three of the judges dissented from that view, and they thought the occupation of a baker was not to such an extent unhealthy as to warrant the interference of the legislature with the liberty of the individual.

We think the limit of the police power has been reached and passed in this case. There is, in our judgment, no reasonable foundation for holding this to be necessary or appropriate as a health law to safeguard the public health or the health of the individuals who are following the trade of a baker. If this statute be valid, and if, therefore, a proper case is made out in which to deny the right of an individual, *sui juris,* as employer or employee, to make contracts for the labor of the latter under the protection of the provisions of the Federal Constitution, there would seem to be no length to which legislation of this nature might not go. . . .

. . . The act is not, within any fair meaning of the term, a health law, but is an illegal interference with the rights of individuals, both employers and employees, to make contracts regarding labor upon such terms as they may think best, or which they may agree upon with the other parties to such contracts. Statutes of the nature of that under review, limiting the hours in which grown and intelligent men may labor to earn their living, are mere meddlesome interferences with the rights of the individual, and they are not saved from condemnation by the claim that they are passed in the exercise of the police power and upon the subject of the health of the individual whose rights are interfered with, unless there be some fair ground, reasonable in and of itself, to say that there is material danger to the public health or to the health of the employees, if the hours of labor are not curtailed. If this be not clearly the case the individuals, whose rights are thus made the subject of legislative interference, are under the protection of the Federal Constitution regarding their liberty of contract as well as of person; and the legislature of the State has no power to limit their right as proposed in this statute. All that it could properly do has been done by it with regard to the conduct of bakeries, as provided for in the other sections of the act above set forth. . . .

It is impossible for us to shut our eyes to the fact that many of the laws of this character, while passed under what is claimed to be the police power for the purpose of protecting the public health or welfare, are, in reality, passed from other motives. We are justified in saying so when, from the character of the law and the subject upon which it legislates, it is apparent that the public health or welfare bears but the most remote relation to the law. The purpose of a statute must be determined from the natural and legal effect of the language employed; and whether it is or is not repugnant to the Constitution of the United States must be determined from the natural effect of such statutes when put into operation, and not from their proclaimed purpose. *Minnesota v. Barber,... Brimmer v. Rebman,...* The court looks beyond the mere letter of the law in such cases. *Yick Wo v. Hopkins,* 118 U.S. 356.

It is manifest to us that the limitation of the hours of labor as provided for in this section of the statute under which the indictment was found, and the plaintiff in error convicted, has no such direct relation to and no such substantial effect upon the health of the employee, as to justify us in regarding the section as really a health law. It seems to us that the real object and purpose were simply to regulate the hours of labor between the master and his employees (all being men, *sui juris*), in a private business, not dangerous in any degree to morals or in any real and substantial degree, to the health of the employees. Under such circumstances the freedom of master and employee to contract with each other in relation to their employment, and in defining the same, cannot be prohibited or interfered with, without violating the Federal Constitution....

Mr. Justice Holmes dissenting.

I regret sincerely that I am unable to agree with the judgment in this case, and that I think it my duty to express my dissent.

This case is decided upon an economic theory which a large part of the country does not entertain. If it were a question whether I agreed with that theory, I should desire to study it further and long before making up my mind. But I do not conceive that to be my duty, because I strongly believe that my agreement or disagreement has nothing to do with the right of a majority to embody their opinions in law. It is settled by various decisions of this court that state constitutions and state laws may regulate life in many ways which we as legislators might think as injudicious or if you like as tyrannical as this, and which equally with this interfere with the liberty to contract. Sunday laws and usury laws are ancient examples. A more modern one is the prohibition of lotteries. The liberty of the citizen to do as he likes so long as he does not interfere with the liberty of others to do the same, which has been a shibboleth for some well-known writers, is interfered with by school laws, by the Post Office, by every state or municipal institution which takes his money for purposes thought desirable, whether he likes it or not. The Fourteenth Amendment does not enact Mr. Herbert Spencer's Social Statics. The other day we sustained the Massachusetts vaccination law. *Jacobson v. Massachusetts,...* United States and state statutes and decisions cutting down the liberty to contract by way of combination are familiar to this court. *Northern Securities Co. v. United States...* Two years ago we upheld the prohibition of sales of stock on margins or for future delivery in the constitution of Califonia. *Otis v. Parker,* 187 U.S. 606. The decision sustaining an eight hour law for miners is still recent. *Holden v. Hardy...* Some of these laws embody convictions or prejudices which judges are likely to share. Some may not. But a constitution is not intended to embody a particular economic theory, whether of paternalism and the organic relation of the citizen to the State or of *laissez faire*. It is made for people of fundamentally differing views, and the accident of our finding certain opinions natural and familiar or novel and even shocking ought not to conclude our judgment upon the question whether statutes embodying them conflict with the Constitution of the United States.

General propositions do not decide concrete cases. The decision will depend on a judgment or intuition more subtle than any articulate major premise. But I think that the proposition just stated, if it is accepted, will carry us far toward the end. Every opinion tends to become a law. I think that the word liberty in the Fourteenth Amendment is perverted when it is held to prevent the natural outcome of a dominant opinion, unless it can be said that a rational and fair man necessarily would admit that the statute proposed would infringe fundamental principles as they have been understood by the traditions of our people and our law. It does not need research to show that no such sweeping condemnation can be passed upon the statute before us. A reasonable man might think it a proper measure on the score of health. Men whom I certainly could not pronounce unreasonable would uphold it as a first instalment of a general regulation of the hours of work. Whether in the latter aspect it would be open to the charge of inequality I think it unnecessary to discuss. . . .

Adair v. United States
208 U.S. 161
1908

On June 1, 1898, Congress passed the Erdman Act which established arbitration procedures in railroad labor disputes. One of the sections of the statute prohibited "yellow dog" contracts as a condition of employment. In this case, the Court, by a vote of 7 to 2, struck down that section of the act as an unreasonable violation of freedom of contract under the Fifth Amendment's due process clause. Justice John Marshall Harlan, who delivered the opinion of the Court, also stated that the statute exceeded the interstate commerce powers of the federal government. Justices Joseph McKenna and Oliver Wendell Holmes dissented. A portion of the latter's dissent follows the majority decision in this selection.

May Congress make it a criminal offense against the United States as by the tenth section of the act of 1898 it does—for an agent or officer of an interstate carrier, having full authority in the premises from the carrier, to discharge an employee from service simply because of his membership in a labor organization?

This question is admittedly one of importance, and has been examined with care and deliberation. And the court has reached a conclusion which, in its judgment, is consistent with both the words and the spirit of the Constitution and is sustained as well by sound reason.

The first inquiry is whether the. . . act of 1898 upon which the first count of the indictment was based is repugnant to the Fifth Amendment of the Constitution declaring that no person shall be deprived of liberty or property without due process of law. In our opinion that section, in the particular mentioned, is an invasion of the personal liberty, as well as of the right of property, guaranteed by that Amendment. Such liberty and right embraces the right to make contracts for the purchase of the labor of others and equally the right to make contracts for the sale of one's own labor; each right, however, being subject to the fundamental condition that no contract, whatever its subject matter, can be sustained which the law, upon reasonable grounds, forbids as inconsistent with the public interests or as hurtful to the public order or as detrimental to the common good. . . .

While, as already suggested, the rights of liberty and property guaranteed by the Constitution against deprivation without due process of law, is subject to such reasonable restraints as the common good or the general welfare may require, it is not within the functions of government—at least in the absence of contract between the parties—to compel any person in the course of his business and against his will to accept or retain the personal services of another, or to compel any person, against his will, to perform personal services for another. The right of a person to sell his labor upon such terms as he deems proper is, in its essence, the same as the right of the purchaser of labor to prescribe the conditions upon which he will accept such labor from the person offering to sell it. So the right of the employee to quit the service of the employer, for whatever reason, is the same as the right of the employer, for whatever reason, to dispense with the services of such employee....

In all such particulars the employer and the employee have equality of right, and any legislation that disturbs that equality is an arbitrary interference with the liberty of contract....

But it is suggested that the authority to make it a crime for an agent or officer of an interstate carrier, having authority in the premises from his principal, to discharge an employee from service to such carrier, simply because of his membership in a labor organization, can be referred to the power of Congress to regulate interstate commerce, without regard to any question of personal liberty or right of property arising under the Fifth Amendment. This suggestion can have no bearing in the present discussion unless the statute, in the particular just stated, is within the meaning of the Constitution a regulation of commerce among the States. If it be not, then clearly the Government cannot invoke the commerce clause of the Constitution as sustaining the indictment against Adair....

This question has been frequently propounded in this court, and the answer has been—and no more specific answer could well have been given—that commerce among the several States comprehends traffic, intercourse, trade, navigation, communication, the transit of persons and the transmission of messages by telegraph—indeed, every species of commercial intercourse among the several States, but not to that commerce "completely internal, which is carried on between man and man, in a State, or between different parts of the same State....

...But what possible legal or logical connection is there between an employee's membership in a labor organization and the carrying on of interstate commerce? Such relation to a labor organization cannot have, *in itself* and in the eye of the law, any bearing upon the comerce with which the employee is connected by his labor and services. Labor associations, we assume, are organized for the general purpose of improving or bettering the conditions and conserving the interests of its members as wage-earners—an object entirely legitimate and to be commended rather than condemned. But surely those associations as labor organizations have nothing to do with interstate commerce as such. One who engages in the service of an interstate carrier will, it must be assumed, faithfully perform his duty, whether he be a member or not a member of a labor organization. His fitness for the position in which he labors and his diligence in the discharge of his duties cannot in law or sound reason depend in any degree upon his being or not being a member of a labor organization. It cannot be assumed that his fitness is assured, or his diligence increased, by such membership, or that he is less fit or less diligent because of his not being a member of such an organization. . . .

Looking alone at the words of the statute for the purpose of ascertaining its scope and effect, and of determining its validity, we hold that there is no such connection between interstate commerce and membership in a labor organization as to authorize Congress to make it a crime against the United States for an agent of an interstate carrier to discharge an employee because of such membership on his part. . . .

Mr. Justice Holmes dissenting.

As we all know, there are special labor unions of men engaged in the service of carriers. These unions exercise a direct influence upon the employment of labor in that business, upon the terms of such employment, and upon the business itself. Their very existence is directed specifically to the business, and their connection with it is, at least, as intimate and important, as that of safety couplers, and, I should think, as the liability of master to servant,—matters which, it is admitted, Congress might regulate so far as they concerned commerce among the states. I suppose that it hardly would be denied that some of the relations of railroads with unions of railroad employees are closely enough connected with commerce to justify legislation by Congress. If so, legislation to prevent the exclusion of such unions from employment is sufficiently near.

The ground on which this particular law is held bad, is not so much that it deals with matters remote from commerce among the states, as that it interferes with the paramount individual rights secured by the 5th Amendment. The section is, in substance, a very limited interference with freedom of contract, no more. It does not require the carriers to employ anyone. It does not forbid them to refuse to employ anyone, for any reason they deem good, even where the notion of a choice of persons is a fiction and wholesale employment is necessary upon general principles that it might be proper to control. The section simply prohibits the more powerful party to exact certain undertakings, or to threaten dismissal or unjustly discriminate on certain grounds against those already employed. I hardly can suppose that the grounds on which a contract lawfully may be made to end are less open to regulation than other terms. So I turn to the general question whether the employment can be regulated at all. I confess that I think that the right to make contracts at will that has been derived from the word "liberty" in the Amendments, has been stretched to its extreme by the decisions; but they agree that sometimes the right may be restrained. Where there is, or generally is believed to be, an important ground of public policy for restraint, the Constitution does not forbid it, whether this court agrees or disagrees with the policy pursued. It cannot be doubted that to prevent strikes and, so far as possible, to foster its scheme of arbitration, might be deemed by Congress an important point of policy, and I think it impossible to say that Congress might not reasonably think that the provision in question would help a good deal to carry its policy along. But suppose the only effect really were to tend to bring about the complete unionizing of such railroad laborers as Congress can deal with, I think that object alone would justify the act. I quite agree that the question what and how much good labor unions do, is one on which intelligent people may differ; I think that laboring men sometimes attribute to combinations of capital, disadvantages, that really are due to economic conditions of a far wider and deeper kind; but I could not pronounce it unwarranted if Congress should decide that to foster a strong union was for the best interests, not only of the men, but of the railroads and the country at large. . . .

Loewe v. Lawlor (Danbury Hatters' Case)

208 U.S. 274

1908

The United Hatters Union of North America boycotted the products of a hat manufacturing corporation known as the Danbury Hatters because the company refused to allow its factory workers to join the union. The Danbury Hatters then sued the union for violation of the anti-trust laws. A unanimous Court, speaking through Chief Justice Melville W. Fuller, ruled in favor of the company, declaring the United Hatters Union of North America an illegal combination in restraint of interstate commerce under the Sherman Anti-Trust Act. Known as the *Danbury Hatters'* case, this decision by the Supreme Court was the first major application of the anti-trust statutes to a labor union.

In our opinion, the combination described in the declaration is a combination "in restraint of trade or commerce among the several States," in the sense in which those words are used in the act, and the action can be maintained accordingly.

And that conclusion rests on many judgments of this court, to the effect that the act prohibits any combination whatever to secure action which essentially obsructs the free flow of commerce between the States, or restricts, in that regard, the liberty of a trader to engage in business.

The combination charged falls within the class of restraints of trade aimed at compelling third parties and strangers involuntarily not to engage in the course of trade except on conditions that the combination imposes; and there is no doubt that (to quote from the well-known work of Chief Justice Erle on Trade Unions) "at common law every person has individually, and the public also has collectively, a right to require that the course of trade should be kept free from unreasonable obstruction." But the objection here is to the jurisdiction, because, even conceding that the declaration states a case good at common law, it is contended that it does not state one within the statute. Thus, it is said that the restraint alleged would operate to entirely destroy plaintiffs' business and thereby include intrastate trade as well; that physical obstruction is not alleged as contemplated; and that defendants are not themselves engaged in interstate trade. . . .

The averments here are that there was an existing interstate traffic between plaintiffs and citizens of other States, and that for the direct purpose of destroying such interstate traffic defendants combined not merely to prevent plaintiffs from manufacturing articles then and there intended for transportation beyond the State, but also to prevent the vendees from reselling the hats which they had imported from Connecticut, or from further negotiating with plaintiffs for the purchase and intertransportation of such hats from Connecticut to the various places of destination. So that, although some of the means whereby the interstate traffic was to be destroyed were acts within a State, and some of them were in themselves as a part of their obvious purpose and effect beyond the scope of Federal authority, still, as we have seen, the acts must be considered as a whole, and the plan is open to condemnation, notwithstanding a negligible amount of intrastate business might be affected in carrying it out. If the purposes of the combination were, as alleged, to prevent any interstate transportation at all, the fact that the means operated at one end before physical transportation commenced and at the other end after the physical transportation ended was immaterial.

Nor can the act in question be held inapplicable because defendants were not themselves engaged in interstate commerce. The act made no distinction between classes. It provided that "every" contract, combination or conspiracy in restraint of trade was illegal. . . .

The subject had so broadened in the minds of the legislators that the source of the evil was not regarded as material, and the evil in its entirety is dealt with. They made the interdiction include combinations of labor, as well as of capital; in fact, all combinations in restraint of commerce, without reference to the character of the persons who entered into them. . . .

That defendants were members of a vast combination called The United Hatters of North America, comprising about 9,000 members and including a large number of subordinate unions, and that they were combined with some 1,400,000 others into another assocation known as The American Federation of Labor, of which they were members, whose members resided in all the places in the several States where the wholesale dealers in hats and their customers resided and did business; that defendants were "engaged in a combined scheme and effort to force all manufacturers of fur hats in the United States, including the plaintiffs, against their will and their previous policy of carrying on their business, to organize their workmen in the departments of making and finishing, in each of their factories, into an organization, to be part and parcel of the said combination known as The United Hatters of North America, or as the defendants and their confederates term it, to unionize their shops, with the intent thereby to control the employment of labor in and the operation of said factories, and to subject the same to the direction and control of persons, other than the owners of the same, in a manner extremely onerous and distasteful to such owners, and to carry out such scheme, effort and purpose, by restraining and destroying the interstate trade and commerce of such manufacturers, by means of intimidation of and threats made to such manufacturers and their customers in the several States, of boycotting them, their product and their customers, using therefor all the powerful means at their command, as aforesaid, until such time as, from the damage and loss of business resulting therefrom, the said manufacturers should yield to the said demand to unionize. . . .

[T]he defendants proceeded to carry out their combination to restrain and destroy interstate trade and commerce between plaintiffs and their customers in other States by employing the identical means contrived for that purpose. . . .

Muller v. Oregon
208 U.S. 412
1908

In 1903, the state of Oregon passed a law making it illegal to employ women in laundries or factories for more than ten hours a day or sixty hours in any week. When the owner of an Oregon laundry violated the act, he was convicted and fined by the Oregon Supreme Court. On appeal to the Supreme Court of the United States, the attorney for the state, Louis D. Brandeis, prepared a brilliant and unusual defense, now referred to as the Brandeis Brief, in which he quickly disposed of the constitutional precedents, but documented his presentation before the Court with a huge variety of statistical, historical, sociological and economic materials. These arguments convinced the Court that the Oregon law was a reasonable exercise of state police power. The unanimous Court opinion, delivered by Justice David J. Brewer, held that the statute in question was constitutional, and did not violate the freedom of contract clause of the Constitution. To some extent, the Court modified its previous position in the *Lochner* case.

The single question is the constitutionality of the statute under which the defendant was convicted so far as it affects the work of a female in a laundry. That it does not conflict with any provisions of the state constitution is settled by the decision of the Supreme Court of the State. The contentions of the defendant, now plaintiff in error, are thus stated in his brief:

"(1) Because the statute attempts to prevent persons, *sui juris,* from making their own contracts, and thus violates the provisions of the Fourteenth Amendment, as follows:

" 'No State shall make or enforce any law which shall abridge the privileges or immunities of citizens of the United States; nor shall any State deprive any person of life, liberty, or property, without due process of law; nor deny to any person within its jursidiction the equal protection of the laws.'

"(2) Because the statute does not apply equally to all persons similarly situated, and is class legislation.

"(3) The statute is not a valid exercise of the police power. The kinds of work proscribed are not unlawful, nor are they declared to be immoral or dangerous to the public health; nor can such a law be sustained on the ground that it is designed to protect women on account of their sex. There is no necessary or reasonable connection between the limitation prescribed by the act and the public health, safety or welfare."

It is the law of Oregon that women, whether married or single, have equal contractual and personal rights with men. . . .

It thus appears that, putting to one side the elective franchise, in the matter of personal and contractual rights they stand on the same plane as the other sex. Their rights in these respects can no more be infringed than the equal rights of their brothers. We held in *Lochner v. New York,* . . . that a law providing that no laborer shall be required or permitted to work in a bakery more than sixty hours in a week or ten hours in a day was not as to men a legitimate exercise of the police power of the State, but an unreasonable, unnecessary and arbitrary interference with the right and liberty of the individual to contract in relation to his labor, and as such was in conflict with, and void under, the Federal Constitution. That decision is invoked by plaintiff in error as decisive of the question before us. But this assumes that the difference between the sexes does not justify a different rule respecting a restriction of the hours of labor.

In patent cases counsel are apt to open the argument with a discussion of the state of the art. It may not be amiss, in the present case, before examining the constitutional question, to notice the course of legislation as well as expressions of opinion from other than judicial sources. In the brief filed by Mr. Louis D. Brandeis, for the defendant in error, is a very copious collection of all these matters, an epitome of which is found in the margin. . . .

The legislation and opinions referred to in the margin may not be, technically speaking, authorities, and in them is little or no discussion of the constitutional question presented to us for determination, yet they are significant of a widespread belief that woman's physical structure, and the functions she performs in consequence thereof, justify special legislation restricting or qualifying the conditions under which she should be permitted to toil. Constitutional questions, it is true, are not settled by even a consensus of present public opinion, for it is the peculiar value of a written constitution that it places in unchanging form limitations upon legislative action, and thus gives a permanence and stability to popular government which otherwise would be lacking. At the same time, when a question of fact is debated and debatable, and the extent to which a special constitutional limitation goes is affected by the truth in respect to that fact, a widespread and long continued belief concerning it is worthy of consideration. We take judicial cognizance of all matters of general knowledge.

It is undoubtedly true, as more than once declared by this court, that the general right to contract in relation to one's business is part of the liberty of the individual, protected by the Fourteenth Amendment to the Federal Constitution; yet is is equally well settled that this liberty is not absolute and extending to all contracts, and that a State may, without conflicting with the provisions of the Fourteenth Amendment, restrict in many respects the individual's power of contract. . . .

That woman's physical structure and the performance of maternal functions place her at a disadvantage in the struggle for subsistence is obvious. This is especially true when the burdens of motherhood are upon her. Even when they are not, by abundant testimony of the medical fraternity continuance for a long time on her feet at work, repeating this from day to day, tends to injurious effects upon the body, and as healthy mothers are essential to vigorous offspring, the physical well-being of woman becomes an object of public interest and care in order to preserve the strength and vigor of the race.

Still again, history discloses the fact that woman has always been dependent upon man. He established his control at the outset by superior physical strength, and this control in various forms, with diminishing intensity, has continued to the present. As minors, though not to the same extent, she has been looked upon in the courts as needing especial care that her rights may be preserved. Education was long denied her, and while now the doors of the school room are opened and her opportunities for acquiring knowledge are great, yet even with that and the consequent increase of capacity for business affairs it is still true that in the struggle for subsistence she is not an equal competitor with her brother. Though limitations upon personal and contractual rights may be removed by legislation, there is that in her disposition and habits of life which will operate against a full assertion of those rights. She will still be where some legislation to protect her seems necessary to secure a real equality of right. Doubtless there are individual exceptions, and there are many respects in which she has an advantage over him; but looking at it from the viewpoint of the effort to maintain an independent position in life, she is not upon an equality. Differentiated by these matters from the other sex, she is properly placed in a class by herself, and legislation designed for her protection may be sustained, even when like legislation is not necessary for men and could not be sustained. It is impossible to close one's eyes to the fact that she still looks to her brother and depends upon him. Even though all restrictions on political, personal and contractual rights were taken away, and she stood, so far as statutes are concerned, upon an absolutely equal plane with him, it would still be true that she is so constituted that she will rest upon and look to him for protection; that her physical structure and a proper discharge of her maternal functions—having in view not merely her own health, but the well-being of the race—justify legislation to protect her from the greed as well as the passion of man. The limitations which this statute places upon her contractual powers, upon her right to agree with her employer as to the time she shall labor, are not imposed solely for her benefit, but also largely for the benefit of all. Many words cannot make this plainer. The two sexes differ in structure of body, in the functions to be performed by each, in the amount of physical strength, in the capacity for long-continued labor, particularly when done standing, the influence of vigorous health upon the future well-being of the race, the self-reliance which enables one to assert full rights, and in the capacity to maintain the struggle for subsistence. This difference justifies a difference in legislation and upholds that which is designed to compensate for some of the burdens which rest upon her. . . .

St. Louis and Iron Mountain Railway v. Taylor
210 U.S. 281
1908

In 1905, Congress increased the liability of employers who were negligent in providing safety equipment for their employees when it enacted the Safety Appliance Law. When the widow of a railroad brakeman sued the St. Louis and Iron Mountain Railway for damages for the death of her husband under the terms of the act, an Arkansas Circuit Court decided the suit in favor of the widow. The railroad appealed the decision to the Supreme Court of the United States, where a unanimous decision, given by Justice William H. Moody, declared the constitutionality of the law on the ground that it was a proper exercise of congressional police power in regulating all aspects of interstate commerce. This decision was an interesting turnabout from the Court's position in the *First Employers' Liability* case heard only five months earlier.

The defendant in error, as administratrix of George W. Taylor, brought, in the Circuit Court of the State of Arkansas, this action at law against the plaintiff in error, a corporation owning and operating a railroad. Damages were sought, for the benefit of Taylor's widow and next of kin, on account of his injury and death in the course of his employment as brakeman in the service of the railroad. It was alleged in the complaint that Taylor, while attempting, in the discharge of his duty, to couple two cars was caught between them and killed. The right to recover for the death was based solely on the failure of the defendant to equip the two cars which were to be coupled with such draw bars as were required by the act of Congress known as the Safety Appliance Law, Act of March 2, 1893.... The defendant's answer denied that the cars were improperly equipped with draw bars, and alleged that Taylor's death was the result of his own negligence. At a trial before a jury upon the issues made by the pleadings there was a verdict for the plaintiff, which was affirmed in a majority opinion by the Supreme Court of the State. The judgment of that court is brought here for reexamination by writ of error. The writ sets forth many assignments of error, but of them four only were relied upon in argument here, and they alone need be stated and considered. It is not, and cannot be, disputed that the questions raised by the errors assigned were seasonably and properly made in the court below, so as to give this court jurisdiction to consider them; so no time need be spent on that. But the defendant in error insists that the questions themselves, though properly here in form, are not Federal questions; that is to say, not questions which we by law are authorized to consider on a writ of error to a state court. For that reason it is contended that the writ should be dismissed. That contention we will consider with each question as it is discussed. . . .

The principles to be derived from the cases are these: Where a party to litigation in a state court insists, by way of objection to or requests for instructions upon a construction of a statute of the United States which will lead, or, on possible findings of fact from the evidence may lead, to a judgment in his favor, and his claim in this respect, being duly set up, is denied by the highest court of the State, then the question thus raised may be reviewed in this court. The plain reason is that in all such cases he has claimed in the state court a right or immunity under a law of the United States and it has been denied to him. Jurisdiction so clearly warranted by the Constitution and so explicitly conferred by the act of Congress needs no justification. But it may not be out of place to say that in no other manner can a uniform construction of the statute laws of the United States be secured, so that they shall have the same meaning and effect in all the States of the Union.

It is clear that these principles govern the case at bar. The defendant, now plaintiff in error, objected to an erroneous construction of the Safety Appliance Act, which warranted on the evidence of a judgment in its favor. The denials of its claims were decisions of Federal questions reviewable here.

The plaintiff in error raises another question, which, for the reasons already given, we think is of a Federal nature. The evidence showed that draw bars which, as originally constructed, are of standard height, are lowered by the natural effect of proper use; that, in addition to the correction of this tendency by general repair, devices called shims, which are metallic wedges of different thickness, are employed to raise the lowered draw bar to the legal standard; and that in the caboose of this train the railroad furnished a sufficient supply of these shims, which it was the duty of the conductor or brakeman to use as occasion demanded. On this state of the evidence the defendant was refused instructions, in substance, that if the defendant furnished cars which were constructed with draw bars of a standard height, and furnished shims to competent inspectors and trainmen and used reasonable care to keep the draw bars at a reasonable height, it had complied with its statutory duty, and, if the lowering of the draw bar resulted from the failure to use the shims, that was the negligence of a fellow servant, for which the defendant was not responsible. In deciding the questions thus raised, upon which the courts have differed *(St. Louis & S.F. Ry. v. Delk,* 158 Fed. Rep. 931), we need not enter into the wilderness of cases upon the common law duty of the employer to use reasonable care to furnish his employee reasonably safe tools, machinery and appliances, or consider when and how far that duty may be performed by delegating it to suitable persons for whose default the employer is not responsible. In the case before us the liability of the defendant does not grow out of the common law duty of master to servant. The Congress, not satisfied with the common law duty and its resulting liability, has prescribed and defined the duty by statute. We have nothing to do but to ascertain and declare the meaning of a few simple words in which the duty is described. It is enacted that "no cars, either loaded or unloaded, shall be used in interstate traffic which do not comply with the standard." There is no escape from the meaning of these words. Explanation cannot clarify them, and ought not to be employed to confuse them or lessen their significance. The obvious purpose of the legislature was to supplant the qualified duty of the common law with an absoute duty deemed by it more just. If the railroad does, in point of fact, use cars which do not comply with the standard, it violates the plain prohibitions of the law, and there arises from that violation the liability to make compensation to one who is injured by it. It is urged that this is a harsh construction. To this we reply that, if it be the true construction, its harshness is no concern of the courts. They have no responsibility for the justice or wisdom of legislation, and no duty except to enforce the law as it is written, unless it is clearly beyond the constitutional power of the law-making body. It is said that the liability under the statute, as thus construed, imposes so great a hardship upon the railroads that it ought not to be supposed that Congress intended it. Certainly the statute ought not to be given an absurd or utterly unreasonable interpretation leading to hardship and injustice, if any other interpretation is reasonably possible. But this argument is a dangerous one, and never should be heeded where the hardship would be occasional and exceptional. It would be better, it was once said by Lord Eldon, to look hardship in the face than break down the rules of law. But when applied to the case at bar the argument of hardship is plausible only when the attention is directed to the material interest of the employer to the exclusion of the interests of the employee and of the public. Where an injury happens through the absence of a safe draw bar there must be a hardship. Such an injury must be an irreparable misfortune to some one. If it must be borne entirely by him who suffers it, that is a hardship to him. If its burden is transferred, as far as it is capable of transfer, to the employer, it is a hardship to him. It is quite conceivable that Congress, contemplating the inevitable hardship of such injuries, and hoping to diminish the economic loss to the community resulting from them, should deem it wise to impose their burdens upon those who could measurably control their causes, instead of upon those who are in the main helpless in that regard. Such a policy would be intelligible, and, to say the least, not so unreasonable as to require us to doubt that it was intended, and to seek some unnatural interpretation of common words. We see no error in this part of the case. But for the reasons before given the judgment must be reversed.

Berea College v. Kentucky
211 U.S. 45
1908

The *Plessy v. Ferguson* decision went a long way toward reestablishing and maintaining a caste system society in the South when it enunciated the "separate but equal" doctrine. This case saw the Court speaking through Justice David J. Brewer, once again apply this rule when it sustained by a vote of 7 to 2 a Kentucky law which prohibited the admission of blacks to all-white private schools in the state. The segregation principle in education was firmly established by the Court in this decision. As he had done in the *Plessy* case, Mr. Justice John Marshall Harlan filed an angry dissent which follows the majority opinion in this selection.

There is no dispute as to the facts. That the act does not violate the Constitution of Kentucky is settled by the decision of its highest court, and the single question for our consideration is whether it conflicts with the Federal Constitution. The court of appeals discussed at some length the general power of the state in respect to the separation of the two races. It also ruled that "the right to teach white and negro children in a private school at the same time and place is not a property right. Besides, appellant, as a corporation created by this state, has no natural right to teach at all. Its right to teach is such as the state sees fit to give to it. The state may withhold it altogether, or qualify it. . . .

Again, the decision by a state court of the extent and limitation of the powers conferred by the state upon one of its own corporations is of a purely local nature. In creating a corporation a state may withhold powers which may be exercised by and cannot be denied to an individual. It is under no obligation to treat both alike. In granting corporate powers the legislature may deem that the best interests of the state would be subserved by some restriction, and the corporation may not plead that, in spite of the restriction, it has more or greater powers because the citizen has. "The granting of such right or privilege [the right or privilege to be a corporation] rests entirely in the discretion of the state, and, of course, when granted, may be accompanied with such conditions as its legislature may judge most befitting to its interests and policy.". . .

Construing the statute, the court of appeals held that "if the same school taught the different races at different times, though at the same place, or at different times at the same place, it would not be unlawful." Now, an amendment to the original charter, which does not destroy the power of the college to furnish education to all persons, but which simply separates them by time or place of instruction, cannot be said to "defeat or substantially impair the object of the grant." The language of the statute is not in terms an amendment, yet its effect is an amendment, and it would be resting too much on mere form to hold that a statute which in effect works a change in the terms of the charter is not to be considered as an amendment, becuse not so designated. The act itself, being separable, is to be read as though it, in one section, prohibited any person, in another section any corporation, and, in a third, any association of persons to do the acts named. Reading the statute as containing a separate prohibtion on all corporations, at least, all state corporations, it substantially declares that any authority given by previous charters to instruct the two races at the same time and in the same place is forbidden, and that prohibition, being a departure from the terms of the original charter in this case, may properly be adjudged an amendment....

Mr. Justice Harlan dissenting.

...If the commonwealth of Kentucky can make it a crime to teach white and colored children together at the same time, in a private institution of learning, it is difficult to perceive why it may not forbid the assembling of white and color children in the same Sabbath school, for the purpose of being instructed in the Word of God, although such teaching may be done under the authority of the church to which the school is attached as well as with the consent of the parents of the children. So, if the state court be right, white and colored children may even be forbidden to sit together in a house of worship or at a communion table in the same Christian church. In the cases supposed there would be the same association of white and colored persons as would occur when pupils of the two races sit together in a private institution of learning for the purpose of receiving instruction in purely secular matters. Will it be said that the cases supposed and the case here in hand are different, in that no government, in this country, can lay unholy hands on the religious faith of the people? The answer to this suggestion is that, in the eye of the law, the right to enjoy one's religious belief, unmolested by any human power, is no more sacred nor more fully or distinctly recognized than is the right to impart and receive instruction not harmful to the public. The denial of either right would be an infringement of the liberty inherent in the freedom secured by the fundamental law....

...Further, if the lower court be right, then a state may make it a crime for white and colored persons to frequent the same market places at the same time, or appear in an assemblage of citizens convened to consider questions of a public or political nature, in which all citizens, without regard to race, are equally interested. Many other illustrations might be given to show the mischievous, not to say cruel, character of the statute in question, and how inconsistent such legislation is with the great principle of the equality of citizens before the law.

Of course, what I have said has no reference to regulations prescribed for public schools, established at the pleasure of the state and maintained at the public expense. No such question is here presented and it need not be now discussed. My observations have reference to the case before the court, and only to the provision of the statute making it a crime for any person to impart harmless instruction to white and colored pupils together, at the same time, in the same private institution of learning. That provision is, in my opinion, made an essential element in the policy of the statute, and, if regard be had to the object and purpose of this legislation, it cannot be treated as separable nor intended to be separated from the provisions relating to corporations. The whole statute should therefore be held void; otherwise, it will be taken as the law of Kentucky, to be enforced by its courts, that the teaching of white and black pupils, at the same time, even in a *private* institution, is a crime against that commonwealth, punishable by fine and imprisonment.

In my opinion the judgment should be reversed upon the ground that the statute is in violation of the Constitution of the United States.

Theodore Roosevelt: Criticism of the Court

1910

During his years as President, Theodore Roosevelt attempted to reconstitute the Supreme Court toward a more liberal philosophy. A long line of Supreme Court decisions during the Progressive Era had negated or substantially weakened congressional measures designed to restrain unethical practices among businessmen and industrialists. Anti-Court sentiment grew as reformers watched the destruction of their "brain children." One of the most vocal critics was Roosevelt. Two years after he had left the presidency, he delivered an address in which he castigated the Court, contending that it should be more attuned to the force of public opinion. Theodore Roosevelt, "Criticism of the Courts," *The Outlook,* XVI (September 24, 1910); 149-153.

On August 29, at Denver, before the Colorado Legislature, I made an address dwelling partly upon the necessity of good government, and specifically upon the need of more coherent work between the state and the national governments, and of action on the part of the legislative, executive, and judicial officers of the country, both national and state, which would prevent the growth and extension of a neutral territory or borderland of ill-defined limits in which neither the nation nor any state should be able to exercise effective control, especially over big corporations, in their relations to the public at large and to their own employees. I spoke in part as follows:—

The courts occupy a position of importance in our government such as they occupy in no other government, because, instead of dealing only with the rights of one man face to face with his fellow-men, as is the case with other governments, they here pass upon the fundamental governmental rights of the people as exercised through their legislative and executive officers. Unfortunately, the courts, instead of leading in the recognition of the new conditions, have lagged behind, and, as each case has presented itself, have tended by a series of negative decisions to create a sphere in which neither nation nor state has effective control, and where the great business interests that can call to their aid the ability of the greatest corporation lawyers escape all control whatsoever. Let me illustrate what I mean by a reference to two concrete cases. Remember that I believe in states' rights wherever states' rights mean the people's rights. On the other hand, I believe in national rights wherever national rights mean the people's rights; and, above all, I believe that in every part of our complicated social fabric there must be either national or state control, and that it is ruinous to permit governmental action, and especially judicial action, which prevents the exercise of such control.

The first case to which I shall refer is the Knight Sugar Trust case. In that case the Supreme Court of the United States handed down a decision which rendered it exceedingly difficult for the people to devise any method of controlling and regulating the business use of great capital in interstate commerce. It was a decision nominally against national rights, but really against popular rights, against the democratic principle of government by the people.

The second case is the so-called New York Bakeshop case. In New York City, as in most large cities, the baking business is likely to be carried on under unhygienic conditions, conditions which tell against the welfare of the general public. The New York Legislature pased, and the New York Governor signed, a bill remedying these unhealthy conditions. New York State was the only body which could deal with them; the nation had no power whatever in the matter. Acting on evidence which to them seemed ample and sufficient, acting in the interest of the public and in accordance with the demand of the public, the only governmental authority having affirmative power in the matter, the Governor and the Legislature of the State of New York took the action which they deemed necessary, after what inquiry and study were needed to satisfy them as to the conditions, and as to the remedy. The Governor and the Legislature alone had the power to remedy the abuse. But the Supreme Court of the United States possessed, and unfortunately exercised, the negative power of not permitting the abuse to be remedied. By a five-to-four vote they declared the action of the State of New York unconstitutional, because, forsooth, men must not be deprived of their "liberty" to work under unhealthy conditions. All who are acquainted with the effort to remedy industrial abuses know the type of mind (it may be perfectly honest, but is absolutely fossilized), which declines to allow us to work for the betterment of conditions among the wage earners on the ground that we must not interfere with the "liberty" of a girl to work under conditions which jeopardize life and limb, or the "liberty" of a man to work under conditions which ruin his health after a limited number of years.

Such was the decision. The Court was of course absolutely powerless to make the remotest attempt to provide a remedy for the wrong which undoubtedly existed, and its refusal to permit action by the state did not confer any power upon the nation to act. The decision was nominally against states' rights, but really against popular rights.

Much exception was taken in the East to this speech as an "attack" on the Supreme Court, some of the critics going so far as to call it an attack upon the judiciary as a whole, an incitement to riot, and an appeal to the passions of the mob. The gloom caused by the "attack" was naturally deepest in that section of the metropolitan press which is owned and edited in the shadow of Wall Street. . . .

PART III

The Justices of the Supreme Court

▪ ▪ ▪ ▪ ▪

1888-1910

Melville W. Fuller

Melville Weston Fuller was born on February 11, 1833 in Augusta, Maine to Catherine Martin Weston and Frederick Augustus Fuller, a respected Augusta attorney. His uncle was also a prominent lawyer, and both of his grandfathers were judges. After primary schooling in Augusta, Fuller attended Bowdoin College, graduating in 1853 with an A.B. He then read law in his uncle's Bangor office, attended Harvard Law School in 1855, and was admitted to the Maine bar toward the end of that year. In 1856, he worked on a local newspaper, was elected to the Augusta common council and was appointed that community's city solicitor. Toward the end of 1856, he moved to Chicago, passed the Illinois bar and practiced law in that state from 1856 to 1888, forming several partnerships during that period.

Fuller became interested in politics, joined the Democratic party in Illinois, and supported Stephen A. Douglas in his senatorial race with Abraham Lincoln (1858). Although only moderately successful as a corporation lawyer, by 1860, Fuller had gained somewhat of a political reputation in Illinois, and in the presidential campaign of that year, again vigorously supported Douglas.

When Civil War came in 1861, Fuller pledged his loyalty to the Union, but did not serve in the army. Instead, he was elected a delegate to the Illinois Constitutional Convention, and two years later (1863), a member of the state legislature, where he remained until 1865. In the Illinois house, he opposed many of President Lincoln's policies including the Emancipation Proclamation. In 1864, his first wife, Calista Ophelia Reynolds, died after bearing him two daughters. Two years later, he remarried; his bride was Mary Ellen Coolbaugh, the daughter of a prominent Chicago banker. From this marriage eight children were born.

With his father-in-law's contacts, Fuller now built a large, influential, and profitable law practice. He specialized in real estate and corporate law. A firm believer in strict construction, he subscribed to the principle that the best government is that which governs least. On May 20, 1888, about a month after the death of Chief Justice Morrison R. Waite, President Grover Cleveland nominated Fuller to become the new Chief Justice of the Supreme Court of the United States. His loyalty to the Democratic party, as well as his impeccable reputation, no doubt influenced the President, despite the fact that he had never served in a judicial capacity. Although many business and political leaders applauded Fuller's appointment, it ran into some opposition in the Senate, based on partisan considerations. Confirmation was delayed for several months, but on July 20, 1888, Melville Fuller became the eighth Chief Justice of the Supreme Court. He took his seat at the head of the supreme bench on October 8, 1888.

Fuller served as Chief Justice for twenty-two years, but could not dominate the Court as John Marshall had done before him, or Edward D. White would do after him. His primary contribution was as a moderator, very efficiently managing the administrative details of the Court and its conflicting personalities. He believed in the sanctity of private property, *laissez faire* economics, and limitations on the expansion of federal power. In short, he was a conservative, and the perfect leader for the Court as it was constituted during this period.

During his tenure, the Court, with his complete approval, methodically destroyed the regulatory authority of the states. In cases such as *Chicago, Milwaukee and St. Paul Railroad Company v. Minnesota* (1890), *Regan v. Farmers' Loan and Trust Company* (1894) and *Smyth v. Ames* (1898), the Court did away with the precedents established in *Munn v. Illinois* (1877), and made the concept of due process under the Fourteenth Amendment continually work on the side of corporate enterprise. This general principle was extended to other areas beyond merely the fixing of railroad rates. It was also applied in the freedom of contract cases such as *Holden v. Hardy* (1898), and *Lochner v. New York* (1905). The Fuller Court's conservatism reached its height in 1895, when it struck down the income tax, *Pollock v. Farmers' Loan and Trust Company,* emasculated the Sherman Anti-Trust Act, *United States v. E.C. Knight Company,* and upheld the use of federal injunctions in labor disputes, *In re Debs.* Fuller, and the Court, were fiercely denounced throughout the nation for these decisions.

Fuller rarely dissented, but when he did, his opinions were always in opposition to the expansion of federal authority. In cases as disparate as *In re Neagle* (1890), *United States v. Wong Kim Ark* (1898), and *McCray v. United States* (1904), the Chief Justice's strict constructionist views on this question were amply displayed. Except for his "unbroken package" concept, introduced in *Leisy v. Hardin* (1890), he added very little else that was original to the jurisprudence of the Court. Despite this fact, Fuller was a highly respected, well-liked man. In 1892, President Cleveland offered him the post of secretary of state, but he declined the appointment, and likewise refused President William McKinley's offer of appointment to the Spanish-American Peace Commission in 1898. He did serve, however, as a member of the Venezuela-British Guiana Border Commission in 1899, and as the American member of the Permanent Court of Arbitration at the Hague (1900-10).

During the last five years of Fuller's Chief Justiceship, the Court slowly began to moderate its positions. With Fuller's general concurrence, a somewhat more liberal view of governmental regulation of business enterprise was expressed. The new President, Theodore Roosevelt, attempted to force Fuller's resignation during this period, but the Chief Justice adamantly refused. However, on July 4, 1910, he died suddenly of a heart attack at his home in Washington.

Samuel F. Miller

Samuel Freeman Miller, one of the greatest Justices in the history of the Supreme Court, was born on April 5, 1816 in the farming village of Richmond, Kentucky. He was the eldest of eight children born to Patsy Freeman and Frederick Miller. He grew up on the Miller farm and went to the local school in Richmond. In 1834, he enrolled at Transylvania University in Lexington from which he was graduated in 1838 with a degree in medicine. For the next ten years, he plied his craft among the farmers of Knox county in southeastern Kentucky. It was there at Barbourville that he met and married Lucy Ballinger, who bore him three children.

By the mid-1840s, Miller tired of medicine and became a lawyer after purchasing law books and reading law in an attorney friend's office. In 1847 he was admitted to the Kentucky bar and practiced law in that state for the next three years. During that time, he became a member of the county court and a justice of the peace. In 1849, he was an unsuccessful candidate for delegate to a Kentucky constitutional convention. Opposing the pro-slavery position of the new Kentucky constitution produced by the convention, Miller moved his family to Keokuk, Iowa, in 1850. Within a year, he had become one of the leading attorneys in the state and had entered a law firm owned by a prominent Keokuk lawyer, Louis Reeves. In 1852, he became Reeves's partner and the firm prospered both in clients and reputation. In 1854, both his wife and his law partner died. Soon after, he married his partner's widow, Eliza Reeves, and opened a new law office in partnership with John Rankin. Again his practice grew both in reputation and prosperity while political affairs began increasingly to occupy more and more of his time.

Politically, Miller was a "moderate." Originally a member of the Whigs, he joined the newly founded Republican party in Iowa following the passage of the Kansas-Nebraska Act of 1854 of which he strongly disapproved. An outspoken anti-slavery man, within two years he had risen to the post of Keokuk Republican county chairman. Although defeated in 1856 for the Iowa state senate, by the eve of the Civil War he had become one of Iowa's leading Republicans and an avid supporter of Abraham Lincoln's presidential candidacy. He devoted much time to Lincoln's campaign in Iowa and when the Civil War began after Lincoln's inauguration, Miller stoutly supported the Union contributing time and money to the Northern cause.

In 1862, when the federal judiciary was in the process of reorganization, President Lincoln recommended Miller's appointment to the Supreme Court of the United States. The Senate confirmed the appointment on July 16, 1862 and Miller took his seat on December 1, 1863 beginning a twenty-eight year tenure on the supreme bench.

During his many years on the Court, Miller supported the needs of the national government rendering decisions protecting its taxing power, and extending its authority over interstate commerce. He believed that only through federal regulation could order be secured. In addition, he fervently defended and protected individual liberty. As a jurist, Miller favored loose construction of the Constitution and the use of implied powers. Yet his judgements were always well reasoned utilizing legal precedent and a good deal of common sense.

In a variety of cases, Miller supported the Union cause in the Court, declaring constitutional such things as greenbacks, blockades and military tribunals. When peace came, he continued his defense of the Union in the *Test Oath Cases, Cummings v. Missouri* and *Ex parte Garland,* (both 1867), the *Legal Tender Cases, Hepburn v. Griswold,* (1870), and the *Confederate Confiscation Cases, Miller v. United States* and *Tyler v. Defrees,* (both 1871).

He, along with other members of the Court also validated congressional reconstuction for the South. Miller was also closely connected with the early judicial interpretations of the newly ratified Fourteenth Amendment. He wrote the majority opinion in the *Slaughterhouse Cases* (1873), declaring that the amendment did not restrict the state's powers to regulate private enterprise, a narrow interpretation which limited the amendment's effectiveness for years to come. Miller also took part in cases involving Granger regulatory legislation, first voting with the majority to sustain state regulation, *Munn v. Illinois,* (1877), and then reversing himself to declare such legislation a violation of the commerce clause of the Constitution, *Wabash v. Illinois,* (1886).

In addition to his judicial responsibilities, Miller served as a member of the Electoral Commission which decided the disputed Tilden-Hayes presidential election of 1876. He voted with the Republican members of the commission on all points at issue, thus helping to make Rutherford B. Hayes President of the United States. Miller also received some consideration for the post of Chief Justice in 1873, and again in 1888. Nothing materialized either time. In 1890, he grew ill while still serving on the bench. On October 13, 1890, at age seventy-four, he died in Washington.

Stephen J. Field

Stephen J. Field was born on November 4, 1816 at Haddam, Connecticut, the sixth child of Submit Dickinson and David Dudley Field. Three years later, the family moved to Stockbridge, where Stephen's father served as a minister in the Congregational Church. Reared in the Puritan tradition, Stephen was educated at Stockbridge's local school, traveled throughout Europe with his sister and brother-in-law in 1829, attended Williams College upon his return, and graduated from that institution with honors in 1837. He then read law in the office of his eldest brother, David Dudley Field, Jr., already a promising attorney in New York City. In 1841, he was admitted to the New York bar and immediately thereafter formed a partnership with his brother that lasted for six years. In 1848, he returned to Europe once more and toured the continent for about six months. Upon his return to New York in 1849, he immediately set out for California to seek his fortune among the thousands searching for the gold that had been recently discovered there. He arrived in San Francisco in December, 1849 and soon established himself in the area helping to found the town of Marysville which he served as its first *alcalde* and chief civil magistrate. This position provided him with his first judicial experience. At the same time, he established a law practice in the town. In 1850, he was elected to the newly formed California legislature, but when defeated in his bid for the state senate in the following year, returned to private practice in Marysville, where he remained for the next six years building both his practice and his political contacts. The effort was rewarded when he ran for and won a seat on the California Supreme Court in 1857. He was elevated to its Chief Justiceship in 1861 and remained in that post for two years. These years proved invaluable to his judicial experience especially in cases dealing with private property. In 1859, he married Sue Virginia Swearingen.

During these California years, Field became friends with a number of California's business leaders including Leland Stanford, owner of the Cental Pacific Railroad, and it was Stanford who recommended his appointment to the Supreme Court to President Lincoln. The President agreed and nominated Field on March 10, 1863. He was confirmed on the same day and took his seat on December 7, 1863 beginning the longest tenure on the Supreme Court of any judge in American history.

Throughout his long tenure, Field was the arch-conservative of the Court and its most ardent defender of *laissez faire.* Believing completely in the Court's right of judicial review of governmental legislation, he consistently defended business against any form of governmental interference. He was a strict constructionist, determined to assert the Court's authority in the face of Radical Republican reconstruction measures following the conclusion of the Civil War. To this end, he struck down Radical Republican reconstruction legislation in *Ex parte Milligan* (1866), and the *Test Oath Cases* (1867). Field continued his opposition to reconstruction measures in a variety of other cases that came before the supreme bench during the 1870s. Very often he found himself among the minority, and on several occasions the lone dissenter.

However, by the 1870s, new constitutional questions concerning private property and *laissez faire* came before the Court. Justice Field was, without doubt, the arch-defender of property rights and private enterprise using the Fourteenth Amendment's due process clause to strike down both state and federal regulatory legislation. The *Slaughterhouse Cases* (1873), *Munn v. Illinois* (1877), and the *Sinking Fund Cases* (dissent, 1879) all illustrate his philosophy.

During these years, Field continued a good friend of a number of "Robber

Barons" who viewed him as potential presidential timber. Various segments of the Democratic party concurred in this assessment especially following his support of Samuel J. Tilden in the disputed election of 1876. As a member of the Electoral Commission of 1877, he voted with the Democratic representatives for Tilden's election to the presidency, but to no avail. As a result, his name was placed in nomination at the Democratic National Nominating Convention in 1880, but nothing came of this attempt by his supporters. Throughout the rest of his life, Field always harbored ambitions for higher office, either the presidency or the Chief Justiceship of the Supreme Court.

Field continued his crusade in behalf of property rights in a number of decisions during the 1880s. Many of his opinions made substantive due process under the Fourteenth Amendment the rule of the conservative Court. Upon his prodding, the Court accepted the concept that corporations were persons within the meaning of the Fourteenth Amendment, and in several cases such as *San Mateo v. Southern Pacific Railroad Company* (1882), *Santa Clara v. Southern Pacific Railroad Company* (1886), and *Chicago, Milwaukee and St. Paul Railway v. Minnesota* (1890), he played an important role when the Court voided the regulatory powers granted to the states in *Munn v. Illinois* (1877).

During this same period, Field was busy presiding over the federal Circuit Court in California. As a result of one of his decisions, *The Terry Case* (1888-89), he was attacked by the plaintiff, David Terry, in a California restaurant. Field's bodyguard, a deputy United States marshal named David Neagle, shot and killed Terry in defense of the Judge. Neagle was arrested for murder, but released on a writ of *habeus corpus* issued by the Circuit Court. The case, *In re Neagle* (1890) was appealed to the Supreme Court, and the decision set a precedent when the majority ruled that the Circuit Court had not unduly interfered with the state's power in this matter.

A wide range of constitutional issues faced the Court during the 1890s, but Field never wavered in his position concerning the judicial protection of property rights. By this time, however, Field found his health failing. Although he was less visible personally, his constitutional ideas were often put forward by his nephew Justice David J. Brewer who had joined him on the Court in 1890. While it was Brewer who spoke for the majority in *Regan v. Farmer's Loan and Trust Company* (1894), and who delivered the dissent in *Budd v. New York* (1892), the ideas and even some of the phraseology were unmistakeably Field's. Again, in *In re Debs* (1895), *United States v. E.C. Knight Company* (1895), and the *Income Tax Case, Pollock v. Farmers' Loan and Trust Company* (1895), Field's defense of property rights rang clear. Old and sick, Field finally agreed to resign from the bench, which he did on December 1, 1897 after serving thirty-four years, eight months and twenty days. He died a year and a half later on April 9, 1899.

Joseph P. Bradley

Joseph P. Bradley was born on March 14, 1813 on a farm near Berne, New York to Mercy Gardner and Philo Bradley. His formal education temporarily came to an end after completion of grade school, because Bradley was needed to work on the farm on a full time basis. However, at the age of nineteen, he left home and went to Albany to seek his fortune. There he was befriended by a clergyman who got him a job, and helped him to enter Rutgers College in New Brunswick, New Jersey. He graduated from that institution in 1836 with an A.B.

Upon leaving Rutgers, Bradley taught school, worked on a Newark, New Jersey newspaper and read law in a Newark attorney's office. By 1839, he was admitted to the New Jersey bar and secured a position in the law firm headed by John P. Jackson, a noted railroad attorney. In 1844, he married Mary Hornblower, the daughter of the Chief Justice of the New Jersey Supreme Court.

Bradley exhibited considerable legal talent and during the 1840s and 1850s counted many important New Jersey business firms among his clients. During this period, he entered politics, joined the Republican party and became an enthusiastic supporter of Abraham Lincoln in the presidential election of 1860. When Lincoln became President, Bradley consistently supported his policies throughout the Civil War. With the war concluded in 1865, Bradley's rise to political prominence was meteoric. By the late 1860s, he had become a nationally recognized figure in Republican party circles and as a result, his name was suggested to President Ulysses S. Grant as a possible nominee to the Supreme Court of the United States. Grant agreed, and on February 8, 1870, he nominated Bradley for the highest tribunal in the nation. There was considerable opposition to Bradley's nomination based on a charge that Grant was seeking to "pack" the Court with two new Justices (Bradley and William Strong of Pennsylvania) in vacancies existing after Congress restored the Court's membership to nine from seven, in order to override the adverse 4-3 ruling given by the Court in the first *Legal Tender Case, Hepburn v. Griswold* (1870). Despite this opposition, he was confirmed by the Senate on March 21, 1870 and took his seat two days later.

Soon after he accepted his commission, Bradley voted with the majority, as his critics expected, to reverse the decision in the *Hepburn Case*. In the second *Legal Tender Case, Knox v. Lee* (1871), the Court gave the federal government control over its own currency. This decision established a pattern which Bradley followed throughout his entire career on the bench, support of federal power.

It is interesting to note that although Bradley had spent a good deal of his legal career as a railroad attorney, he became one of the Court's strongest supporters of state, and later federal railroad regulation. In cases such as *Munn v. Illinois* (1877), *The Wabash Case* (1886), and *Chicago, Milwaukee and St. Paul Railroad v. Minnesota* (1890), he consistently favored state regulation, either voting with the majority, or dissenting from its opinion when the Court struck down state control.

Bradley also played the key role in the decision of the Electoral Commission of 1877 which determined the outcome of the disputed presidential election of 1876. Having replaced Judge David Davis as the so-called "neutral" member of the commission, Bradley proceeded to vote with its Republican members on every disputed point, giving the Republicans an 8-7 majority and helping to make Rutherford B. Hayes President. For his actions in this matter, Bradley was criticized in many quarters for the rest of his life.

With Electoral Commission tensions behind him, Bradley spent the next fifteen years devoting most of his time to the question of governmental regulation of business. Although he voted in favor of governmental control over interstate commerce most of the time, there were occasions when he invalidated this same form of authority. Bradley had the unique gift of being able to clearly judge each case on its own merits, and for this type of approach few Justices of the Court have surpassed him.

While Bradley is not thought of as a dissenter, some of his finest opinions were delivered in opposition to a majority ruling. Many of these dissenting opinions later became law. For example, his dissent in *Collector v. Day* (1871), was sustained seventy years later in *Graves v. O'Keefe* (1939). Dissent at first characterized Bradley's opinions in defense of civil rights. In *Blyew v. United States* (1872), he appeared as a champion of rights for blacks according to the provisions of the Fourteenth Amendment, but later in the *Civil Rights Cases* (188e), and others concerned with this question, he voted with the majority to invalidate the Civil Rights Act of 1875. This was the only real instance of inconsistency in Bradley's record.

Unlike many of his colleagues, Bradley refrained from politics, living quietly with his family in Washington. A diligent worker and a meticulous lawyer, he had few, if any peers. His opinions were masterpieces of logic and realism. In many ways, he was in a class by himself. He died in his home in Washington on January 22, 1892, one of the finest Justices ever to grace the Supreme Court.

John M. Harlan

John Marshall Harlan was born on June 1, 1833 in Boyle County, Kentucky, the son of James Harlan a leading lawyer in the state. James greatly admired Chief Justice John Marshall for whom he named his son. John attended the local county grammar school, entered Centre College in 1847 and was graduated from that institution in 1850 with an A.B. He then studied law in his father's office, the offices of other Kentucky attorneys, attended Transylvania Law School for about a year, and was admitted to the Kentucky bar in 1853. He opened his own office in Frankfort where he practiced from 1853 to 1860. During this period, he joined the Know-Nothing party, became Frankfort's city attorney, worked in the office of the adjutant-general of Kentucky (1856-58) and served a term as a county judge (1858-59).

In 1860, with the Civil War imminent, he supported the Constitutional Union party's candidate, John Bell, in the presidential election of that year; its program of preservation of the Union through compromise seemed most sensible to him. When the war broke out, however, he became a staunch Union supporter and participated in a number of military engagements fighting with the Tenth Kentucky Volunteers. However, in 1863, his father died and he returned home to care for his family. The following year he was elected to the position of attorney general of the state of Kentucky. As a loyal Democrat, he opposed Lincoln's reelection in 1864, as well as most of the President's policies including the Emancipation Proclamation and the passage of the Thirteenth Amendment. However, once the war was ended, he rejected the dictates of the more reactionary members of the Democratic party in his state, and instead cast his political lot with the Radical Republicans entering into a law partnership with one of that party's leaders, Benjamin Bristow, in 1867. The following year, he followed his new party's choice and supported Ulysses S. Grant's candidacy for President.

Once a loyal Republican, Harlan became an ardent supporter of civil rights before the law and a staunch defender of the Thirteenth, Fourteenth and Fifteenth Amendments. In 1871, he unsuccessfully ran for governor on the Republican ticket. Following this political defeat, Harlan returned to private practice in Frankfort where he remained until 1876. In that year, he tried unsuccessfully to gain the Republican presidential nomination for his friend and partner, Bristow, but when that effort fizzled, he swung his support to Rutherford B. Hayes of Ohio. When Hayes finally became President after the Electoral Commission decision, he appointed Harlan to the Louisiana Reconstruction Commission (1877), which peacefully settled the gubernatorial election in that state. As a result of his loyalty to and efforts in behalf of his party, on October 17, 1877, President Hayes nominated Harlan for the Supreme Court to replace Judge David Davis who had resigned earlier in the year. Senatorial confirmation was secured on November 29, and Harlan took his seat on December 10, 1877, beginning one of the most controversial tenures the Supreme Court has ever seen.

Harlan served on the Court for thirty-four years and participated in 14,226 cases. He is best known for his eloquent, to-the-point dissents which numbered no less than 316. His total number of written decisions was 1,161, an all-time high for the Court. Early in his career, Harlan's judicial philosophy was clearly enunciated. He firmly believed in the checks and balances system of the Constitution, and as such, vehemently opposed the usurpation of legislative authority by the judiciary. During the following three-and-a-half decades he never wavered from that position.

This philosophy was clearly demonstrated in his many dissents in cases arising under the Interstate Commerce Act and the Sherman Anti-Trust Act, where the majority decisions removed much of the teeth from these statutes. Differing from his colleagues, he expressed a marked distrust of monopoly in any form. Harlan was never predictable in his opinions, but always exciting. One of his most dramatic dissents came in the *Income Tax Case, Pollock v. Farmers' Loan and Trust Company* (1895), where a 5 to 4 majority declared the income tax provision in the Wilson-Gorman Tariff of 1894 unconstitutional. He dissented again in a series of cases dealing with civil rights. In the *Civil Rights Cases* (1883), *Plessy v. Ferguson* (1896), and *Berea College v. Kentucky* (1908), he strongly supported the equal protection clauses of the Fourteenth and Fifteenth Amendments. During the *Plessy* dissent, he brilliantly attacked segregation and discrimination with a phrase that has become legendary; "Our Constitution is color-blind, and neither knows nor tolerates classes among citizens." Years later, it was Harlan's arguments that formed the basis for the legal destruction of segregation.

Dissent again characterized his opinions in the so-called *Insular Cases, De Lima v. Bidwell* (1901), *Downes v. Bidwell* (1901), and *Hawaii v. Mankichi* (1903), where he stated each time that the American Constitution did indeed follow the flag. While Harlan is usually considered a liberal, there were some cases in which his decisions were considerably less than that. In *In re Debs* (1895), and *Adair v. United States* (1908), he sided with the majority in sustaining federal injunctions in labor disputes, and helped to strike down that part of a federal act which had outlawed "yellow dog" contracts. Yet, he always defended the Sherman Anti-Trust Act, as in *United States v. E.C. Knight Company* (1895), and a state's authority to enact legislation beneficial to the health and welfare of its citizens in *Lochner v. New York* (1905).

Despite a few inconsistencies, Harlan's record on the bench was truly remarkable and would certainly qualify this "great dissenter" from Kentucky as one of the finest Justices of his time. On October 14, 1911, at age seventy-eight, he died in his home in Washington.

Stanley Matthews

Stanley Matthews was born on July 21, 1824, at Transylvania University in Lexington, Kentucky, where his father, Thomas Johnson Matthews, was a mathematics professor. In 1832, the family moved to Cincinnati, Ohio, when Professor Matthews became the principal of Woodward High School in that city. It was there that Stanley went to school, graduating from Woodward in 1837. He then attended Kenyon College in Ohio, receiving his A.B. from that institution in 1840. One of his classmates at Kenyon was another Ohioan named Rutherford B. Hayes with whom Matthews established a lifelong friendship.

Following his college graduation, Matthews returned to Cincinnati, read law in several local attorneys' offices and in an attorney's office in Columbia, Tennessee, edited a local newspaper, and married Mary Black, the daughter of a wealthy farmer in Columbia. He then opened a small practice in Columbia, but returned to Cincinnati by the end of 1844 where he practiced law intermittently for the next four years (1844-48). At the same time, he worked for an antislavery newspaper, the *Cincinnati Herald,* and through his work became friends with a number of Cincinnati's antislavery advocates. With their help, he secured the post of clerk to the Ohio house of representatives (1848-49). In 1851, he was elected to the Hamilton County Court of Common Pleas remaining a judge until 1853. Two years later, he was elected to the Ohio senate (1855-57). In 1858, President James Buchanan appointed Matthews United States attorney for the Southern District of Ohio. At about the same time, he joined the Ohio Republican party as did his old college friend Hayes.

When the Civil War began, Matthews resigned his post, and he and Hayes joined the Union army together. Matthews saw considerable action with both the Twenty-third Ohio Infantry and the Fifty-first Ohio Volunteers. He rose to the rank of colonel, was wounded at the battle of Chickamauga, but resigned his commission in 1863 having been elected a Superior Court Judge in Cincinnati while he was in military service. He sat on that bench for two years, but when his term was concluded, he returned to private practice in the "Queen City," and for the next twelve years worked as a railroad attorney. During this decade, he became a leader of the Ohio bar and was widely respected throughout the state. A loyal Republican, he did yeoman work in behalf of his party in statewide and national elections, especially helping his old friend and comrade in arms become President of the United States in 1876. He also played a leading role as Hayes's personal representative in negotiating the Compromise of 1877 which finally ended Radical Reconstruction in the South, and cemented Hayes's election to the presidency. For all of his prodigious efforts in behalf of his party, Matthews was elected a United States senator by the Republican dominated Ohio legislature to fill out the unexpired term of Senator John Sherman whom Hayes had recently appointed secretary of the treasury. During his two years in the senate (1877-81), he accomplished little, but he did go on record as opposed to the Chinese Exclusion Act of 1880 and in favor of a system of bimettalism. Finally, during the waning days of his administration, President Hayes, on January 26, 1881, nominated his old friend to the Supreme Court to replace Justice Noah H. Swain. The Senate, however, refused to act on the nomination claiming it was nothing more than a political accommodation. After James A. Garfield was inaugurated as President, he resubmitted Matthews's nomination on March 14, 1881, making his selection of Matthews a test of party loyalty. Through Garfield's influence senatorial confirmation was secured by a single vote (24-23) on May 12, 1881. Five days later, on May 17, Matthews took his seat on the Court.

Despite the fact that he was a hard worker, honest, skillful and basically impartial, his eight years on the Supreme Court were relatively undistinguished. There is not a single case, either decision or dissent, that clearly stands out to mark the record of Justice Matthews. A strict constructionist, his conservative tendencies were amply demonstrated in a variety of cases ranging from civil rights to state regulation of railroads and private enterprise in general. He always voted to limit the effectiveness of the Fourteenth Amendment as it applied to civil rights, and to use its due process clause to reduce or negate state legislation and control. He made little, if any, contribution to the Court's procedures or major pronouncements, and never introduced any original concepts. In only one case, however, did he stray from his usual conservative path. In *Yick Wo. v. Hopkins* (1886), he voted to extend equal protection of the laws to Chinese citizens. This seems to be in keeping with his earlier senatorial ideas concerning the Chinese.

By the middle of 1888, Matthews had become quite ill and was unable to fulfill his duties on the supreme bench. The end came on March 22, 1889, when he died in his sleep at his home in Washington. As one expert has written, "Matthews played an honorable if secondary role in the generally conservative Supreme Court of the 1880s."

Horace Gray

Horace Gray was born on March 24, 1828 at Boston, Massachusetts, into a family prominent in shipping and commerce. After attending private schools in the city, he enrolled at Harvard College from which he was graduated in 1845 with an A.B. Following a three year hiatus, he entered Harvard Law School, receiving his LL.B. a year later. He then read law in several Boston attorneys' offices, passed the Massachusetts bar in 1851, and began a private law practice in Boston almost immediately thereafter. Gray soon earned a reputation as a lawyer-scholar, a label that stuck with him throughout his entire career. He practiced in Boston intermittently between 1851 and 1864, serving, at the same time, as reporter to the Massachusetts

Supreme Court. In 1861, he published sixteeen volumes of that court's proceedings and enhanced his already notable reputation as a legal scholar. During his years as court reporter, he met many of the state's leading lawyers and established a law partnership with one of them, Ebenezer Rockwood Hoar, who later became attorney general of the United States. George F. Hoar, Ebenezer's brother, and later United States senator from Massachusetts, also became close friends with Gray. It was Senator Hoar who later urged Gray's appointment to the Supreme Court.

Politics and national affairs also interested Gray during these years. He joined the Free Soil party in the 1840s and became a member of the Republican party in 1855. While he performed no military service during the Civil War, he was a strong Unionist and acted as one of Massachusetts Governor John A. Andrew's legal advisors during the conflict. In 1864, Andrew appointed him to the state supreme court, where he served until 1881, becoming its Chief Justice in 1873. His seventeen years on the state bench were far more distinguished than his subsequent years of service on the Supreme Court of the United States. Despite his low-key approach, Gray was widely respected and admired throughout the state by colleagues and attorneys alike. A strict constructionist, his decisions in the Massachusetts court already reflected a strong concern for the sanctity of property rights. His knowledge of legal history and precedent was always held in the highest esteem by everyone with whom he came in contact.

As a result of these factors, and through the urging of his friend Senator Hoar, President James A. Garfield was ready to appoint Gray to the Supreme Court; Garfield's assassination in early 1881 delayed his elevation to the high tribunal. However, the new President, Chester A. Arthur nominated Gray on December 19, 1881, and senate confirmation came the next day. Gray took his seat on the bench on January 9, 1882. Gray's appointment marked the climax of the "rehabilitation" of the Supreme Court after its disastrous decline in public regard during the Reconstruction Era.

Gray served twenty-one years on the Court, and while his record may not have always been consistent, it was nonetheless fairly important. Gray's judicial philosophy was essentially conservative, but at the same time he was an ardent nationalist. It was this nationalism which colored many of his decisions, especially his majority opinion in *Julliard v. Greenman* (1884), where he upheld the government's control over national currency regulation. Inconsistency, however, was expressed in his decisions concerning civil rights in general, and equal rights for blacks in particular. In the *Civil Rights Cases* (1883), he voted to strike down the Civil Rights Act of 1875, but a year later in *Ex parte Yarbrough,* another civil rights case, he reversed himself and came to the defense of black civil liberties.

Not known as a dissenter, Gray, nevertheless, would take issue with the majority's decision on occasion. Two of his most famous dissents were given in the *Wabash Case* (1886), and *Leisy v. Hardin* (1890), when he spoke out in favor of a state's right to reasonably exercise its police powers.

Perhaps the most controversial and confusing decision with which Gray was associated was the *Income Tax Case, Pollock v. Farmers' Loan and Trust Company* (1895), which aroused great passion throughout the country. The Court, in a rehearing of this case struck down the two-percent income tax provision included within the Wilson-Gorman Tariff Act of 1894. Gray voted with the majority in declaring the income tax unconstitutional. For the so-called nationalist, his vote against a federal government measure was in itself unusual, but what is even more confusing is the belief by some scholars of constitutional history that it was Gray, rather than Justice George Shiras, Jr., as traditionally thought, who changed his vote on the question, first voting aye in the original hearing and then voting nay in the rehearing. Why Gray would shift his position on the income tax remains a matter of conjecture as does the actual identity of the Justice who shifted his vote from one side to the other.

A bachelor for sixty years of his life, Gray married Jane Matthews, the daughter of Justice Stanley Matthews, in 1889. But, during the last ten years of his tenure on the Court, he was plagued by a variety of illnesses which limited his participation in Court business. As a result of his physical condition, Gray resigned from the bench on July 9, 1902. Several months later, on September 15, 1902, the venerable scholar-judge from Massachusetts died.

Samuel Blatchford

Samuel Blatchford was born on March 9, 1820, in New York City to Julia Ann Mumford and Richard Blatchford, a prominent Manhattan attorney. Samuel was educated at private schools and entered Columbia University in 1833 at the age of thirteen. He received his A.B. from that institution in 1837, graduating first in his class. From 1837 to 1841, he read law in the office of New York state governor William H. Seward, prepared for and passed the New York bar in 1842, and entered his father's law firm in the same year. In 1844, he struck out on his own establishing a law partnership in Auburn, New York, and a few months later married Caroline Appleton of Lowell, Massachusetts. He remained in Auburn for the next ten years, moving back to New York City in 1854, where he opened a new law office specializing in international, admiralty and commercial cases. He was a competent attorney, and his practice and income both grew steadily.

During this period, he began collecting and officially reporting federal court decisions. In 1852, he published the first of twenty-four volumes of *Blatchford's Circuit Court Reports,* which covered cases from 1845 to 1877; most of them were admiralty cases. Subsequently, he also published *Blatchford's and Howland's Reports* (1855), and *Blatchford's Prize Cases* (1861-65).

In 1867, he was appointed a federal judge for the Southern District of New York, a post he held until 1872, when he was promoted to circuit court judge for the Second Circuit which encompassed the same region. In the mid-1850s, he had joined the Republican party and was regarded as a moderate in his political beliefs. He commanded great respect, was widely admired for his judicial qualities, and was a man of impeccable reputation. These attributes apparently convinced President Chester A. Arthur to nominate Blatchford to the Supreme Court on March 13, 1882. Senate confirmation came on March 27, and he took his seat on the bench on April 3, 1882.

Blatchford served eleven years on the Court, and was known as a procedural expert rather than a true molder of constitutional precedent. His specialities were bankruptcy, maritime and patent law, and as a result he was rarely assigned important cases. He contributed little to constitutional jurisprudence. Despite his moderate views, Blatchford was involved in a series of volatile cases that came before the bench during his decade on the supreme tribunal. Most of them concerned the Court's conservative interpretation of the due process clause of the Fourteenth Amendment. His most important decision came in 1890, when he delivered the majority opinion in *Chicago, Milwaukee and St. Paul Railway Company v. Minnesota,* in which the Court held that railroad rate regulation was subject to judicial review. This opinion further weakened the precedents established in *Munn v. Illinois* (1877), and greatly reduced the effectiveness of the newly enacted Interstate Commerce Act (1887). Most liberal elements throughout the nation severely criticized Blatchford's opinion in this case. Yet, two years later in *Budd v. New York* (1892), Blatchford, again speaking for the majority, reversed himself and affirmed the "public interest" doctrine of *Munn.* Blatchford stated that the issues in the two cases were totally different, and therefore believed he had not really changed his position. Upon investigation of the substance of these cases, his reasoning seems rather spurious.

Blatchford also participated in several important civil liberties cases, among them *United States v. Ah Lung* (1888), *O'Neil v. Vermont* (1892), and *Councilman v. Hitchcock* (1892). His liberal outlook concerning civil rights was reflected in all three cases, with the latter usually considered his finest hour in defense of civil liberties, and the most impressive moment of his

Court tenure. In *Councilman v. Hitchcock,* his opinion for the Court broadly interpreted the Constitution's Fifth Amendment privilege against self-incrimination.

During the early spring of 1893, Blatchford became ill. He barely finished the spring session of the Court, and on July 7, 1893, at age seventy-three, he died in Washington. Never a great jurist of the Court, his career might best be described in the words of Seymour D. Thompson, the editor of the *American Law Review,* Blatchford was "...a better reporter than a Judge."

Lucius Q.C. Lamar

Lucius Quintus Cincinnatus Lamar was born on September 17, 1825, in Putnam County, Georgia. His family was of French Huguenot ancestry. He attended the Georgia Conference Manual-Labor School for his primary education, and in 1841 enrolled at Emory College in Atlanta from which he was graduated in 1845 with an A.B. Soon after graduation, he married Virginia Longstreet of Atlanta, read law in a Macon, Georgia attorney's office, was admitted to the Georgia bar in 1847, and opened a law office in Covington, Georgia in the same year. In 1849, his father-in-law became president of the University of Mississippi, and Lamar took a position as a mathematics instructor at the university in Oxford. He was admitted to the

Mississippi bar in 1849 and opened a new law office near the university. He practiced law and taught mathematics until 1852, when he returned to Covington, where he went into partnership with E.C. Walthall in a new law firm. There, his practice and reputation grew, and in 1853 he was elected to the Georgia state legislature on the Democratic ticket. In 1854, he dissolved his partnership, moved to Macon and established a new law office. In Macon, he ran unsuccessfully for the Democratic congressional nomination from that district (1854). Lamar returned to Mississippi in 1855, purchased a plantation and slaves, and opened another law office. In 1856, he was elected to Congress, serving for two terms until 1860. His four years in the House clearly marked him as an extremist on the question of states rights.

In 1860, he attended the Democratic National Nominating Convention, but eventually walked out with the other southern delegates, when Stephen A. Douglas of Illinois gained the Democratic nomination for President. He then ardently supported the candidacy of John C. Breckenridge of Kentucky, the choice of the southern Democrats. However, when the Republican candidate, Abraham Lincoln was elected President in 1860, he attended the Mississippi secession convention, and personally wrote the ordinance of secession that took Mississippi out of the Union in January, 1861.

When the Civil War began, Lamar served as a colonel in a Confederate infantry regiment and participated in several military engagements. However, in 1862, he was appointed the Confederate commissioner to Russia and temporarily resigned his military commission. By 1863, he was back in the army serving as judge advocate in the Confederate army, where he remained for the duration of the war.

Soon after the war ended, Lamar returned to Mississippi, opened another law office, and took a position as professor of law at the University of Mississippi, where he remained until 1870, when he resigned to devote full time to his law practice. In 1872, he was again elected to Congress after the federal government removed his disqualification from holding public office. Once back in the House, Lamar became a leading spokesman for southern states' rights, but was clever enough to soften his position by also making a number of speeches in behalf of reconciliation. As a result, he gained a national reputation, and earned the sobriquet of the Great Pacificator. By 1875, Lamar had grown so powerful in Mississippi politics that he came to dominate the state.

Lamar also played an important role in resolving the disputed presidential election of 1876. He helped to work out the Compromise of 1877, which not only made Rutherford B. Hayes President, but also ended Radical Reconstruction in the South. In 1876, he was elected to the United States Senate where he remained until 1885. He continued to support southern states rights, but at the same time again advocated sectional reconciliation. In late 1884, President-elect Grover Cleveland appointed him secretary of the interior, where his record was an outstanding one. Finally, on December 6,

1887, Cleveland nominated him for the Supreme Court, provoking a heated debate over confirmation. In the end, however, Lamar was confirmed by the Senate on January 16, 1888, by a close vote of 32 to 28, and took his seat on the bench on January 18.

Lamar served only five years on the Court, becoming well-known for his strict constructionist views and traditional interpretations. He believed in a limited application of the Fourteenth Amendment's protection clauses, and in cases dealing with the regulation of interstate commerce, tended not only to side with the carriers, but also to favor judicial scrutiny of state railroad rate schedules. In *McCall v. California* (1890), *Leisy v. Hardin* (1890), and *Norfolk and Western Railroad Company v. Pennsylvania* (1890), these views were clearly expressed. Yet, he was flexible enough to sometimes sustain state regulation over interstate commerce when the "public interest" doctrine of *Munn v. Illinois* (1877) conformed to his own philosophy. Usually regarded as his most outstanding opinion was his dissent in *In re Neagle* (1890), in which he challenged the unlimited expansion of executive prerogatives. In 1892, he again dissented in *Field v. Clark,* speaking out once more in opposition to the unwarranted delegation of congressional powers to the executive. During that year, Lamar's health began to fail, and he was able to write only two other opinions. He returned to Georgia late in the year, and there he died on January 23, 1893.

David J. Brewer

David Josiah Brewer was born on June 20, 1837, in Smyrna, Asia Minor, to Emilia Field, the sister of Justice Stephen J. Field, and Josiah Brewer, a Congregationalist missionary. The Brewers returned home in 1838 and settled in Wethersfield, Connecticut. Local schools provided Brewer's early education. In 1852, he entered Wesleyan College, but transferred to Yale in 1854 from which he was graduated in 1856 with an A.B. He then read law in an uncle's office (David Dudley Field), attended Albany Law School (1858), and was admitted to the New York bar in the same year. In late 1858, he moved to Leavenworth, Kansas, passed the Kansas bar in 1859, worked as a notary public and served a term on the Leavenworth school board. Two years later, he married Louise R. Landon of Burlington, Vermont, and shortly thereafter was appointed commissioner of the Kansas federal Circuit Court. He practiced law intermittently between 1859 and 1861, but in 1862 was elected probate judge of Leavenworth County, serving in that post until 1865, when he was appointed county attorney. In 1870, Brewer was elected to the Kansas Supreme Court and remained there for the next fourteen years (1870-84). During his years on the Kansas bench, he already exhibited a judicial conservatism that would become more pronounced when he reached the United States Supreme Court. First, however, he put in a five year (1884-89) stint as Judge of the Eighth Circuit Court having been appointed to that position by President Chester A. Arthur. On the Circuit Court, he manifested a strong position in defense of *laissez faire* and private property.

In 1889, following the death of Justice Stanley Matthews, President Benjamin Harrison nominated Brewer to the Supreme Court on December 4. Senate confirmation came on December 18, and he took his seat on January 6, 1890, thus joining his uncle, Justice Field. Together, they would form the most formidable conservative combination in the history of the Court.

During this time, Brewer was also a much sought-after guest speaker, a frequent contributor to legal journals, and an author of several books on the law. A prodigious worker, his writings seem to reflect quantity rather than quality. From his speeches, articles, books and Court opinions, there can be no doubt concerning Brewer's ultra-conservatism, and he very soon became the chief spokesman for the rights of property in the face of state and federal regulation. In addition, he was regarded as somewhat of an expert on international law, and served as chairman of the congressional committee that investigated the Venezuela Boundary Dispute (1895-97), and later as one of the American members of the International Border Commission that settled the conflict (1897-99).

His right wing judicial conservatism was expressed in such cases as *Chicago, Milwaukee and St. Paul Railway Company v. Minnesota* (1890), *Regan v. Farmers' Loan and Trust Company* (1894), *United States v. E.C. Knight Company* (1895), *Pollock v. Farmers' Loan and Trust Company* (1895), and *In re Debs* (1895). In all of these cases, he either wrote or concurred with the majority decisions sustaining substantive due process under the Fourteenth Amendment, and the prerogatives of judicial review over state and congressional legislation. Although the Court in subsequent years began to modify some of its more conservative views, Brewer steadfastly continued in his ultra-conservative posture, even though his uncle had retired in 1897. Very often he found himself alone in dissent as the Progressive Era moved inexorably forward. In a variety of different types of cases he stuck to his antiquated thinking. In *Keller v. United States* (1909), for example, he opposed a congressional statute which afforded protection to alien women who were being used for the purposes of prostitution. In *Holden v. Hardy* (1898), and *Lochner v. New York* (1905), he refused to validate protective state labor legislation arguing that freedom of contract was being negated. However, in a complete reversal of character, he not only voted to sustain an Oregon statute establishing a ten hour day for women working in laundries and factories, *Muller v. Oregon* (1908), but also wrote the opinion for a unanimous Court. Brewer's simplistic legalisms and rhetorical mumbo-jumbo never fully explained why he so completely reversed himself on this freedom of contract question, except for his statement espousing special considerations for women because of their physical characteristics. Brewer remained on the Court for two more years after the *Muller Case,* but on March 28, 1910 he died suddenly of a heart attack at age seventy-three. He had served a total of twenty-one years on the high tribunal. He probably never realized that his opinion in *Muller v. Oregon* would be his most lasting and important piece of work on the Court in its establishment of a major precedent that would be used in future progressive legislation.

Henry B. Brown

Henry Billings Brown was born on March 21, 1836, at South Lee, Massachusetts. Following a prep school education, he entered Yale in 1852 and was graduated from that institution in 1856 with an A.B. After a year of European travel, he read law in an Ellington, Connecticut attorney's office, attended Yale then Harvard Law Schools, and in 1859 moved to Detroit, Michigan. He continued reading law in a Detroit lawyer's office and passed the Michigan bar in 1860. In the same year he opened a practice in Detroit, and was appointed a deputy United States marshal. Brown's major field of expertise was admiralty law. Soon after his arrival in Detroit, he joined the Republican party.

When the Civil War began in 1861, Brown avoided the army by hiring a substitute, a common practice at the time if one could afford it. In 1863, he was appointed an assistant United States attorney, and in 1864 he married Caroline Pitts of Detroit. By 1868, he had been appointed to the Michigan Circuit Court to fill out an unexpired term, but when he tried to win a full term to the Circuit Court in the regular election of that year, he was unsuccessful. Brown returned to private practice forming a partnership, and intermittently handled cases for the next seven years (1868-75). Politics, however, consumed more and more of his time. Though he failed to gain the Republican nomination for Congress from Detroit in 1872, three years later he was appointed United States District Court judge for eastern Michigan, and served honorably in that post until 1890. During these years, he was much in demand as an after-dinner speaker, published a collection of admiralty cases, and became a part-time lecturer at the University of Michigan Law School.

In late 1890, he was nominated for the Supreme Court by President Benjamin Harrison on December 23. Senate confirmation was given on December 29, and he took his seat on the Court on January 6, 1891. Since Brown was considered a technical expert on the law, he was most often assigned cases of a procedural nature dealing with admiralty, patent, and bankruptcy law. During his sixteen years on the Court, he made no major contribution to the development of federal jurisprudence. Brown was considered a "moderate conservative," usually taking a slightly right of center position, and rarely dissented from the majority opinion. He seems to have desired consistency and equanimity among his colleagues on the bench, and apparently strove to achieve these goals. Yet, interestingly enough, his three most important decisions contradicted this cherished aim. For example, he dissented in the *Income Tax Case, Pollock v. Farmers' Loan and Trust Company* (1895), voted with the majority in *Holden v. Hardy* (1898), and delivered the majority opinion in the very controversial *Plessy v. Ferguson* case (1896). Each of these cases provoked heated debate, not only among the Justices, but also throughout the country at large. But Brown always wished to be, as one expert has put it, "within the mainstream" of the political and judicial thinking of his time.

Brown's voting record on questions concerned with substantive due process and freedom of contract is a mixed bag. In *Budd v. New York* (1892), for example, he opposed the majority when it affirmed the "public interest" doctrine established in *Munn v. Illinois* (1877), but two years later, in *Lawton v. Steele* (1894), he reversed himself and voted in favor of that same doctrine. On freedom of contract, he sustained a state law establishing an eight hour day for miners, *Holden v. Hardy* (1898), but in *Lochner v. New York* (1905), he refused to sanction a ten hour day state statute for bakers. Perhaps it was Brown's "mainstream" philosophy which conditioned his reasoning in these cases, as well as so many others, where his record seems confused. During the last few years that he sat on the bench, Brown experienced increasing problems with his eyesight. As a result, on May 28, 1906, he resigned his seat on the Court. During his retirement years, he lectured, dabbled in Republican party politics and wrote a bit. Seven-and-a-half years after he left the Court, he died in New York City on September 4, 1913, at age seventy-seven.

George Shiras, Jr.

George Shiras, Jr. was born on January 26, 1832, in Pittsburgh, Pennsylvania, to Eliza Herron and George Shiras, a wealthy brewer. George, Jr., however, was brought up on the family farm located on the outskirts of the city. He attended a private academy near Pittsburgh for his primary schooling, entered Ohio University in 1849, transferred to Yale in 1851, and graduated from that institution in 1853 with an A.B. He immediately enrolled at the Yale Law School, but returned to Pittsburgh after a few months, and read law in a local attorney's office (1853-55). He passed the Pennsylvania bar in 1855, opened a practice with his brother in Dubuque, Iowa (1855-58), but returned to Pittsburgh in 1858, to become a junior partner in the law firm headed by Judge Hopewell Hepburn. In 1859, he married Lillie Kennedy of Pittsburgh and from this union two children were born. By 1862, he had opened his own office, preferring not to serve in the Union army when the Civil War broke out. During this time, he joined the Republican party, but did not take an active role in the politics of the period. In 1881, he refused appointment to the United States Senate by the Pennsylvania legislature, and except for his service as a presidential elector in 1888, he never held any public office, and never served as a judge.

Despite his lack of any judicial experience, President Benjamin Harrison nominated Shiras for the Supreme Court on July 19, 1892. His reputation, prominent background, and political affiliation made him a seemingly perfect choice for the seat opened by the death of Justice Joseph P. Bradley. Although some opposition to his nomination arose in the Senate, Shiras was confirmed on July 26, 1892, and he took his seat on October 10, promising to retire from the Court in ten years.

During his decade on the Court, Shiras did not particularly distinguish himself as a Justice. He wrote about 260 opinions and only 14 dissents. He would be considered a "moderate conservative," and was usually assigned cases dealing with procedural matters. His opinions were logical, well-crafted and extraordinarily boring. Although he sustained state regulatory powers during his first two years on the bench, he normally voted in favor of private enterprise, using the due process clause of the Fourteenth Amendment. Yet, at times, he could be quite independent minded, as illustrated by his vote in *Holden v. Hardy* (1898), which validated a state maximum working hours statute. However, in most cases dealing with substantive due process and freedom of contract, Shiras invariably sided with the conservatives on the Court. In *United States v. E.C. Knight Company* (1895), *Pollock v. Farmers' Loan and Trust Company* (1895), *Interstate Commerce Commission v. Alabama Midlands Railway Company* (1897), and others, he helped to curtail the Sherman Anti-Trust Act, void the income tax, and limit the effectiveness of the Interstate Commerce Act. Shiras also showed his conservatism, when he voted with the majority in *Plessy v. Ferguson* (1896), which established the "separate but equal" doctrine. Yet, in certain instances, he sided with the Court's liberal wing in defense of civil rights, *Wong Wing v. United States* (1896).

Despite his active, if not spectacular participation in Court affairs, Shiras, unfortunately, is chiefly remembered as the Justice who allegedly shifted his vote in the *Income Tax Case* of 1895, *Pollock v. Farmers' Loan and Trust Company*. It has been believed, but never proven, that he voted to sustain the income tax in the original hearing of the case, but in the rehearing, called a month later, he changed his mind and voted to declare the income tax unconstitutional. No real evidence existed at that time, or now, to prove Shiras's reversal, but he was blamed for killing the tax, and was severely castigated by those elements throughout the nation who had supported this progressive measure. Some modern scholars are of the opinion that it was not Shiras, but actually Justice Horace Gray, who changed his mind between the first and second hearings of the *Income Tax Case*. Be that as it may, Shiras continues to be remembered as the man who wrecked the income tax.

True to his word, Shiras retired from the Court on February 23, 1903, after serving a little more than ten years. He lived in quiet retirement with his family until his death on August 21, 1924 at the age of ninety-two.

Howell E. Jackson

Howell Edmunds Jackson was born on April 8, 1832, at Paris, Tennessee, the son of Mary Hunt and Dr. Alexander Jackson. After the usual primary schooling, Jackson entered West Tennessee College in 1847, and was graduated from that institution in 1850 with an A.B. He attended the University of Virginia Law School for two years (1851-53), read law for a year in the office of a relative, Judge H.O.W. Totten, completed his legal preparation at Cumberland University Law School in Lebanon, Tennessee (1855-56), and passed the Tennessee bar in 1856. In that year, he moved to Jackson, Tennessee, and opened a law office, but two years later, he relocated in Memphis where he entered into a law partnership with William Currin.

This firm was dissolved when the Civil War came, and Jackson accepted the post of custodian of sequestered property for the Confederate government in Western Tennessee (1861-65). Just prior to the outbreak of the war, Jackson married Sophia Mallory of Memphis, and four children were born before Sophia died in 1873. In 1876, he married Mary E. Harding, the daughter of a wealthy Tennessee landowner, and this union produced three more children. He also came into possession of a large horse-breeding farm through his wife's inheritance.

After the Civil War ended, Jackson resumed his practice in Memphis, and began specializing in corporate and banking law. He also joined the Democratic party at this time. In 1875, he was appointed to the Provisional Court of Arbitration for Western Tennessee, and was reappointed to this court in 1876, serving until its dissolution in 1877. In that year, he tried, unsuccessfully, for the Democratic nomination for judge of the Tennessee Supreme Court. He continued in private practice in Memphis for the next three years, during which time, he enhanced his reputation among Tennessee Democratic party leaders. In 1880, he was elected to the Tennessee house of representatives, where he remained until 1881, when the legislature elected him to the United States Senate. Jackson served as a senator from 1881 to 1886, and was known as a hard worker, and a devoted supporter of President Grover Cleveland's policies. He also became close friends with the junior senator from Indiana, Benjamin Harrison. In 1886, Cleveland appointed him to the Sixth Circuit Court, where he served until 1893. As a Circuit Court judge, Jackson built a reputation for scholarship and attention to detail. Most of his Circuit Court opinions dealt with patent litigation. When a vacancy opened on the Supreme Court because of the death of Justice Lucius Quintus Cincinnatus Lamar, his old friend, now President of the United States, Benjamin Harrison, nominated him for that seat on February 2, 1893. The Senate gave its approval on February 18, and Jackson took his seat on March 4, 1893.

Due to recurring illnesses, Jackson spent only a little over two years on the Court. It is estimated that his active service amounted to fifteen months, during which time he wrote less than 50 opinions and 4 dissents. Only three of his written opinions dealt with constitutional law, the remainder concerned with patents and banking. Even during his short tenure on the bench, Jackson displayed definite conservative tendencies. He supported substantive due process under the Fourteenth Amendment, opposing the majority view in both *Brass v. North Dakota* (1894), and *Budd v. New York* (1892), when the Court sustained the "public interest" doctrine of *Munn v. Illinois* (1877). Because of his illnesses, he did not participate in many of the other landmark cases of these years such as *United States v. E.C. Knight Company* (1895), and *In re Debs* (1895), but it is likely that he would have voted with the conservative faction of the Court if he had been present.

Yet, interestingly enough, if Jackson has any claim to fame as a Supreme

Court Justice, it comes from his dissent in the *Income Tax Case, Pollock v. Farmers' Loan and Trust Company* (1895), when the Court struck down the income tax in the Wilson-Gorman Tariff. Because Jackson was ill when the case was first heard, the Court had deadlocked 4-4 on the constitutionality of the income tax and scheduled a rehearing on the matter. When the rehearing took place about a month later, a visibly ill Jackson was present. It was believed that Jackson favored the tax and that his vote would now break the deadlock. But, as it turned out, Jackson's vote was not crucial, as one of the Justices who had originally voted to sustain the tax, switched his vote to declare it unconstitutional. Jackson, thus found himself merely one dissenter among three others, rather than the key figure in one of the most important cases of the period. Despite this unforseen turn of events, Jackson delivered an eloquent and moving dissent, probably the best opinion he had given during his time on the Court. It was the last speech he was to make in the Court, for a few days later, he returned to Tennessee, and there he died on August 8, 1895.

Edward D. White

Edward D. White was born on November 3, 1845, at Thibodeaux, Louisiana. One of five children, he was the son of Edward D. White, lawyer, politician, judge, five term congressman, and Louisiana's seventh governor. White received his primary school training at a Jesuit institution in New Orleans, and at St. Mary's Preparatory School in Emmitsburg, Maryland. In 1857, he entered Georgetown College in Washington, but when the Civil War broke out, he left college and enlisted in the Confederate army. Between 1861 and 1863, he served as an aide-de-camp at various army headquarters, but in the summer of 1863 he was taken prisoner at the battle of Port Hudson. After a short period as a Union prisoner, he returned home and sat out the remaining years of the war. By 1865, he had begun to read law in the office of a New Orleans attorney, then attended the University of Louisiana School of Law (1865-68), and passed the Louisiana bar in 1868. He then opened an office in New Orleans, and simultaneously plunged into Democratic politics in his state. In 1874, he was elected to the Louisiana senate, and having established himself as a power in state politics, was appointed to the state Supreme Court in 1879, serving there until 1881. He then returned to private practice, and for the next ten years (1881-91) became a pillar of the New Orleans community. He was a member of the New Orleans Law Association, and Chairman of the Board of Trustees of Tulane University (1884).

During this period, White continued to be active in Democratic party politics, and in 1891, he was appointed to the United States Senate, where he served from 1891 to 1894. There he was known as a loyal Cleveland Democrat, supporting all administration policies with the exception of presidential tariff reform. This attitude naturally brought him into conflict with Cleveland, who had made tariff revision in a downward direction, one of his chief priorities when he assumed office for the second time. Despite this fact, Cleveland nominated White for the Supreme Court on February 19, 1894, immediately after Senators David Hill and Edward Murphy of New York had invoked "senatorial courtesy" in rejecting the President's first choice for the seat, Wheeler H. Peckham of the Empire State because of Peckham's militant independence of regular party organization in New York. So great was White's reputation, however, that he was confirmed by his colleagues on the same day, and he took his seat on March 12, 1894. Eight months after he was appointed to the Court, he married Virginia Montgomery Kent of Alabama. White would serve on the Court for the next twenty-seven years, the final ten as Chief Justice.

Basically White was a conservative, believing in *laissez faire* and the limitation of both federal and state power expansion. Like the majority of his colleagues, he supported substantive due process under the Fourteenth Amendment. Yet his record on this question was not always consistent. In cases such as *Holden v. Hardy* (1898), *Hawkes v. New York* (1898), *Austin v. Tennessee* (1900), *Reid v. Colorado* (1902), *Lochner v. New York* (1905), and *Muller v. Oregon* (1908), he exhibited liberal tendencies in validating state police powers in the interests of the public. Yet, in other cases dealing with the same subject, he voted to apply due process under the Fourteenth Amendment, thereby denying the states the use of this power. On questions concerning freedom of contract, White's attitudes were decidedly conservative. He voted to extend freedom of contract to its greatest extreme in *Allgeyer v. Louisiana* (1897), and in *Adair v. United States* (1908), and *Coppage v. Kansas* (1915), he sided with the majority to validate "yellow dog" contracts under the same freedom of contract concept. In those cases involving the federal government's regulatory powers under the commerce clause, White's decisions again reflected ambivalence. In *Champion v. Ames*

(1903), and *McCray v. United States* (1904), he upheld federal police powers in regulating lottery tickets, and the sale of artificially colored oleomargarine, but in *Hammer v. Dagenhart* (1918), and *United States v. Doremus* (1919), he denied that same power in cases dealing with child labor and the narcotics traffic. He seems to have been far more consistent in cases concerned with the Interstate Commerce Act, where he normally voted to restore the teeth to this emasculated federal statute (1887). White was also intimately involved in the so-called *Insular Cases, De Lima v. Bidwell,* (1901), *Downes v. Bidwell* (1901), *Dooley v. United States* (1901), *Hawaii v. Mankichi* (1903), and *Dorr v. United States* (1904), in which he introduced the "incorporation" concept denying automatic and immediate constitutional guarantees to the newly acquired colonial possessions of the United States. White apparently did not believe that the Constitution automatically followed the American flag.

When Chief Justice Melville W. Fuller died in July, 1910, President William Howard Taft, insecure in his own political future, and harboring designs on the Chief Justiceship himself when his presidential term was concluded, decided to appoint a man of advanced years to the post, with the belief that such an individual would be able to serve in that capacity for only a short time. Taft would then be able to gain the Chief Justiceship for himself. Thus, on December 12, 1910, the President nominated the 65 year old White for the post of Chief Justice of the Supreme Court. Senatorial confirmation was secured on the same day, and White took his seat atthehead of the chief tribunal as the ninth Chief Justice in American history on December 19, 1910. White remained in that position for a little more than a decade, and during that period he tried to mold the Court to his own will. Early in 1911, he introduced his "rule of reason" dictum, and successfully persuaded the majority of his colleagues to use this new concept in many of the anti-trust cases that came before them. In the year this new idea was introduced, the Court applied the "rule of reason" in two landmark cases, *Standard Oil Company v. United States* and *United States v. American Tobacco Company,* both of which set the pattern for the Court's future actions in anti-trust litigation. Utilizing White's doctrine, the Supreme Court severely limited the Sherman Anti-Trust Act's effectiveness, and was denounced by Justice John Marshall Harlan as "judicial usurpation." Conservatism was the rule of the Court during White's tenure as it had been during his predecessors' stewardship.

White's conservative attitude toward increasing governmental authority softened somewhat during the last few years of his Chief Justiceship, but his strict constructionist viewpoint was never really abandoned. By 1920, the Chief Justice's eyesight began to deteriorate because of a steadily worsening cataract condition. His resignation was sought by some, chiefly ex-President Taft, whose ambitions for the Chief Justiceship were now stronger than ever, and whose goals had been frustrated by White's longevity. At first, the old Chief Justice refused to resign, but on May 13, 1921, he became gravely ill and had to be hospitalized. He lingered on for six days, finally succombing on May 19, 1921. Taft got his wish in October of the same year when he was appointed the tenth Chief Justice of the Supreme Court of the United States.

Rufus W. Peckham

Rufus Wheeler Peckham was born on November 8, 1838, at Albany, New York. His father, Rufus Peckham, was a successful attorney, had served as district attorney of Albany County, as a one term congressman, and as a judge on both the New York State Supreme Court and the Court of Appeals. Peckham was educated in private schools and in several European universities. When he returned home in 1858, he read law in his father's office and was admitted to the New York bar in 1859. He then entered his father's firm where he remained in practice until the mid-1860s when he opened a law partnership in Albany. In 1869, he became district attorney of Albany County, serving in that post until 1872. At the same time, he worked as a special assistant to the state attorney general. In 1872, he returned to private practice where he remained until 1881. During this period, he married, was elected to the board of trustees of Albany Hospital, and to the boards of several Albany banks. It was also during these years that he manifested a lively interest in Democratic party politics, becoming by the mid-1870s head of the Albany County Democratic Committee. In this position, he was a leading spokesman for upstate Democrats, an avid supporter of Samuel J. Tilden's bid for the presidency in 1876, and an ardent opponent of New York City's Tammany Hall. As a result of his work in behalf of his party, in 1881, he was appointed Albany corporation counsel, and during the following year, he was elected to the New York Supreme Court where he remained until 1886 when he was elected to the Court of Appeals, serving on that bench until 1895.

Peckham's tenure on the Court of Appeals was distinguished. It was there that he honed his conservative judicial philosophy which, in most cases, protected *laissez faire* and private property from governmental interference. On occasion, he was known to support measures designed to protect the public welfare, but not very often. These ideas conditioned his thinking when he was elevated to the Supreme Court of the United States.

That event transpired in 1895, ending a patronage debacle between President Grover Cleveland and Senator David Hill of New York. In both 1893 and 1894, Hill had blocked Cleveland's attempts to name a successor to the seat opened by the death of Justice Samuel Blatchford. Through Hill's influence, the Senate had twice rejected Cleveland appointees (William Hornblower and Wheeler H. Peckham), forcing Cleveland to appoint Edward D. White to the Court. In 1895, another vacancy occurred when Justice Howell Jackson died. After some wrangling, and with Senator Hill's acquiescence, the President nominated Rufus Peckham on December 3, 1895. Confirmation was secured on December 9, and he took his seat on January 6, 1896.

Peckham served on the Court for thirteen years, and with his already established conservative attitudes had no difficulty fitting in with the majority of his colleagues. Like them, he most often supported substantive due process in the interests of private enterprise. He was not an innovator and contributed little to the Court's jurisprudence. He simply "went along" with his conservative colleagues. This was illustrated in such cases as *Allgeyer v. Louisiana* (1897), *Holden v. Hardy* (1898), *Jacobson v. Massachusetts* (1905), and *Lochner v. New York* (1905), for which he wrote the majority opinion. In all of these cases and others, he applied either freedom of contract, or due process under the Fourteenth Amendment to their greatest extremes in limiting the reach of state authority over interstate business. His "go along" philosophy was seen again in *Muller v. Oregon* (1908), when he joined the unanimous Court in sustaining an Oregon maximum working hours law for women. We shall never know why Peckham changed his mind in this instance for he voted without giving an opinion. Most likely, he was again simply "going along" with his colleagues.

While devotedly conservative in freedom of contract matters, Peckham's record is much more liberal in the anti-trust cases of his day. On a number of occasions, he voted to sustain the Sherman Anti-Trust Act. These cases included, *United States v. Trans-Missouri Freight Association* (1897), *Addyston Pipe and Steel Company v. United States* (1899), and *United States v. Joint Traffic Association* (1898). These decisions partially rehabilitated the Sherman Act after the extreme decision in the 1895 *Sugar Trust Case.* On all other matters, however, he expressed his conservative attitudes, once again opposing the extension of any other type of federal police power. For example, he opposed the majority in *Champion v. Ames* (1903), when the Court validated a federal police power not recognized up to that time, and in *Adair v. United States* (1908), he voted to uphold "yellow dog" contracts in an interstate railroad case. Peckham continued to hold to his outworn beliefs during his final years on the bench and remained a strict constructionist to the end. That came on October 24, 1909, while he was still a member of the Court.

Joseph McKenna

Joseph McKenna was born on August 10, 1843, in Philadelphia, Pennsylvania, to Mary Ann Johnson and John McKenna, recent immigrants. In 1851, young Joseph was sent to a Philadelphia Catholic school, remaining there until 1855 when the family moved to the town of Benicia, California. Three years later, McKenna's father died, and Joseph went to work to support the family. Yet, he did manage to attend Benicia Collegiate Institute from which he was graduated in 1865. He read law at the Institute, passed the California bar in 1865, and opened a law practice in Benicia. Although he practiced law intermittently between 1865 and 1885, he was more interested in politics, believing that politics was the road to upward escalation. During the 1860s, he joined the Republican party, and with its help, was elected district attorney of Solano County in 1866, and reelected in 1868. In 1870, McKenna married Amanda Bornemann of San Francisco and moved to Suisan City, California, where he practiced law for the next five years. In 1875, he was elected to the state assembly from Solano County. In 1876, and again in 1878, he ran unsuccessfully for Congress, but in 1884, with the Republican party's political machine behind him, he was finally elected to the House of Representatives. Proving himself loyal to his party and faithful to his constituents, McKenna was returned to Congress in 1886, 1888, and 1890. During his four terms in Congress, he served on the House Ways and Means Committee, becoming a close friend and advisor to its chairman, William McKinley of Ohio. A shrewd politician, he continuously built his political alliances throughout the nation during these years.

These contacts paid off in 1892, when President Benjamin Harrison appointed him to the ninth Circuit Court of Appeals. Despite protests over his lack of judicial experience, and charges of patronage, McKenna's appointment was approved, and he sat on the Court of Appeals bench from 1892 until 1897. His tenure there was less than exciting.

When McKinley was elected President, he appointed McKenna attorney general of the United States, but this job lasted less than a year because the President nominated him for the Supreme Court on December 16, 1897, two weeks after the resignation of Justice Stephen J. Field. McKenna's nomination was denounced in the press, around the nation, and in the Senate itself, as nothing more than a political accommodation. However, after some debate, confirmation was secured on January 21, 1898, and McKenna took his seat on January 26.

McKenna served twenty-seven years on the Court. He was among the least qualified and least prepared men in the Court's history. As a result of his judicial inexperience and the lack of a solid legal background, McKenna never fully developed any consistent judicial philosophy, and his decisions often conflicted with each other in cases involving similar legal principles. For example, in *German Alliance Insurance Company v. Lewis* (1913), he ruled that state legislation regulating corporations was valid only when a state could show a "broad and definite public interest." This declaration became known as the "McKenna Principle." However, when Justice Oliver Wendell Holmes attempted, in the following year, to apply the "McKenna Principle" to a similar case, *The Pipeline Cases,* McKenna rejected his own arguments and was the lone dissenting Justice. In several other cases concerned with the same principle, he again dissented.

Yet, McKenna did not oppose all increases in federal police power, and in *Champion v. Ames* (1903), *Hipolite Egg Company v. United States* (1911), and *Hoke v. United States* (1913), he voted to sustain that power under the commerce clause. Moreover, in the notorious *Child Labor Case, Hammer v. Dagenhart* (1918), he dissented vigorously when the majority struck down a federal statute banning the shipment of products made by child labor in interstate commerce.

His inconsistency is again illustrated in his decisions concerning interstate commerce and manufacturing. McKenna invariably supported the Interstate Commerce Act, but just as invariably opposed the application of the Sherman Anti-Trust Act. Contrary to all logic, his decisions swung back and forth from case to case and from year to year. In several cases testing labor and social legislation, McKenna's record is difficult to comprehend. In *Adair v. United States* (1908), he again dissented from the majority's validation of "yellow dog" contracts, but in *Coppage v. Kansas* (1915), he reversed himself and declared "yellow dog" contracts constitutional. He opposed state maximum working hours legislation in *Lochner v. New York* (1905), but approved legislation of this type in *Muller v. Oregon* (1908), and *Bunting v. Oregon* (1917). McKenna's total record on the bench is filled with these inconsistencies and reversals. By 1922, McKenna was seventy-nine years old, the senior member of the Court and senile. He refused to retire when this was suggested to him, but he finally gave in and resigned his seat on January 25, 1925. He lived in Washington until he died on November 21, 1926, at age eighty-three.

Oliver Wendell Holmes, Jr.

Oliver Wendell Holmes, Jr., was born on March 8, 1841, in Boston, Massachusetts to Amelia Lee Jackson, the daughter of a Massachusetts Supreme Court Justice, and Oliver Wendell Holmes, a physician, and the acknowledged leader of a noted group of Massachusetts literati known as the Boston Brahmins. Young Oliver attended private school in Boston, and Harvard University (1857-1861), from which he was graduated in 1861 just as the Civil War began. Holmes enlisted in the Union army, served as second-lieutenant with the Twentieth Massachusetts Regiment, fought with distinction in several campaigns, was wounded three times, and rose to the rank of lieutenant colonel before being discharged in 1864. In that year, he entered

Harvard Law School, and received his law degree from that institution in 1866. He passed the Massachusetts bar in 1867, opened an office in Boston, and like his father before him, joined a group of young Boston intellectuals known as the Metaphysical Club. In 1870, while still in private practice, he was appointed instructor in Constitutional Law at Harvard, and became the editor of the *American Law Review* (1870-73). Through his position, he attained a reputation for research and scholarship. In 1873, he edited the twelfth edition of Kent's *Commentaries* and in 1880, he was invited to give a series of lectures at Lowell Institute in Boston, which were subsequently published as the classic study, *The Common Law* (1881). This work brought him even greater respect as a legal scholar both in the United States and Europe. Following the publication of his book, Holmes was promoted to the rank of professor of law at Harvard (1882), and was tendered a newly created chair of law at the university. In 1872, he had married Fanny Bowdich Dixwell, but they had no children.

In 1883, Holmes was appointed to the Massachusetts Supreme Court where he served for nearly twenty years, becoming its Chief Justice in August, 1899. During his tenure on that bench, he wrote almost 1,300 opinions, most of which reflected the liberalism and progressivism with which his name was soon to be associated upon his appointment to the Supreme Court of the United States. That appointment came on August 11, 1902, when President Theodore Roosevelt nominated Holmes on an interim basis. The nomination was resubmitted on December 2, 1902, after Congress had reconvened, and confirmation was secured two days later. Holmes took his seat on December 8, 1902, and remained there for the next twenty-nine years. He became the Court's most famous dissenter, and the leader of its growing wing of liberal Justices. Since the Court was decidedly conservative during these years, Holmes's liberalism often appeared forlorn. However, the Court, later in the twentieth century, shaped many of its precedents upon the dissents delivered by Holmes in an earlier period.

Holmes was an innovator and a molder of judicial opinion. He was never reluctant to speak his mind, and some of his most choice invective was reserved for those whom he believed were obstacles in the way of progress. His voting record throughout his almost three decades on the bench was always on the side of liberalism. He was an unmistakeable supporter of the Sherman Anti-Trust Act, yet in *Northern Securities v. United States* (1904), he criticized the statute on the grounds that it should have been designed to distinguish between "reasonable" and "unreasonable" business combinations. In another anti-trust case, *Swift and Company v. United States* (1905), he introduced his "current of commerce" concept. His dissent in the freedom of contract case, *Lochner v. New York* (1905), was among his most famous, when he criticized the majority reasoning on the grounds that the Constitution was not intended to embody an specific economic theory. He again dissented in *Adair v. United States* (1908), and *Coppage v. Kansas* (1915), when the Court validated "yellow dog" contracts. Both of his dissenting opinions were masterpieces of economic liberalism. One of his most well-known dissents came in *Hammer v. Dagenhart* (1918), when he attacked the Court's decision which had struck down the Keating-Owen Child Labor Act of 1916, by castigating the majority for its callousness in regard to "the evil of premature and excessive child labor." In several cases arising out of World War I, primarily those involving freedom of speech, Holmes's views differed. While he introduced his "clear and present danger" dictum in *Schenck v. United States* (1919), he refused to apply it in *Abrams v. United States* (1919), because he believed that there were degrees within the bounds of the "Schenck Rule," and that there should be a "free trade in ideas." His liberalism in regard to the First Amendment was clearly illustrated by his dissent in this case.

In other opinions, he condemned the majority's interpretation of the Fourteenth Amendment in *Truax v. Corrigan* (1921), when the Court invalidated an Arizona anti-picketing statute, argued, curiously enough, against the Court's decision in *Meyer v. Nebraska* (1923), which struck down a Nebraska act which prohibited the teaching of foreign languages below the high school level, and attacked the majority opinion in *Olmstead v. United States* (1928), which sanctioned wiretapped evidence in a case. Holmes called wiretapping "a dirty business." Holmes never believed that the common law was a "fundamental all-pervasive set of principles," and denied it was "a brooding omnipresence in the sky," a view that has become an important part of American constitutional law.

On January 12, 1932, two months before his ninety-first birthday, Holmes retired from the Supreme Court. Three years later, on March 6, 1935, the "great dissenter" died in Washington and was buried in Arlington National Cemetery.

William R. Day

William Rufus Day was born on April 17, 1849, at Ravenna, Ohio, to Emily Spaulding, the daughter of an Ohio Supreme Court Justice, and Luther Day, a prominent attorney, who would some day become Chief Justice of the Ohio Supreme Court (1874). Day went to the all-purpose schoolhouse in Ravenna, and then attended the University of Michigan from which he was graduated in 1870 with an A.B. He read law in a Ravenna attorney's office (1870), but in 1871 enrolled at the University of Michigan Law School. He left law school in 1872, and moved to Canton, Ohio, where he took and passed the Ohio bar (1872). He then opened an office in Canton in partnership with another young attorney, William S. Lynch. Within a few years, the firm became Canton's leading law office, and counted among its clients many of Ohio's largest corporations. In 1875, Day married Mary Elizabeth Schaefer of Canton, and, at about the same time, met and became very close friends with another young Canton attorney, William McKinley. Both men joined the Republican party and became actively engaged in political affairs. Day continued in private practice for the next ten years, but in 1886, he was elected to the Court of Common Pleas. However, he resigned from this bench six months later because of its poor salary. In 1889, President Benjamin Harrison appointed Day to the United States District Court, but Day was forced to decline the appointment because of ill-health.

During these years, Day continued to manifest a lively interest in politics, helping to make his friend McKinley governor of Ohio in 1892, and President of the United States in 1896. He was one of McKinley's inner circle of advisers, and in 1897, the President appointed him to the post of first assistant secretary of state where he remained until 1898, when he was elevated to secretary of state. Day led the State Department during the four active months of the Spanish-American War, but in August, 1898, resigned to become head of the American peace delegation at the Paris Peace Conference. Upon his return to the United States, McKinley appointed Day to the United States Court of Appeals for the Sixth Circuit (1899), where he remained until 1903. During those four years, he became close friends with two of his colleagues, William Howard Taft, the Court's presiding officer, and Judge Horace Lurton of Tennessee. All three men would eventually sit on the Supreme Court of the United States.

Day became the first of the three to achieve this honor, when President Theodore Roosevelt nominated him to the Court on February 19, 1903 to fill the vacancy created by Justice George Shiras's resignation. Confirmation was secured on February 23, and Day took his seat on March 2, 1903. Day spent nineteen years on the bench. Although he was a strict constructionist, he would be considered a "moderate-liberal," favoring the use of federal police power in many anti-trust and interstate commerce questions. However, he held the same narrow definition of the word *commerce* as the Court had expressed in the *Sugar Trust Case* of 1895, and many of his opinions in anti-trust cases were based upon that precedent, *Hammer v. Dagenhart* (1918). Nevertheless, Day saw a difference between *commerce* and *transportaion,* and thus was able to support certain aspects of governmental regulation of interstate commerce. As a result, he voted to sustain the Interstate Commerce Act in several cases including *Armour Packing Company v. United States* (1908), *Atchison, Topeka and Santa Fe Railway Company v. United States* (1914), *Pittsburgh Melting Company v. Totten* (1918), and others.

Day was also a firm believer in a state's ability to take care of itself, and as a result, he consistently voted to sustain state police powers in the regulation of social and economic matters. In cases such as *Lochner v. New York* (1905),

Barrett v. Indiana (1914), and *Minnesota ex rel. Whipple v. Martinson* (1921), this philosophy was clearly expressed. Never fully convinced by Chief Justice White's "rule of reason" dictum, he favored, instead, enforcement of both the Sherman and Clayton Anti-Trust Acts as proper exercises of the federal government's commerce powers. Perhaps his most famous dissent on this question came in the *Steel Trust Case,* when the Court dismissed the long pending anti-trust suit against United States Steel Corporation, *United States v. United States Steel Corporation* (1920).

In 1922, Day served as an umpire on the Mixed Claims Commission, but in May, 1923, he resigned from the Court at the age of seventy-three complaining of ill-health. Two months later, on July 9, 1923, he died on Mackinac Island, Michigan, where he had gone to rest and recover his strength.

William H. Moody

William Henry Moody was born on December 23, 1853, at Newbury, Massachusetts, to Melissa Emerson and Henry L. Moody. He grew up on the family farm, went to the local grammar school, then to Phillips Academy at Andover, and in 1872 entered Harvard University from which he was graduated in 1876 with a *cum laude* A.B. He then enrolled at Harvard Law School, but left after one semester, and went to work as a law clerk in the office of Richard Henry Dana, a Boston attorney and the author of the novel *Two Years Before the Mast.* He spent eighteen months reading law in Dana's office, and in 1878, passed the Massachusetts bar, and immediately thereafter opened a legal practice in the town of Haverhill, Massachusetts where he specialized in corporate law cases. During the next ten years, Moody established a reputation as one of the state's finest attorneys. In 1888, Moody served a term on the Haverhill school board, and from 1888 to 1890, he was Haverhill's city solicitor. Politics also attracted him, and he joined the Republican party, soon being appointed through its influence, district attorney for eastern Massachusetts (1890). He served competently in that position for five years, gaining a national reputation as the prosecuting attorney in the spectacular Lizzie Borden murder case. By 1895, he had become one of the most prominent lawyers in Massachusetts, and one of the rising stars in the Massachusetts Republican party, impressing such stalwarts as Henry Cabot Lodge and Theodore Roosevelt whom he met at a Republican club dinner in Boston (1895). The two men developed a close personal and political relationship thereafter.

In November, 1895, Moody was elected to Congress from eastern Massachusetts. He remained in the House until 1902, when his friend, President Theodore Roosevelt appointed him secretary of the navy. Some opposition to Moody's appointment arose in the Senate because of his lack of experience, but Roosevelt prevailed and senatorial confirmation was extended. Roosevelt and Moody were both strong advocates of American naval power, and their combined efforts forged a modern navy for the United States. Moody also streamlined his department eliminating much of the waste and bureaucratic inefficiency. In 1904, Roosevelt moved Moody to the Justice Department, appointing him the attorney general, a post he retained until 1906. At justice, Moody instituted dozens of anti-trust suits against the railroads and other giant corporations in pursuit of Roosevelt's progressive reform program and his "trustbusting" activities. He led the fight to enforce the Interstate Commerce Act, the Sherman Anti-Trust Act, the Elkins Act (1903), and the Hepburn Act (1906). His most successful prosecution came in *Swift and Company v. United States* (1905), which he argued before the Supreme Court.

In line with Roosevelt's progressive policies was his desire to reconstitute the conservative Fuller Supreme Court. To this end, he had appointed the liberal jurists Oliver Wendell Holmes, Jr., and William R. Day, and in 1906 he added a third liberal to the Court, William H. Moody. On December 3, 1906, he nominated Moody, and nine days later confirmation was given by the Senate. Moody took his seat on December 17, 1906, and remained a justice until 1910. Unfortunately, Moody never really emerged as a commanding Justice because of a debilitating illness which limited his participation in Court business. Because of crippling rheumatism, he actually spent just over two years (1907-08) in active service. Yet, during that short time, he was involved in about a thousand cases, but he wrote only sixty-seven decisions, all of which reflected a liberal judicial philosophy. For example, in 1908, he dissented from the majority in the *First Employers' Liability Case,* where the Court invalidated a federal statute protecting interstate railroad employees who were injured or killed working for the carriers (Federal Employers' Liability Act, 1906). In another employee safety case, *St. Louis, Iron Mountain and Southern Railway Company v. Taylor* (1908), he wrote the majority opinion sustaining the Safety Appliance Act of 1905. In these and other cases, Moody consistently supported the expansion of the federal government's police powers. *Continental Wall Paper Company v. Voight* (1909), and *Bobbs-Merrill Company v. Ruth Macy* (1908), are good examples of his judicial philosophy on this question.

Moody rarely agreed with his more conservative colleagues. yet, uncharacteristically, in *Twining v. New Jersey* (1908), he delivered the Court's opinion which rejected an argument that a state law permitting judges to comment on the failure of defendants to testify in their own defense denied them the rights of national citizenship. Moody declared that the Fourteenth Amendment did not automatically apply the first eight Amendments of the Bill of Rights to the states. In short, the liberal Moody stated that the states might abridge the self-incrimination exemption.

By the spring of 1909, Moody's rheumatic condition had so worsened that he left Washington, returning to his home in Haverhill where he was bedridden. His rapidly declining health compelled him to resign from the Court on November 20, 1910. He remained at home a cripple for the rest of his life, which finally ended on July 2, 1917.

Horace H. Lurton

Horace Harmon Lurton was born on February 26, 1844, in the town of Newport, Kentucky to Sarah Ann and Dr. Lycurgus Lurton. In the early 1850s, the Lurton family moved to Clarksville, Tennessee, where Horace was raised and went to the local school for his primary education. In 1859, he enrolled at Douglas College in Chicago, but returned home two years later when the Civil War broke out and enlisted in the Confederate army. He served with the Fifth Tennessee Infantry Regiment, fought bravely in a number of engagements and was promoted to the rank of sergeant. In early 1862, he returned home to Tennessee to recuperate from an illness contracted while in service, but after a few weeks returned to the army, joining the

Second Kentucky Infantry, and was taken prisoner with that unit at the battle of Ft. Donnelson. Sent to a Union prison camp at Camp Chase, Ohio, he soon escaped, joined General John H. Morgan's guerilla forces, and was again captured at the battle of Vicksburg. He spent a year-and-a-half as a prisoner on Johnson's Island in Lake Erie, but was allowed to go home in early 1865 when his mother obtained his release from President Abraham Lincoln personally.

Once back in Clarksville, Lurton decided to become a lawyer and entered Cumberland Law School at Lebanon, Tennessee from which he was graduated in 1867. He passed the Tennessee bar (1867), and later in the year married Mary Frances Owen of Lebanon. This union produced five children. He then returned to Clarksville, entered into a law partnership, and remained in practice until 1875, gaining a state-wide reputation as an outstanding attorney. In July, 1875, he was appointed on an interim basis as presiding judge of the Sixth Chancery Division of Tennessee, and was continued in that office on a regular basis until 1878, when he resigned to enter into a new law partnership. He remained in private practice for the next eight years (1878-87).

In 1886, he ran successfully for the Tennessee Supreme Court, and served on that bench until 1893, becoming its Chief Justice in his final year. On the Tennessee Court, he was known as a conservative with the uncanny ability to reconcile the opposing views of his fellow jurists. Within a few months of his election as Chief Justice of the Tennessee Supreme Court, President Grover Cleveland appointed him to the United States Court of Appeals for the Sixth Circuit, a post he held for seventeen years (1893-1910). During that time, he became close friends with two colleagues, William R. Day and William Howard Taft, whom he replaced as presiding judge of the Court in 1900, when Taft was appointed governor-general of the newly acquired Philippine Islands. On the Court of Appeals, his conservative judicial philosophy was amply demonstrated. A strict constructionist, he relied on old precedents for his decisions, and was not quite able to adjust his legal principles to the rapidly changing times. Nevertheless, he was well-liked by his colleagues and respected by all with whom he came in contact, especially attorneys who argued cases before the court. In 1898, while serving on the Court of Appeals, he was appointed an adjunct professor of law at Vanderbilt University. In 1905, he became dean of the Vanderbilt Law School, a post he retained until 1910.

In 1906, President Theodore Roosevelt bypassed Lurton, choosing the more liberal William H. Moody as his nominee for the Supreme Court, but on December 3, 1909, Lurton's old friend and colleague, William Howard Taft, now President of the United States, nominated him for the Court. Some opposition to his appointment was voiced because of his known conservatism, but Senate confirmation was obtained on December 20, 1909, and Lurton took his seat on January 3, 1910. Once seated, Lurton belied the fears of those who had been apprehensive of his conservative tendencies. In two famous cases in 1911, *Standard Oil Company v. United States,* and *United States v. American Tobacco Company,* he joined a unanimous Court in sustaining the Sherman Anti-Trust Act, although in these cases, and others like them, he followed Chief Justice Edward D. White's "rule of reason" concept. Nevertheless, in a variety of decisions, he voted with the Court's liberal wing in validating increased regulatory powers for the federal government, *Hipolite Egg Company v. United States* (1911), *Second Employers' Liability Case* (1912), and *Hoke v. United States* (1913). In cases involving the Interstate Commerce Act, he likewise voted with the liberals, *Minnesota Rate Cases* (1913).

Toward the end of 1913, Lurton, now seventy years old, grew ill, and was forced to spend several weeks away from the Court. He vacationed in Florida to recuperate, and returned in the spring of 1914 to resume his duties, completing the spring session of the Court. At its conclusion, he and his wife went to Atlantic City, New Jersey for another vacation: there, on July 12, 1914, he suffered a fatal heart attack. His body was taken to Tennessee, where he was buried in a Clarksville cemetery.

The Justices of the United States Supreme Court, 1789—1986

Justice	State	Appointed by	Replaced	Term	Life Span
John Jay	N.Y.	Washington	—	1789-1795	1745-1829
John Rutledge	S.C.	Washington	—	1789-1791	1739-1800
William Cushing	Mass.	Washington	—	1789-1810	1732-1810
James Wilson	Pa.	Washington	—	1789-1798	1742-1798
John Blair	Va.	Washington	—	1789-1796	1732-1800
James Iredell	N.C.	Washington	—	1790-1799	1751-1799
Thomas Johnson	Md.	Washington	Rutledge	1791-1793	1732-1819
William Paterson	N.J.	Washington	Johnson	1793-1806	1745-1806
John Rutledge	S.C.	Washington	Jay	1795	1739-1800
Samuel Chase	Md.	Washington	Blair	1796-1811	1741-1811
Oliver Ellsworth	Conn.	Washington	Rutledge	1796-1800	1745-1807
Bushrod Washington	Va.	John Adams	Wilson	1798-1829	1762-1829
Alfred Moore	N.C.	John Adams	Iredell	1799-1804	1755-1810
John Marshall	Va.	John Adams	Ellsworth	1801-1835	1755-1835
William Johnson	S.C.	Jefferson	Moore	1804-1834	1771-1834
H. Brockholst Livingston	N.Y.	Jefferson	Paterson	1806-1823	1757-1823
Thomas Todd	Ky.	Jefferson	—	1807-1826	1765-1826
Gabriel Duval	Md.	Madison	Chase	1811-1835	1752-1844
Joseph Story	Mass.	Madison	Cushing	1811-1845	1779-1845
Smith Thompson	N.Y.	Monroe	Livingstone	1823-1843	1768-1843
Robert Trimble	Ky.	John Quincy Adams	Todd	1826-1828	1777-1828
John McLean	Ohio	Jackson	Trimble	1829-1861	1785-1861
Henry Baldwin	Pa.	Jackson	Washington	1830-1844	1780-1844
James M. Wayne	Ga.	Jackson	Johnson	1835-1867	1790-1867
Roger B. Taney	Md.	Jackson	Marhsall	1836-1864	1777-1864
Philip P. Barbour	Va.	Jackson	Duval	1836-1841	1783-1841
John Catron	Tenn.	Van Buren	—	1837-1865	1786-1865
John McKinley	Ala.	Van Buren	—	1837-1852	1780-1852
Peter V. Daniel	Va.	Van Buren	Barbour	1841-1860	1784-1860
Samuel Nelson	N.Y.	Tyler	Thompson	1845-1872	1792-1873
Levi Woodbury	N.H.	Polk	Story	1845-1851	1784-1851
Robert C. Grier	Pa.	Polk	Baldwin	1846-1870	1794-1870
Benjamin R. Curtis	Mass.	Fillmore	Woodbury	1851-1857	1809-1874
John A. Campbell	Ala.	Pierce	McKinley	1853-1861	1811-1889
Nathan Clifford	Maine	Buchanan	Curtis	1858-1881	1803-1881
Noah H. Swayne	Ohio	Lincoln	McLean	1862-1881	1804-1884
Samuel F. Miller	Iowa	Lincoln	Daniel	1862-1890	1816-1890
David Davis	Ill.	Lincoln	Campbell	1862-1877	1815-1886
Stephen J. Field	Cal.	Lincoln	—	1863-1897	1816-1899
Salmon P. Chase	Ohio	Lincoln	Taney	1864-1873	1808-1873
William Strong	Pa.	Grant	Grier	1870-1880	1808-1895
Joseph P. Bradley	N.J.	Grant	—	1870-1892	1813-1892
Ward Hunt	N.Y.	Grant	Nelson	1872-1882	1810-1886
Morrison R. Waite	Ohio	Grant	Chase	1874-1888	1816-1888
John Marshall Harlan	Ky.	Hayes	Davis	1877-1911	1833-1911
William B. Woods	Ga.	Hayes	Strong	1880-1887	1824-1887
Stanley Matthews	Ohio	Garfield	Swayne	1881-1889	1824-1889
Horace Gray	Mass.	Arthur	Clifford	1881-1902	1828-1902
Samuel Blatchford	N.Y.	Arthur	Hunt	1882-1893	1820-1893
Lucius Q.C. Lamar	Miss.	Cleveland	Woods	1888-1893	1825-1893
Melville W. Fuller	Ill.	Cleveland	Waite	1888-1910	1833-1910
David J. Brewer	Kan.	Benjamin Harrison	Matthews	1889-1910	1837-1910
Henry B. Brown	Mich.	Benjamin Harrison	Miller	1890-1906	1836-1913

(Chief Justices in Italics)

Justice	State	Appointed by	Replaced	Term	Life Span
George Shiras	Pa.	Benjamin Harrison	Bradley	1892-1903	1832-1924
Howell E. Jackson	Tenn.	Benjamin Harrison	Lamar	1893-1895	1832-1895
Edward D. White	La.	Cleveland	Blatchford	1894-1910	1845-1921
Rufus W. Peckham	N.Y.	Cleveland	Jackson	1895-1909	1838-1909
Joseph McKenna	Cal.	McKinley	Field	1898-1925	1843-1926
Oliver Wendell Holmes	Mass.	Theodore Roosevelt	Gray	1901-1932	1841-1935
William R. Day	Ohio	Theodore Roosevelt	Shiras	1903-1922	1849-1923
William H. Moody	Mass.	Theodore Roosevelt	Brown	1906-1910	1853-1917
Horace H. Lurton	Tenn.	Taft	Peckham	1909-1914	1844-1914
Charles E. Hughes	N.Y.	Taft	Brewer	1910-1916	1862-1948
Edward D. White	La.	Taft	Fuller	1910-1921	1845-1921
Willis Van Devanter	Wy.	Taft	White	1910-1937	1859-1941
Joseph R. Lamar	Ga.	Taft	Moody	1910-1916	1857-1916
Mahlon Pitney	N.J.	Taft	Harlan	1912-1922	1858-1924
James C. McReynolds	Tenn.	Wilson	Lurton	1914-1941	1862-1946
Louis D. Brandeis	Mass.	Wilson	Lamar	1916-1939	1856-1941
John H. Clarke	Ohio	Wilson	Hughes	1916-1922	1857-1945
William H. Taft	Conn.	Harding	White	1921-1930	1857-1930
George Sutherland	Utah	Harding	Clarke	1922-1938	1862-1942
Pierce Butler	Minn.	Harding	Day	1922-1939	1866-1939
Edward T. Sanford	Tenn.	Harding	Pitney	1923-1930	1865-1930
Harlan F. Stone	N.Y.	Coolidge	McKenna	1925-1941	1872-1946
Charles E. Hughes	N.Y.	Hoover	Taft	1930-1941	1862-1948
Owen J. Roberts	Pa.	Hoover	Sanford	1930-1945	1875-1955
Benjamin N. Cardozo	N.Y.	Hoover	Holmes	1932-1938	1870-1938
Hugo L. Black	Ala.	Franklin D. Roosevelt	Van Devanter	1937-1971	1886-1971
Stanley F. Reed	Ky.	Franklin D. Roosevelt	Sutherland	1938-1957	1884-1980
Felix Frankfurter	Mass.	Franklin D. Roosevelt	Cardozo	1939-1962	1882-1965
William O. Douglas	Conn.	Franklin D. Roosevelt	Brandeis	1939-1975	1898-1980
Frank Murphy	Mich.	Franklin D. Roosevelt	Butler	1940-1949	1890-1949
James F. Byrnes	S.C.	Franklin D. Roosevelt	McReynolds	1941-1942	1879-1972
Harlan F. Stone	N.Y.	Franklin D. Roosevelt	Hughes	1941-1946	1872-1946
Robert H. Jackson	N.Y.	Franklin D. Roosevelt	Stone	1941-1954	1892-1954
Wiley B. Rutledge	Iowa	Franklin D. Roosevelt	Byrnes	1943-1949	1894-1949
Harold H. Burton	Ohio	Truman	Roberts	1945-1958	1888-1964
Fred M. Vinson	Ky.	Truman	Stone	1946-1953	1890-1953
Tom C. Clark	Tex.	Truman	Murphy	1949-1967	1899-1977
Sherman Minton	Ind.	Truman	Rutledge	1949-1956	1890-1965
Earl Warren	Cal.	Eisenhower	Vinson	1953-1969	1891-1978
John Marshall Harlan	N.Y.	Eisenhower	Jackson	1955-1971	1899-1971
William J. Brennan, Jr.	N.J.	Eisenhower	Minton	1956-	1906-
Charles E. Whittaker	Mo.	Eisenhower	Reed	1957-1962	1901-1973
Potter Stewart	Ohio	Eisenhower	Burton	1958-1981	1915-1985
Byron R. White	Colo.	Kennedy	Whittaker	1962-	1917-
Arthur J. Goldberg	Ill.	Kennedy	Frankfurter	1962-1965	1908-
Abe Fortas	Tenn.	Lyndon B. Johnson	Goldberg	1965-1969	1910-1980
Thurgood Marshall	Md.	Lyndon B. Johnson	Clark	1967-	1908-
Warren E. Burger	Minn.	Nixon	Warren	1969-	1907-
Harry A. Blackmun	Minn.	Nixon	Fortas	1970-	1908-
Lewis F. Powell, Jr.	Va.	Nixon	Black	1972-	1907-
William R. Rehnquist	Ariz.	Nixon	Harlan	1972-	1924-
John Paul Stevens	Ill.	Ford	Douglas	1975-	1920-
Sandra Day O'Connor	Ariz.	Reagan	Stewart	1981-	1930-

Bibliography

Abernathy, M. Glenn. *Civil Liberties Under the Constitution.* New York: Dodd, Mead & Company, 1968. Excellent case study book, tracing the various Court cases that have taken place involving the question of civil liberties.

Abraham, Henry J. "John Marshall Harlan: A Justice Neglected." 41 *Virginia Law Review* 871 (November 1955). A brilliant article taking a very positive stance in favor of Harlan's work on the Court.

———. *Justices and Presidents: A Political History of Appointments to the Supreme Court.* New York: Oxford University Press, Inc., 1974. A well-written short survey of the political considerations which have determined the Court's composition.

———. *The Judiciary: The Supreme Court in the Governmental Process.* Boston: Allyn & Bacon, Inc., 1973.

Acheson, Patricia. *The Supreme Court: America's Judicial Heritage.* New York: Dodd, Mead & Company, 1961.

Allen, Richard C.; Ferster, Elyce Z.; and Rubin, Jessee. *Readings in Law and Psychiatry.* Baltimore: The Johns Hopkins University Press, 1968. Fascinating and novel approach to understanding the minds and decisions of Supreme Court Justices.

Anderman, Nancy. *United States Supreme Court Decisions: An Index to Their Locations.* Metuchen, N.J.: The Scarecrow Press, Inc., 1976. As the title indicates, a very handy book to locate hundreds of landmark cases.

Anderson, Donald F. *William Howard Taft: A Conservative's Conception of the Presidency.* Ithaca, N.Y.: Cornell University Press, 1973. Attempts to explain Taft's failure as a chief executive.

Anderson, Oscar E. "The Pure Food Issue: A Republican Dilemma, 1906-1912." *American Historical Review* LXI (April 1956). Politics and law surrounding the act are discussed in detail.

Angle, Paul, ed. *By These Words: Great Documents of American Liberty.* New York: Rand McNally & Company, 1954. Excellent selection of primary documents, including a number of excerpts from Supreme Court decisions with introductions and commentary.

Bander, E.J., ed. *Justice Holmes Ex Cathedra: Wisdom and Humor of and About Justice Oliver Wendell Holmes.* Charlottesville, Va.: University of Virginia Press, 1966. Very rewarding book, containing quotations from, and anecdotes about, the Justice.

Barker, Lucius J., and Twiley W. Barker, Jr. *Civil Liberties and the Constitution: Cases and Commentaries.* Englewood Cliffs, N.J.: Prentice-Hall, Inc., 1970.

Barth, Alan. *Prophets With Honor: Great Dissents and Great Dissenters in the Supreme Court.* New York: Vintage, 1975. Excellent work detailing some of the great dissenting opinions in Supreme Court history with excerpts.

Bartholomew, Paul C. *Summaries of Leading Cases of the Constitution.* Ames, Iowa: Littlefield, Adams & Co., 1956. Excellent summation of many of the leading cases heard by the Supreme Court throughout its history presented in a very readable fashion.

Bell, Derrick. *Race, Racism and American Law.* Boston: Little, Brown and Company, 1973.

Belz, Herman. "The Constitution in the Gilded Age: The Beginnings of Constitutional Realism in American Scholarship." *American Journal of Legal History* XIII (January 1969). Challenges traditional notions about the nature of the Constitution and constitutional thought in the decades after Reconstruction.

———. "The Realist Critique of Constitutionalism in the Era of Reform." *American Journal of Legal History* XV (October 1971). Useful examination of early twentieth-century legal and constitutional thought.

Bergan, F. "Mr. Justice Brewer: Perspective of a Century." 25 *Albany Law Review* 191 (June 1961).

Bernstein, Barton J. "Plessy v. Ferguson." *Journal of Negro History,* v. 47 (Fall 1962). Interesting discussion of this landmark case and its implications.

Beth, Loren. *The Development of the American Constitution, 1877-1917.* New York: Harper & Row, Publishers, 1971. Broad survey, topically organized which discusses all aspects of national and state constitutional development between the end of Reconstruction and American entry into World War I.

Biddle, Francis. *Justice Holmes, Natural Law and the Supreme Court.* New York: Macmillan Publishing Co., Inc., 1961.

Black, C.F., and Smith, S.B., eds. *Some Account of the Work of Stephen J. Field. . . With an Introductory Sketch by John N. Pomeroy.* New York: Privately Published. 1881. This was intended as a campaign biography of the Justice when he harbored ambitions for the presidency. Highly laudatory.

Blake, Harlan M., and Pitofsky, Robert. *Cases and Materials on Antitrust Law.* Mineola, N.Y.: Foundation Press, 1967.

Blum, John M. *The Republican Roosevelt.* New York: Atheneum Publishers, 1962. One of the best biographies written about Roosevelt with a great deal of information on the Progressive period.

Boles, Donald. *Two Swords: Commentaries and Cases in Religion and Education.* Ames, Iowa: Iowa State University Press, 1967.

Boudin, Louis. *Government by Judiciary,* 2 vols. New York: Godwin Press, 1932. Very partisan study of the practice of judicial review.

Bowen, Catherine Drinker. *Yankee from Olympus: Justice Holmes and His Family.* Boston: Little, Brown and Company, 1944. Extremely entertaining popular biography of the Justice.

Bowers, Claude. *Beveridge and the Progressive Era.* Boston: Houghton Mifflin Company, 1932. Colorful study of Progressive personalities and issues.

Bowie, Robert R.; Rostow, Eugene V.; and Bork, Robert. *Government Regulation of Business.* Mineola, N.Y.: Foundation Press, 1963.

Bradley, Charles, ed. *Miscellaneous Papers.* Newark: Privately Published, 1901. A number of Justice Joseph Bradley's papers were published by his son shortly after the death of the Justice. Some good insights provided.

Breckenridge, Adam C. *Congress Against the Court.* Lincoln, Neb.: University of Nebraska Press, 1970. Details the struggles between the legislative and judicial branches of government in the area of judicial review.

Brown, Henry B. "Writings." 17 *Yale Law Journal* 223. A compilation of a number of out-of-court speeches and papers of the Justice.

———. "Writings." 44 *American Law Review* 321.

Brown, Ray A. "Police Power—Legislation for Health and Personal Safety." *Harvard Law Review* XLII (May 1929). Valuable study of the balance between police power and state social legislation.

Carson, Hampton. *The Supreme Court of the United States: Its History.* Philadelphia: University of Pennsylvania Press, 1892. Old, but still useful general history of the Court and its work.

Cassidy, Lewis C. "An Evaluation of Chief Justice White." 10 *Mississippi Law Journal* 136. Short, but important sketch of White's career as Chief Justice of the Supreme Court.

Cate, Wirt A. *Lucius Q.C. Lamar: Secession and Reunion.* Chapel Hill, N.C.: University of North Carolina Press, 1935. A discerning biography of the Justice from Georgia.

Choate, Joseph. "Choate on Fuller." 19 *Harvard Graduate Magazine* 11 (1910). Short laudatory piece by an ex-classmate of the Chief Justice.

Christopher, Thomas W., and Goodrich, William. *Cases and Materials on the Food and Drug Law: A Study in Consumer Legislation.* New York: Commerce Clearing House, 1973.

Clark, Floyd B. "The Constitutional Doctrines of Justice Harlan." Ph.D. dissertation, Johns Hopkins University, 1915. Interesting study dealing primarily with Justice Harlan's nationalism.

Clayton, James E. *The Making of Justice: The Supreme Court in Action.*

New York: E.P. Dutton & Co., 1964.

Cohn, Sherman L. *Materials in Constitutional Law.* Part I, *The Federal Judiciary.* Washington, D.C.: Lerner Law Book Co., 1968.

Congressional Quarterly. *Historic Documents.* Washington, D.C.: Government Printing House. 1900-1980. Official publication of complete texts of Supreme Court cases and congressional statutes.

Cook, Paul W. *Cases in Antitrust Policy.* New York: Holt, Rinehart and Winston, 1964.

Cooley, Thomas M. *A Treatise on the Constitutional Limitations.* 2d rev. ed. American History, Politics and Law Series. New York: Plenum Publishing Corporation, 1969.

Coolidge, L.A. "The New Secretary of the Navy." 54 *Independent* 744. (Spring 1902). Contains some biographical material on Justice William Moody during his days at the Navy Department.

Cord, Robert L. *Protest, Dissent and the Supreme Court.* Cambridge, Mass.: Winthrop Publishers, 1971.

Corwin, Edward S. *Court Over Constitution.* Princeton, N.J.: Princeton University Press, 1938. Excellent study of the Supreme Court's use of judicial review in blocking or controlling congressional legislation.

———. *The Commerce Power Versus States Rights.* New York: Oxford University Press, Inc., 1936. This work analyzes certain theoretical limitations on the commerce power.

———. *The Constitution and What it Means Today.* Princeton, N.J.: Princeton University Press, 12th ed., 1958. Brillian presentation of a general statement on each article and amendment to the Constitution.

———. *The Doctrine of Judicial Review.* Princeton, N.J.: Princeton University Press, 1914.

———. *The President: Office and Powers.* New York: New York University Press, 1948. Discusses Theodore Roosevelt's stewardship theory.

———. "The Supreme Court's Construction of the Self-Incrimination Clause." 29 *Michigan Law Review* 1.

———. *Twilight of the Supreme Court.* Hamden, Conn.: Shoe String Press, 1970.

Cummings, Homer, and McFarland, Carl. *Federal Justice.* New York: Charles Scribner's Sons, 1937. Interesting work on the role of the attorney general and the solicitor general in the handling of government cases.

Cushman, Robert F. *Cases in Civil Liberties.* New York: Appleton-Century-Crofts, 1968.

———. *Leading Constitutional Decisions.* 15th ed. New York: Appleton-Century-Crofts, 1975. One of the most outstanding case books with detailed explanations of selected decisions of the Court.

Cushman, Robert E. "Social and Economic Controls Through Federal Taxation." *Minnesota Law Review* XVIII (June 1934). Presents a survey of taxation as an instrument of federal power.

———. "The Social and Economic Interpretation of the Fourteenth Amendment." *Michigan Law Review* XX (May 1922). Discusses the role of due process in the new judicial review.

Davis, Elbridge B., and Davis, Harold A. "Mr. Justice Gray: Some Aspects of His Judicial Career." 41 *American Bar Association Journal* 421. Presents some interesting material on the life and career of the Justice.

Dishman, Robert B. "Mr. Justice White and the Rule of Reason." 13 *The Review of Politics* 229 (Fall 1951). Interesting reappraisal of the origins of White's concept and several of its applications.

Doak, H.M. "Howell Edmunds Jackson." 1897 *Procedings of the Bar Association of Tennessee* 76. With a full-scale biography on Justice Jackson lacking, this is about the most informative piece of work that now exists, but it is really quite superficial.

———. "Howell Edmunds Jackson." 5 *Green Bag* 209 (Spring 1893). Earlier version of the same material presented in the above article.

Dumbauld, Edward. *The Constitution of the United States.* Norman, Okla.: University of Oklahoma Press, 1964.

Dunham, Allison, and Kurland, Philip B., eds. *Mr. Justice.* Chicago: University of Chicago Press, 1964. Authorities in the field have written short biographies for this work, which treats selected members of the Supreme Court as prototypes of various periods and philosophy.

Durden, R.F. *The Climax of Populism: The Election of 1896.* Lexington, Ky.: University of Kentucky Press, 1965. Superior study of the forces that created Populism and the culmination of this movement in the McKinley-Bryan election.

Eggert, Gerald G. *Richard Olney: Evolution of a Statesman.* University Park, Pa.: Pennsylvania State University Press, 1974. Especially valuable for Olney's years as attorney general detailing both the *Debs* and *Income Tax* cases.

Emerson, Thomas I.; Haber, David; and Dorsen, Norman. *Political and Civil Rights in the United States: A Collection of Legal and Related Materials.* 2 vols. Boston: Little, Brown and Company, 1967.

Fairman, Charles. *Mr. Justice Miller and the Supreme Court, 1862-1890.* Cambridge, Mass.: Harvard University Press, 1939. Rich account of the Justice, the Court, and constitutional development.

———. "Justice Samuel Miller: A Study of a Judicial Statesman." 50 *Political Science Quarterly* 15.

———. "Samuel F. Miller, Justice of the Supreme Court." 10 *Vanderbilt Law Review* 193.

———. "The Education of a Justice: Justice Bradley and Some of His Colleagues." 1 *Stanford Law Review* 217. Interesting article, giving some biographical material on Bradley, but more important for its discussion of Bradley's relationship with Justices Brewer, Field, and Miller.

———. "The So-Called Granger Cases, Lord Hale, and Justice Bradley." *Stanford Law Review* V (July 1953).

———. "What Makes a Great Justice? Mr. Justice Bradley and the Supreme Court, 1870-1892." 30 *Boston University Law Review* 49. Excellent article on Bradley's work on the Court and a detailed discussion of his judicial philosophy.

Farrelly, David G. "Justice Harlan's Dissent in the Pollock Case." 24 *Southern California Law Review* 175. Looks at Harlan's attitudes toward the income tax, civil rights, and other vital issues of the day.

Faulkner, Harold U. *Politics, Reform and Expansion, 1890-1900.* New York: Harper & Row Publishers, 1959. Excellent general study of this crucial decade, containing much background material on the early era of national economic regulation.

———. *The Quest for Social Justice, 1898-1914.* New York: Macmillan Publishing Co., Inc., 1931. Very good study of the Progressive era. Detailed discussion of the passage of the Pure Food and Drug and Livestock acts.

Field, Stephen J. *The Opinions and Papers of Stephen J. Field.* New York: Privately Published, undated.

———. *Personal Reminiscences of Early Days in California.* Field Papers in California State Library, Sutro Branch.

Fisher, Joe A. "The Knight Case Revisited." *Historian* XXXV (May 1973). Blames the Sugar Trust decision on the incompetence of the government attorney who handled the case rather than the bias of the Court.

Frank, John P. "Supreme Court Appointments." 1941 *Wisconsin Law Review* 351. Discusses the circumstances surrounding the confirmation of Melville Fuller as Chief Justice.

Frankfurter, Felix. "Hours of Labor and Realism in Constitutional Law." *Harvard Law Review* XXIX (February 1916). Detailed survey of maximum hours cases before 1916.

———., ed. *Mr. Justice Holmes.* New York: Coward, McCann & Geoghegan, Inc., 1931. A compilation of Justice Holmes's writings with commentary.

———. *Mr. Justice Holmes and the Supreme Court.* Cambridge, Mass.: Harvard University Press, 1939, 1961. Excellent short study of Holmes's legal and constitutional philosophy.

Fruend, Ernst. *The Police Power.* Chicago: University of Chicago Press, 1904. Includes a detailed discussion of the *Munn* case and its later implications.

Freund, Paul A., ed. *The History of the Supreme Court of the United States.* 11 vols. Washington, D.C.: The Oliver Wendell Holmes, Jr. Devise, 1971-. . . Extremely detailed, comprehensive, massive work on the history of the Court from the eighteenth century to 1941. Each volume is being written by a specialist on that period of the Court's history.

Friedman, Lawrence. *A History of American Law.* New York: Simon & Schuster, Inc., 1973.

Friedman, Leon, and Fred L. Israel, eds. *The Justices of the United States Supreme Court, 1789-1969, Their Lives and Major Opinions.* 4 vols. New York: Chelsea House, 1969. Detailed series of ninety-seven detailed biographical sketches, containing much information about the lives, careers, and judicial philosophy of the Justices. Also contains major opinions of the individual Justices with short introductions. A must for students of the Court.

Fusilier, H. Lee, and Darnell, Jerome C. *Competition and Public Policy; Cases in Antitrust.* Englewood Cliffs, N.J.: Prentice-Hall, Inc., 1971.

Gaedecke, Walter R. "Rights, Interests and the Court: The Jurisprudence of Mr. Justice Stephen J. Field." Ph.D. dissertation, University of Chicago, 1958. Only full-length study of Justice Field. While informative, needs greater development.

Galloway, John. *The Supreme Court and the Rights of the Accused.* New York: Facts on File, 1973.

Gamer, R.E. "Justice Brewer and Substantive Due Process: A Conservative Court Revisited." 18 *Vanderbilt Law Review* 615. Well constructed article explaining the Court's philosophy toward interpreting due process under the Fourteenth Amendment with Justice Field as the leader in this move.

Garraty, John A., ed. *Quarrels that Have Shaped the Constitution.* New York: Harper & Row Publishers, 1964.

———. *The New Commonwealth, 1877-1896.* New York: Harper & Row Publishers, 1968. Well-written survey of this crucial period in American history, beginning with the Granger Movement and concluding with the election of 1896.

Gould, Lewis L., ed. *The Progressive Era.* Syracuse, N.Y.: Syracuse University Press, 1974. Collection of essays on this period by scholars who do not take the New Left approach.

Graham, Howard J. "Justice Field and the Fourteenth Amendment." 52 *Yale Law Journal* 851. Investigates Justice Field's approach to due process under the Fourteenth Amendment.

Gregory, Charles O. *Labor and the Law.* New York: W.W. Norton & Company, Inc., 1946. Very useful discussion on the *Debs* case and the use of the federal injunction in labor disputes.

———. *Samuel Freeman Miller: A Biography.* Iowa City, Iowa: University of Iowa Press, 1906. Old, but valuable biography on the Justice, with an appendix of year by year opinions.

Greve, Charles T. "Stanley Matthews." In *Great American Lawyers,* edited by William D. Lewis. (Philadelphia 1909). One of the few pieces of literature on this Justice, containing some useful biographical material.

Grossman, Joel B., and Wells, Richard. *Constitutional Law and Judicial*

Policy Making. New York: John Wiley & Sons, Inc., 1972.

Hacker, Louis. *The Shaping of the American Tradition*. New York: Columbia University Press, 1947. Classic study of the development of rights and privileges under the Constitution.

Hagemann, Gerard. *The Man on the Bench*. South Bend, Ind.: University of Notre Dame Press, 1962. An informative biography about Justice Edward D. White's career on the Court.

Haines, Charles G. "Judicial Review Implied Limitations on Legislatures." 2 *Texas Law Review* 257, 387. Authoritative survey of the growth of substantive due process as a technique of conservative judicial review.

———. "Judicial Review of Legislation in the United States and the Doctrine of Vested Rights." *Texas Law Review* II, III (June, December 1924).

———. *The American Doctrine of Judicial Supremacy*. Berkeley: University of California Press, 1932. Good general study of judicial review as a constitutional, political, and social institution.

Hale, R.L. "Judicial Review Versus Doctrinaire Democracy." *American Bar Association Journal* (1924). Interesting article written from a pro-Court point of view.

Hall, A. Oakey. "Rufus W. Peckham," 8 *Green Bag* (1896). Although old, this still remains the most valuable short piece on the Justice's life and career, written by the ex-mayor of New York City during the Tweed Ring days.

Halsell, W.D. "L.Q.C. Lamar, Associate Justice of the Supreme Court." 5 *Journal of Mississippi History* 59. Contains some valuable biographical information especially about Lamar's years in Mississippi.

Handler, Milton. *Cases and Materials on Trade Regulation*. Mineola, N.Y.: Foundation Press, 1967.

———, and Hays, Paul. *Cases and Materials on Labor Law*. St. Paul, Minn.: West Publishing Co., 1963.

Hartman, Harold F. "Constitutional Doctrines of Edward D. White." Ph.D. dissertation, Cornell University, 1936. Very good examination of several of the novel concepts introduced by White on the bench, especially his "rule of reason."

Hartz, Louis. "John M. Harlan in Kentucky, 1855-1877." 14 *Filson Club Historical Quarterly* 17. Solid study concerning Harlan's Kentucky years and his transformation from states rights Southerner to ardent nationalist.

Helfman, M. "The Contested Confirmation of Stanley Matthews to the United States Supreme Court." 8 *Bulletin of the Historical and Philosophical Society of Ohio in the War* II (1868). Old, but very useful article detailing the Senate fight over Matthews's appointment to the Court.

Henkin, Louis. *Foreign Affairs and the Constitution*. Mineola, N.Y.:

Foundation Press, 1972. Fascinating study of the Supreme Court's role in the conduct of foreign affairs and its application of judicial review to administrative policies connected with diplomacy.

Hicks, John D. *The Populist Revolt.* Minneapolis, Minn.: University of Minnesota Press, 1930. Best study of this agrarian movement with special emphasis on the passage of the income tax law of 1894.

Higham, John. *Strangers in the Land.* New Brunswick, N.J.: Rutgers University Press, 1955. Solid work on American immigration and the problems created by it in the period prior to World War I.

Hirschfield, Robert S. *The Constitution and the Court: The Development of the Basic Law Through Judicial Interpretation.* New York: Random House, Inc., 1962. Well-written, erudite study of the development of legal principles through the process of judicial review.

Hoar, George F. "Memoir of Horace Gray." 18 *Proceedings Massachusetts Historical Society,* second series (1903-5). Interesting piece on the Justice, written in a very laudatory manner by a very old friend.

Hockett, H.C. *Constitutional History of the United States.* 2 vols. New York: Macmillan Publishing Co., Inc., 1939. One of the classic studies on the Court and constitutional development. Needs to be updated, but very good on the Fuller years.

Hoffman, P.T. "Theodore Roosevelt and the Appointment of Mr. Justice Moody." 18 *Vanderbilt Law Review* 545. Excellent article on the relationship between Moody and the President and the motivating factors in Roosevelt's appointment of Moody to the Court.

Hoogenboom, Ari, and Hoogenboom, Olive. *A History of the I.C.C.: From Panacea to Palliative.* New York: W. W. Norton & Company, 1976. One of the best general surveys on the act and its uses.

Howe, Mark DeWolfe., ed. *Later Years at the Saturday Club, 1870-1920.* Boston: Little, Brown and Company, 1927. Contains some interesting sketches of several of the Justices.

———. *Oliver Wendell Holmes: The Proving Years, 1870-1882.* Cambridge, Mass.: Harvard University Press, 1963. The best biography written about the great Justice from Massachusetts.

———. *Oliver Wendell Holmes: The Shaping Years, 1841-1870.* Cambridge, Mass.: Harvard University Press, 1957. The first volume of the definitive work on Holmes. The author died before he could produce the projected final volumes of this massive biography.

———., ed. *The Holmes-Pollock Letters.* 2 vols. Cambridge, Mass.: Harvard University Press, 1941. Very useful collection revealing much of the judicial philosophy of the Justice.

———., ed, *The Occasional Speeches of Justice Oliver Wendell Holmes.* Cambridge, Mass.: Harvard University Press, 1962. Excellent collection of out-of-court addresses of Holmes.

Joyce, W.E. "Edward White: The Louisiana Years." 41 *Tulane Law Review*

751. Excellent on the early years of White's early life and career.

Jones, Alan. "Thomas M. Cooley and Laissez-Faire Constitutionalism: A Reconsideration." *Journal of American History* LIII (March 1967).

Jones, Peter d'A. *The Consumer Society: A History of American Capitalism.* Baltimore: Penguin Books, 1969.

———. *The Robber Barons Revisited.* Boston: D.C. Heath & Company, 1968. Eminently readable volume on the great industrialists of the nineteenth century, the trusts they created, and the reactions to their monopolistic practices.

Kales, A.M. "New Methods in Due Process Cases." *American Political Science Review* XII (May 1918). Discusses the Court's new uses for the Fourteenth Amendment's due process clause by the end of World War I.

Kauper, Paul G. *Constitutional Law: Cases and Materials.* Boston: Little, Brown and Company, 1972. An excellent case study volume, very well recognized by experts in the field.

———. *Frontiers of Constitutional Liberty.* Ann Arbor, Mich.: University of Michigan Press, 1956. Interesting book which examines the development of a number of judicial precedents.

Kelly, Alfred H., and Harbison, Winfred A. *The American Constitution: Its Origins and Development.* 6th ed. New York: W.W. Norton & Company, Inc., 1983. One of the best general surveys on constitutional history. A standard book in the field, very readable and well organized.

Kent, Charles A. *Memoir of Henry Billings Brown.* New York: Charles Scribner's Sons, 1915. Brief study, but the only book length treatment of the Justice to date.

King, Willard L. *Melville Weston Fuller, Chief Justice of the United States, 1888-1910.* New York: Macmillan Publishing Co., Inc., 1950. The sole full-length biography of the Chief Justice primarily concentrates on his Court career.

Klinkhamer, Marie C. *Edward Douglas White, Chief Justice of the United States.* Washington, D.C.: Catholic University of America Press, 1943. Probably the most complete and informative work about Justice White. Written originally as a doctoral dissertation.

———. "Joseph P. Bradley: Private and Public Opinions of a Political Justice," 38 *University of Detroit Law Journal* 150. Very interesting study of the New Jersey Justice.

———. "The Legal Philosophy of Edward Douglas White." 35 *University of Detroit Law Journal* 174.

Kolko, Gabriel. *Railroads and Regulation, 1877-1916.* New York: W.W. Norton & Company, Inc., 1965. Contains valuable information on the *Munn* case through the prosecutions of the carriers under the Interstate Commerce and the Sherman Anti-Trust acts.

———. *The Triumph of Conservatism: A Reinterpretation of American History, 1900-1916.* New York: Macmillan Publishing Co., Inc., 1963.

Very interesting work detailing the victory of conservatism in America prior to the outbreak of World War I and the role the Court played in this triumph.

Konefsky, Samuel J. *The Legacy of Holmes and Brandies: A Study in the Influence of Ideas.* New York: Macmillan Publishing Co., Inc., 1956. Erudite, well-written book on the impact these two liberal Justices had on the development of constitutional law.

Konvitz, Milton R. *Bill of Rights Reader: Leading Constitutional Cases.* Ithaca, N.Y.: Cornell University Press, 1973.

Koretz, Robert F. *Statutory History of the United States: Labor Organization.* New York: Chelsea House, 1970. Detailed history of the major acts passed by Congress pertaining to labor in this country with excerpts from selected statutes.

Krislow, Samuel. "Oliver Wendell Holmes: The Ebb and Flow of Judicial Legendry." 52 *Northwestern University Law Review* 514.

Kutler, Stanley I., ed. *The Supreme Court and the Constitution: Readings in American Constitutional History.* Boston: Houghton Mifflin Company, 1969. Well-done volume of select cases, topically organized, with readable explanatory introductions.

La Feber, Walter. *The New Empire.* Ithaca, N.Y.: Cornell University Press, 1959. Deals with American imperialism and the Spanish-American War. Contains a good description of the relationship between Justice William Day and President McKinley.

Lardner, Lynford A. "The Constitutional Doctrines of Justice David Josiah Brewer." Princeton University, Ph.D. dissertation, 1938. Solid study of the "great conservative's" Supreme Court career. One of the only full-length works on Brewer.

Leavitt, Donald C. "Attitude Change on the Supreme Court, 1910-1920." *Michigan Academician* IV (Summer 1971). Analysis of judicial voting patterns to explain the Court's response to Progressive legislation.

Lee, R. Alton. *A History of Regulatory Taxation.* Lexington, Ky.: University Press of Kentucky, 1973. Interesting treatment of taxation as an instrument of federal police power.

Leech, Margaret. *In the Days of McKinley.* New York: Harper & Row Publishers, 1959. Popular treatment of the McKinley administration and the colorful history of that period.

Legislative Reference Service of the Library of Congress. *The Constitution of the United States of America.* Washington, D.C.: Government Printing Office, 1965, 1972. Excellent reference work on the statutes and federal court cases of the United States. Periodic supplements are also available.

Leif, Alfred, ed. *Dissenting Opinions.* New York: Vanguard Books, 1929. A series of selected dissents primarily delivered by Justice Holmes. With introductions and commentary.

———., ed. *Representative Opinions of Justice Holmes.* New York: Vanguard Books, 1931.

Lerner, Max. "Constitution and Court as Symbols." *Yale Law Journal* XLVI (June 1937).

———. *The Mind and Faith of Justice Holmes.* Boston: Little, Brown and Company, 1943. Superior semibiography examining the personal and judicial philosophy of the Justice.

Levy, Leonard., ed. *American Constitutional Law: Historical Essays.* New York: Harper & Row Publishers, 1966. Notable essays in history and constitutional law gathered from a large variety of the nation's legal periodicals.

Lucey, Francis E. "Holmes—Liberal—Humanitarian—Believer in Democracy?" 39 *Georgetown Law Journal* 523. Revisionist interpretation of the work of Justice Holmes.

Magreth, C. Peter. *Constitutionalism and Politics: Conflict and Consensus.* Glenview, Ill.: Scott, Foresman and Company, 1968.

Mann, Arthur. *The Progressive Era.* New York: Holt, Rinehart and Winston, 1963. One of the best and most comprehensive works on the subject.

———. *Yankee Reformers in the Urban Age.* Chicago: University of Chicago Press, 1974. Superb study of the motivations behind the Progressive reformers from small town and rural backgrounds in an increasingly urbanizing America.

Marcosson, Issac F. "Attorney General Moody and His Work." 13 *World's Work* 8140 (January 1906). Very complimentary article about the future Supreme Court Justice during his successful tenure as Roosevelt's attorney general.

Martin, Albro. "The Troubled Subject of Railroad Regulation in the Gilded Age." *Journal of American History* XLI (September 1974). Well-balanced article exploring the difficulties involved in prosecuting common carriers who violated the Interstate Commerce and Sherman acts.

Mason, Alpheus T., ed. *American Constitutional History.* New York: Harper & Row Publishers, 1964. Solid case book study with introductions and commentary.

———., and William M. Beaney, eds. *American Constitutional Law: Introductory Essays and Selected Cases.* Englewood Cliffs, N.J.: Prentice-Hall, Inc., 1972. Well-regarded case book, containing much valuable and interesting material.

———. *The Supreme Court in a Free Society.* New York: W.W. Norton & Company, 1959. Uses an historical-analytical approach to explaining constitutional law.

May, Ernest R. *American Imperialism: A Speculative Essay.* New York: Atheneum Publishers, 1968.

Mayes, Edward. *Lucius Q.C. Lamar: Life, Times and Speeches.* Nashville, Tenn.: 1896. Repro. AMS Press, 1970. Old, but still valuable biography of Justice Lamar by his son-in-law.

McAllister, B.P. "Lord Hale and Business Affected With a Public Interest." *Harvard Law Review* XLIII (March 1930). Well-developed article discussing the relationship of *Munn v. Illinois* to the public interest doctrine.

———. "Public Purpose in Taxation." *California Law Review.* XVIII (January, March 1930).

McCloskey, Robert G. *American Conservatism in the Age of Enterprise.* New York: Oxford University Press, Inc., 1951. Very fine work explaining the development of conservative attitudes in the United States during the last two decades of the nineteenth century.

———. *The American Supreme Court.* Chicago: University of Chicago Press, 1960.

McDevitt, Matthew. "Joseph McKenna: Associate Justice of the United States." Ph.D. dissertation, Catholic University of America, 1945. Only full-length study on the Justice from California. Fairly interesting and well done.

McLaughlin, Andrew C. *A Constitutional History of the United States.* New York: Appleton-Century-Crofts, 1935. Classic text on the subject.

McLean, Joseph E. *William Rufus Day, Supreme Court Justice from Ohio.* Baltimore: Johns Hopkins University Press, 1946. The only study of significance on the Justice.

Meador, Daniel J. "Lamar and the Law at the University of Mississippi." 23 *Mississippi Law Journal* 227. Very interesting article of Lamar's teaching days at the University of Mississippi, where he began to formulate his constitutional jurisprudence.

Mendelson, Wallace. "Mr. Justice Field and Laissez Faire." 36 *Virginia Law Review* 45. Descriptive article detailing Field's antigovernmental interference with American enterprise.

———. *The Constitution and the Supreme Court.* New York: Dodd, Mead & Company, 1965.

Merrill, Maurice H. "Jurisdiction to Tax—Another World." *Yale Law Journal* XLIV (February 1935). Fascinating article describing the growth of the federal taxing power from the *Income Tax* case to the 1930's.

Meyer, B.H. *History of the Northern Securities Case.* 1906. Reprint. New York: Da Capo Press, 1972. Although old, a very detailed and scholarly work on this precedent-setting case.

Miller, Charles. *The Supreme Court and the Uses of History.* Cambridge, Mass.: Harvard University Press, 1969. Intelligent and provocative analysis of the types of historical inquiries in which Justices of the Supreme Court have engaged and the purposes for which they have used history in their opinions.

Miller, George H. "Origins of the Iowa Granger Laws." *Mississippi Valley Historical Review* XL (March 1954).

———. *Railroads and the Granger Laws.* Madison, Wis.: University of Wisconsin Press, 1973. Good study of state regulatory legislation.

Miller, Samuel F. *The Constitution and the Supreme Court of the United States.* 1889. Reprint. New York: Rothman Publishers, 1981. Quite short, but interesting treatise by the Justice, containing a good deal of his own judicial philosophy.

———. *Lectures on the Constitution.* 1891. Reprint. New York: Rothman Publishers, 1981. Justice Miller's own posthumously published speeches.

Mitchell, Stephen R. "Mr. Justice Horace Gray." Ph.D. dissertation, University of Wisconsin, 1961. Only full-length study presently available on the entire career of the Justice.

Morgan, H. Wayne. *The Gilded Age: A Reappraisal.* Syracuse, N.Y.: Syracuse University Press, 1970. Lively, colorful study of turn of the century America.

Morrison, Elting E., and Blum, John., eds. *The Letters of Theodore Roosevelt.* 8 vols. Cambridge, Mass.: Harvard University Press, 1951-1954. Brilliantly edited books containing all the known correspondence of the Progressive Period President, with introductions and commentary.

Mott, I.R.L. *Due Process of Law.* Indianapolis: The Bobbs-Merrill Co., Inc., 1926. Some very useful chapters on the development of early due process.

Mowry, George E. *The Era of Theodore Roosevelt, 1900-1912.* New York: Harper & Row Publishers, 1958. Superior study of the President and his national Progressive policies.

Murphy, Walter F. "In His Own Image: Mr. Justice Taft and Supreme Court Appointments." 1961 *Supreme Court Review* 159.

Myers, Gustavus. *History of the Supreme Court of the United States.* Chicago: Kerr Publishing Co., 1925. Contains a certain amount of factual data not readily found elsewhere, particularly for the Fuller Court of the 1890s.

Nevins, Allan. *Grover Cleveland: A Study in Courage.* New York: Dodd, Mead, 1932. The definitive biography on the President.

Parker, Courtlandt. *Mr. Justice Bradley of the United States Supreme Court.* Newark, N.J.: Privately Published, 1893. Early, very complimentary biography written by an old friend of the Justice.

Paul, Arnold M. *Conservative Crisis and the Rule of Law: Attitudes of Bar and Bench, 1887-1895.* Ithaca, N.Y.: Cornell University Press, 1960. One of the foremost accounts of the Court and of constitutional development during the Fuller years particularly in respect to the growth of the new judicialism in its relationship to social tensions.

Pfeffer, Leo. *This Honorable Court: A History of the United States Supreme Court*. Boston: Beacon Press, 1965. Well-written, fast-paced, general history of the Court. Contains many anecdotes.

Pollak, Louis H. *The Constitution and the Supreme Court: A Documentary History*. 2 vols. Cleveland: World Publishing Co., 1966. Excellent, fairly comprehensive piece of work with commentary and introductions.

Pollack, Norman. *The Populist Response to Industrialism*. Cambridge, Mass.: Harvard University Press, 1962. Solid study of the Populist movement, its philosophy and goals.

Pollock, Sir Frederick. "The New York Labor Law and the Fourteenth Amendment." *Law Quarterly Review* XXI (Fall 1906). A perceptive contemporary critique of the 1905 *Lochner v. New York* case.

Pound, Roscoe. "Liberty of Contract." *Yale Law Journal* XVIII (May 1909). Brilliant contemporary account of the development of the constitutional principle of freedom of contract and judicial interpretation of this concept.

———. "The New Feudal System." *Kentucky Law Journal* XIX (November 1930). The social and economic implications of the new force of judicial review are treated in this article.

Pratt, Julius W. *Expansionists of 1898*. Baltimore: The Johns Hopkins University Press, 1936. One of the best books written on the Spanish-American War and its ramifications.

Pringle, Henry F. *The Life and Time of William Howard Taft: A Biography*. 2 vols. 1938. Reprint. Hamden, Ct.: Shoe String Press, 1965. Probably the most complete work on the life and career of Taft.

———. *Theodore Roosevelt: A Biography*. New York: Harcourt, Brace, Jovanovitch, Inc., 1931. Presents a good general account of the first Roosevelt administration.

Pritchett, Charles H. *American Constitutional Issues*. New York: McGraw-Hill Book Company, 1962.

———. *The American Constitution*. New York: McGraw-Hill Book Company, 1968. Employs an historical-analytical approach to the development of constitutional law.

———., and Westin, Alan F., eds. *The Third Branch of Government: Eight Cases in Constitutional Politics*. New York: Harcourt, Brace, Jovanovitch, Inc., 1963. Very interesting approach. Looks at these selected cases from a political rather than a judicial point of view.

Purcell, E.A. "Ideas and Interests: Businessmen and the Interstate Commerce Act." *Journal of American History* LIV (December 1967).

Ratner, Sidney. *American Taxation*. New York: W.W. Norton & Company, 1942. Good general treatment with much information on the 1894 income tax law and subsequent litigation concerned with the tax.

Read, Conyears, ed. *The Constitution Reconsidered*. New York: Columbia University Press, 1938. Interesting work dealing with due process of law and its development.

Reeder, Robert F. "Chief Justice Fuller." 59 *University of Pennsylvania Law Review* 1. Primarily a review of Fuller's more prominent judicial opinions and dissents.

Regier, Cornelius C. *The Era of the Muckrakers.* Chapel Hill, N.C.: University of North Carolina Press, 1932. Contains much valuable information on the background of federal police acts.

Roche, John P., and Levy, Leonard W. *The Judiciary.* New York: Harcourt, Brace, Jovanovitch, Inc., 1964.

Rosenblum, Victor, and Castberg, A. Diderick. *Cases on Constitutional Law; Political Roles of the Supreme Court.* Homewood, Ill.: Dorsey Press, 1965. Interesting study dealing with the political considerations which influence the Justices in making decisions on the Court.

Scheiber, Harry N. "The Road to Munn: Eminent Domain and the Concept of Public Purpose in the State Courts." *Perspectives in American History* V (March 1971). Brilliant article which examines the antecedents of the public interest doctrine.

Schubert, Glendon A. *Constitutional Politics: The Political Behavior of Supreme Court Justices and the Constitutional Policies They Make.* New York: Holt, Rinehart and Winston, 1960. Scholarly, detailed work on the political factors that influence Justices of the Court in coming to their decisions.

Schwartz, Bernard. *A Basic History of the United States Supreme Court.* Princeton, N.J.: D. Van Nostrand Company, 1968.

———. *A Commentary on the Constitution of the United States.* 5 vols. New York: Macmillan Publishing Co., Inc., 1963-1968. This massive work comprises three parts: Part One is entitled *The Powers of the Government,* consisting of two volumes; vol. I, *Federal and State Powers* (1963) and vol. II, *The Powers of the President* (1963). Part Two is entitled *The Rights of Property* (1965). Part Three is entitled *The Rights of the Individual* consisting of two volumes; vol. I, *Sanctity, Privacy, and Expression* (1968) and vol. II, *Equality, Belief, and Dignity* (1968). It is probably the most substantial work of this type yet to appear in the twentieth century.

———. *Statutory History of the United States: The Economic Regulation of Business and Industry.* 5 vols. New York: Chelsea House, 1973.

———. *The Reigns of Power: A Constitutional History of the United States.* New York: Hill & Wang, 1963. Solid, scholarly general work, tracing the entire history of the Court.

Schwartz, Louis B. *Free Enterprise and Economic Organization: Antitrust Regulatory Controls.* Mineola, N.Y.: Foundation Press, 1972. Very detailed work containing explanations of antitrust statutes, their application, and the litigation that arose as a result of their violation.

Shapiro, Martin M. *The Supreme Court and Public Policy.* Glenview, Ill.:

Scott, Foresman and Company, 1969.

Sharfman, I.L. *The Interstate Commerce Commission.* 5 vols. Boston: Commonwealth Fund, 1931-1937. Detailed and technical work on the early history of the commission.

Sheldon, Charles H. *The Supreme Court: Politicians in Robes.* Beverly Hills, Calif.: Glencoe Press, 1970. Excellent study, concentrating on the political nature of many of the Justices.

Shippee, B. Lester, and Ways, Royal B. "William Rufus Day." In *The American Secretaries of State and Their Diplomacy,* edited by Samuel Flagg Bemis, vol. ix, pp. 27-112. New York: Pageant Book Co. Fairly comprehensive treatment of Day's career in the State Department prior to his appointment as a Justice of the Supreme Court.

Shipman, George A. "Constitutional Doctrines of Stephen J. Field." Ph.D. dissertation, Cornell University, 1931. Solid discussion of Field's conservatism.

Shiras, Winfield, ed. *Justice George Shiras, Jr. of Pittsburgh.* Pittsburgh: University of Pittsburgh Press, 1953. The papers of Justice Shiras, collected and published by his son.

Smith, James M., and Murphy, Paul, eds. *Liberty and Justice: A Historical Record of American Constitutional Development.* 2 vols. New York: Alfred A. Knopf, Inc., 1965-1968. A well-written, well-organized basic documentary history.

Smith, John M. "Mr. Justice Gray of the United States Supreme Court." 6 *South Dakota Law Review* 221. Contains some significant material on the life and career of the Justice.

Stelzer, Irwin M. *Selected Antitrust Cases: Landmark Decisions.* Homewood, Ill.: Irwin, 1972.

Strong, Frank R. "The Economic Philosophy of Lochner: Emergence, Embrasure and Emasculation." *Arizona Law Review* XV (March 1973). Interesting article on the implications of the Court's decision in *Lochner v. New York* (1905).

Sweet, Esther C. *Civil Liberties in America: A Casebook.* Princeton, N.J.: Van Nostrand Reinhold Company, 1966. Very good study of Supreme Court cases involving civil liberties and civil rights, including an excellent discussion on the *Plessy* case.

Swindler, William F. *Court and Constitution in the Twentieth Century: The Old Legality, 1889-1932.* Indianapolis: Bobbs-Merrill Co., Inc., 1969. Excellent study of this period in the Court's history, relating politics and the work of the Court in an effective style. Contains a number of very valuable appendices including about one hundred landmark cases in synopsis form.

Swisher, Carl B. *American Constitutional Development.* Boston: Houghton Mifflin Company, 1954. Very good study providing much material on early twentieth-century constitutional problems.

———. *Historic Decisions of the Supreme Court.* New York: Van Nostrand Reinhold Company, 1969. Presents a number of selected landmark cases with introductions and commentary in a well-organized format.

———. *Stephen J. Field, Craftsman of the Law.* Hamden, Ct.: Shoe String Press, 1963. The definitive biographical study on the conservative Justice from California dealing with Field's role in the emergence of substantive due process among other things.

Thorelli, Hans B. *The Federal Antitrust Policy: Origination of an American Tradition.* Baltimore: The Johns Hopkins University Press, 1955. Excellent scholarly study primarily dealing with the Sherman Antitrust Act of 1890.

Tompkins, Dorothy C. *The Supreme Court of the United States: A Bibliography.* Berkeley: University of California Press, 1959. While almost twenty-five years old, this work is still a handy reference book on the Court published by the Bureau of Public Administration at the University.

Tresolini, Rocco J. *These Liberties: Case Studies in Civil Rights.* Philadelphia: J.B. Lippincott Company, 1968. Excellent case book with a well-balanced discussion of *Plessy v. Ferguson.*

Umbreit, Kenneth B. *Our Eleven Chief Justices.* New York: Harper & Row Publishers, 1938. Includes an extremely critical evaluation of Chief Justice Fuller's years at the center of the bench.

United States Supreme Court Reports. Washington, D.C.: Government Printing House, Yearly bound volumes. Available in three principal editions: *United States Reports, The Supreme Court Reporter,* and *The Lawyers Edition.*

Waite, Edward F. "How Eccentric Was Mr. Justice Harlan?" 37 *Minnesota Law Review* 173. Extremely interesting article which takes a very positive view of Harlan's positions on the Court.

Walker, A.H. *History of the Sherman Law.* New York: Baker Publishing, 1910. Early study of the Sherman Antitrust Act, its application, and the cases that arose under it.

Walz, William E. "Chief Justice Fuller, the Individualist on the Bench." 10 *Maine Law Review* 77. Very complimentary appraisal of Fuller's performance as Chief Justice.

Warren, Charles. "The New Liberty Under the Fourteenth Amendment." *Harvard Law Review* XXXIX (February 1926).

———. *The Supreme Court in United States History.* 2 vols. Boston: Little, Brown and Company, 1960. Contains a wealth of material on the Court's role in politics and history.

Watt, Richard F., and Orlikoff, Richard M. "The Coming Vindication of Mr. Justice Harlan." 44 *Illinois Law Review* 13. Brilliant article praising Harlan's work on the Court, and making a plea for the proper recognition for the controversial Justice from Kentucky.

Weinstein, James. *The Corporate Ideal in the Liberal State, 1900-1918.* Boston: Beacon Press, 1968.

Westin, Alan F., ed. *An Autobiography of the Supreme Court.* New York: Macmillan Publishing Co., Inc., 1963. Excellent collection of out-of-court commentaries by individual Justices with short, explanatory introductions.

———. "John Marshall Harlan and the Constitutional Rights of Negroes: The Transformation of a Southerner." 66 *Yale Law Journal* 637. One of the best articles written about Harlan. Contains much more material than the title indicates.

———. "Stephen J. Field and the Headnote to O'Neill v. Vermont: A Snapshot of the Fuller Court at Work." 67 *Yale Law Journal* 363.

Wiebe, R.H. *The Search for Order, 1877-1920.* New York: Hill & Wang, 1967. Good general description of the period, with excellent coverage of the various reform movements from the Grangers through the Progressives.

Williston, Samuel. "Horace Gray." In *Great American Lawyers,* edited by W.D. Lewis. Philadelphia: University of Pennsylvania Press, 1909. Brief, but valuable sketch of the Justice.

Wood, Stephen B. *Constitutional Politics in the Progressive Era: Child Labor and the Law.* Chicago: University of Chicago Press, 1968. An excellent work on the subject, detailing the various Supreme Court cases dealing with attempts at the regulation of child labor. Particularly good for *Hammer v. Dagenhart.*

Wright, Benjamin F. *The Contract Clause of the Constitution.* Cambridge, Mass.: Harvard University Press, 1938. The doctrine of vested rights and the obligations of the contract clause are thoroughly discussed.

Ziegler, Benjamin M. *Desegregation and the Supreme Court.* Boston: D.C. Heath & Company, 1958.